IMAGES
of America

BATTLESHIP COVE

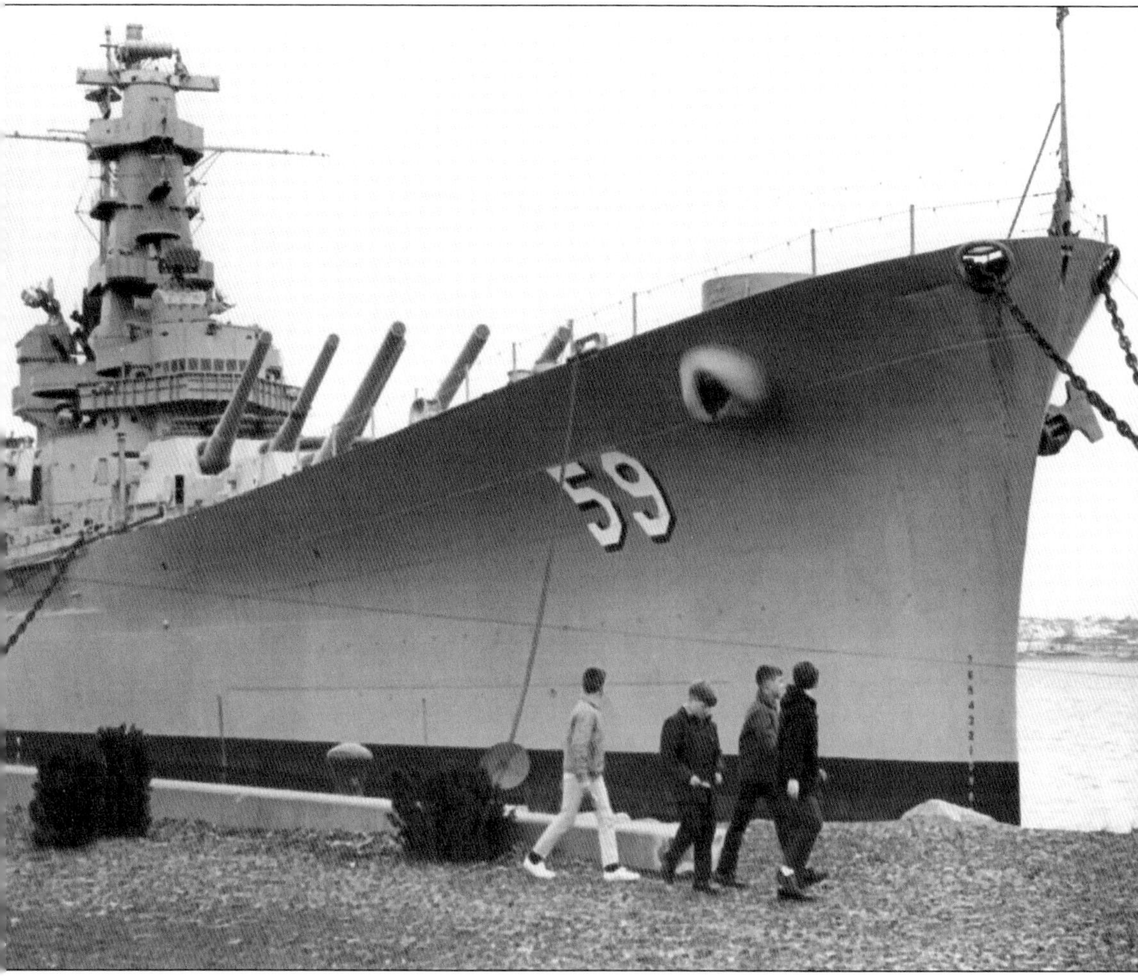

In this 1967 photograph, a few children head for the exit of Battleship Cove after touring the *Massachusetts*. (Courtesy of Battleship Cove.)

On the Cover: As seen from the Fall River waterfront in early evening in 1970, the *Massachusetts* is at her deep-water mooring. At the time, she was the only exhibit at the museum. In a few years, the *Lionfish* and *Joseph P. Kennedy, Jr.* would join her. (Courtesy of Battleship Cove.)

IMAGES
of America

BATTLESHIP COVE

James A. Gay

ARCADIA
PUBLISHING

ISBN 978-1-4671-2149-1

Published by Arcadia Publishing
Charleston, South Carolina

Printed in the United States of America

Library of Congress Control Number: 2013949632

For all general information, please contact Arcadia Publishing:
Telephone 843-853-2070
Fax 843-853-0044
E-mail sales@arcadiapublishing.com
For customer service and orders:
Toll-Free 1-888-313-2665

Visit us on the Internet at www.arcadiapublishing.com

To the sailors of the Massachusetts, Lionfish, *and* Joseph P. Kennedy, Jr. *and for those who have crossed the bar.*

Contents

Acknowledgments

I would like to thank all the employees, staff, and volunteers at Battleship Cove. Thanks in particular go to Brad King, executive director; Chris Nardi, curator; Rich Angelini, *Joseph P. Kennedy* curator; and Don Shannon, PT-boat curator. I also wish to thank Tin Can Sailors Inc. and PT Boats Inc. for their restoration and preservation efforts, along with being excellent resources on destroyer and PT-boat history.

I need to acknowledge the thousands of volunteers who have given so much over the decades to preserve these historic ships and boats for future generations. I am grateful to the former crew members of the *Joseph P. Kennedy, Jr.* who I have had the pleasure to meet. It is an honor knowing you; thanks for sharing your personal experiences on the *JPK* with me.

Thanks to Ed Zajkowski, Rich Angelini, and the JPK volunteers for their hard work and dedication to restoring and preserving the *Kennedy*. Thanks also to the *JPK*'s Division of Sea Cadets for their dedication and service, and for representing the next generation of volunteers. Thanks to Chris Nardi and Tom Lowney for their preservation efforts on the *Massachusetts*.

A thank-you to Ted Hayes for providing excellent photographs for this book, and to the following individuals who submitted personal photographs: Joe Hesson, Tom Martin, Thomas Howard, Catherine Marx, Braid Strait, Dr. Peter N. Mikhalevsky, and Steve Wallace.

Thanks to Brinkley Gary and Lissie Cain for introducing me to the world of Arcadia Publishing, and my editor on this project, Rebekah Collinsworth.

Finally, I would like to thank my parents, Eldon and Margaret, who first introduced me to Battleship Cove and instilled in me the values of duty, honor, and country. Thanks to my wife, Becky Rizoli, my mother-in-law, Connie Rizoli, and Tracy Pace, for their editing.

Unless otherwise noted, all images appear courtesy of the archives of Battleship Cove.

INTRODUCTION

One of the most famous slogans of the US Navy is "Don't give up the ship." Uttered by dying Capt. James Lawrence aboard the *Chesapeake* in the War of 1812, it has echoed down to every sailor who has served in the American Navy ever since. It was heard loud and clear by former crew members of the *Massachusetts* when they learned that their ship was about to be destroyed. Today, those words are ingrained in the hearts of every employee and volunteer at Battleship Cove.

The battleship USS *Massachusetts* (BB-59) was built in Quincy, Massachusetts, and was commissioned in South Boston on May 12, 1942. In October, she joined up with the Western Naval Task Force and fought in the naval battle of Casablanca during the invasion of North Africa. Firing what is believed to have been the first 16-inch shell of World War II, she destroyed the *Jean Bart* and several other ships. Arriving in the Pacific in March 1943, the *Massachusetts* steamed with the fast carrier task forces as they attacked the Japanese in the Gilbert Islands. In January 1944, she protected the carriers of Task Force 58 as they drove the Japanese from the Marshall Islands. After she blasted Kwajalein Atoll at the end of the month, she next turned her guns on Truk. For the next several months, she steamed with the fast carrier task forces in strikes against the Marianas and Caroline Islands. In May, she headed to the Puget Sound Naval Shipyard for overhaul and repairs.

The veteran battleship returned to the war zone and was with Adm. William Halsey during the Battle of Leyte Gulf. In December, she survived a typhoon that sank three destroyers, killing almost 800 sailors. Alternating with the famous Third and Fifth Fleets, she protected the carriers from kamikazes and bombarded Iwo Jima and Okinawa prior to their invasion in 1945. After steaming through another typhoon in June, she shelled Kamaishi, Honshu. The *Massachusetts* destroyed factories on Hamamatsu two weeks later and then returned to bombard Kamaishi on August 9. It was in this action that she is believed to have fired the last 16-inch shell of World War II.

From her commissioning in 1942, the *Massachusetts* steamed more than 225,000 miles, took part in 35 engagements, sank several enemy ships, shot down 18 enemy aircraft, saved the lives of seven pilots, and never lost a man. In 1946, she was reassigned to the East Coast and arrived at Norfolk, Virginia, in April. With the war over, she was decommissioned on March 27, 1947, and entered the Atlantic Reserve Fleet at Norfolk. For the next 18 years, "Big Mamie" sat idle in Norfolk, patiently waiting to serve her country again. Old and technically obsolete, she was struck from the Naval Register on June 1, 1962, and was planned to be scrapped. When former crew members learned in early 1963 that the Navy was going to scrap their Big Mamie, they began the fight to save her. They asked Massachusetts governor Endicott Peabody for financial support, but he refused.

Determined to save their ship, former crewmembers created the USS *Massachusetts* Memorial Committee Inc. on February 10, 1964. Through tremendous effort, hard work, and perseverance, the committee raised enough money and support to bring the veteran battleship back to her home state in June 1965. Officially opening to the public in August, she became the commonwealth's official World War II memorial in 1968.

The submarine USS *Lionfish* (SS-298) was commissioned on November 1, 1944, and her first commanding officer was Lt. Cmdr. Edward D. Spruance, son of the famous commander of the Fifth Fleet in the Pacific, Adm. Raymond Spruance. She headed to the Pacific on January 8, 1945, and left for her first war patrol on March 19. On April 11, a Japanese submarine fired two torpedoes at her, but through evasive action, both of them missed. The *Lionfish* fired upon a Japanese submarine on July 10. When her captain looked through the periscope, he noticed a cloud of smoke. In addition, a sonar man reported hearing noises concurrent with a submarine imploding. The *Lionfish* was decommissioned on January 16, 1945, and entered the Pacific Reserve Fleet. She received one Battle Star for her service in World War II.

On January 31, 1951, the *Lionfish* was recommissioned for training purposes in Key West, Florida, and New London, Connecticut. On October 18, 1952, she departed for a Mediterranean cruise in which she participated in NATO exercises and had liberty calls at Taranto and Naples, Italy. Decommissioned in 1971, she became a permanent memorial to all submariners at Battleship Cove on August 30, 1972.

Lt. Joseph P. Kennedy Jr. (USNR), the oldest son of Joseph and Rose Kennedy, was killed when the drone aircraft he was piloting exploded prematurely over England on August 12, 1944. He was posthumously awarded the Navy Cross, and the US Navy would honor and perpetuate his memory by naming a destroyer after him. The *Joseph P. Kennedy, Jr.* was built in Quincy, Massachusetts, and was christened by Jean Kennedy on July 26, 1945. The destroyer was commissioned at the Boston Navy Yard on December 15, 1945, with Cmdr. Harry G. Moore as her first commanding officer. Based at Newport, Rhode Island, she spent several years making deployments with the Sixth Fleet in the Mediterranean and operating on the East Coast and in the Caribbean. On August 23, 1949, she served as flagship for Destroyer Squadron 8 on a deployment with the Sixth Fleet in the Mediterranean.

With the outbreak of the Korean War, the *Joseph P. Kennedy, Jr.* left Newport on January 3, 1951, and arrived off Korea in February. For the next several months, she provided direct fire support to the troops ashore, screened aircraft carriers, and provided plane guard duties. She served a stint in the Formosa Patrol, and helped bombard the city of Wonsan from May 20 until June 13. With the other destroyers of Squadron 8, she steamed west to complete a circuit of the globe and returned to Newport on August 8, 1951.

The "Jay Pee," as nicknamed by the crew, served as a school ship for the Fleet Training School in Newport, made several deployments to the Mediterranean with the Sixth Fleet, and, in 1955, steamed for Arctic maneuvers off Northern Europe. After visiting Washington, DC, for the inauguration of Pres. John F. Kennedy, brother of the ship's namesake, in January 1961, she entered the Brooklyn Navy Yard for her fleet rehabilitation and modernization overhaul. Her entire steel superstructure was rebuilt with aluminum, she received a more modernized bridge, and she was fitted with the latest weapons systems, Anti-Submarine Rocket (ASROC) and Drone Anti-Submarine Helicopter (DASH).

After serving as a viewing platform for President Kennedy and First Lady Jacqueline Kennedy during the America's Cup races in 1962, she left Newport to defend America during the Cuban Missile Crisis. Both she and another destroyer, the USS *Pierce*, stopped and boarded the freighter *Marucla* on October 26, 1962. In 1965, the *Kennedy* helped qualify two new Polaris missile submarines, and at the end of the year participated in the afloat recovery teams for Gemini 6 and 7. Throughout the late 1960s, she continued in astronaut recovery and made deployments with the Sixth Fleet in the Mediterranean. In 1970, Jackie Kennedy and her children, Caroline and John, were on board to watch the America's Cup races off Newport. Decommissioned in 1973, she opened to the public in 1974 and is the official Massachusetts memorial to those killed in the Korean and Vietnam Wars.

In the ensuing years, the museum and its exhibits continued to grow. PT Boats Inc. founder Jimmy "Boats" Newberry was instrumental in bringing a unique craft and two PT-boats to Battleship Cove in the 1970s. The *Massachusetts*, *Lionfish*, *Kennedy*, and PT-boats *796* and *617* are National Historic Landmarks and represent different periods of naval history. In addition, two of them memorialize those who have given their lives for the nation. Battleship Cove's exhibits include the National Destroyermen's Museum, the National PT Museum, and the new Pearl Harbor Experience. Receiving visitors from all over the world, Battleship Cove is one of Southeastern Massachusetts's most popular attractions. With nearly six million visitors, it stands at the threshold of a new era in its ambitions to modernize for the 21st century. Through new exhibitions about the ships and those who served aboard them, new generations of visitors will learn the meaning of duty, honor, and country and will be reminded of those who paid the ultimate price to preserve our freedom.

One

USS *Massachusetts* (BB-59)

The battleship USS *Massachusetts* (BB-59) was built at the Fore River Shipyard in Quincy, Massachusetts, and was commissioned on May 12, 1942. While supporting the invasion of North Africa in November 1942, she was the first US Navy ship to fire a 16-inch shell in World War II. Arriving in the Pacific in March 1943, "Mighty Mamie" helped drive the Japanese back. Her big guns blasted enemy troops ashore, and her anti-aircraft guns shot down Japanese planes.

She fought in the famous naval battle of Leyte Gulf in 1944 and survived a typhoon that killed close to 800 sailors. Throughout 1945, she blasted her way to the home islands of Japan and fired the last 16-inch shell of World War II. Soon after Japan surrendered, the *Massachusetts* headed home with the proud distinction of never losing a man. In 1946, she was reassigned to the East Coast and arrived at Norfolk, Virginia, in April. With the war over and military budgets slashed, she was decommissioned on March 27, 1947, and entered the Atlantic Reserve Fleet at Norfolk.

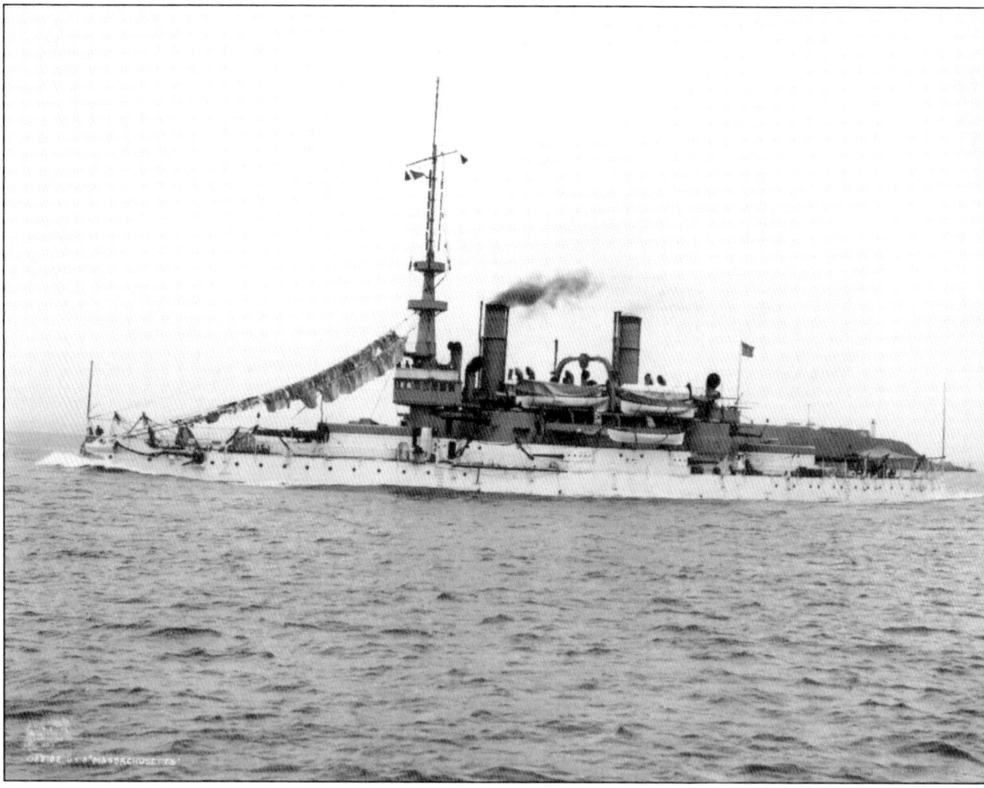

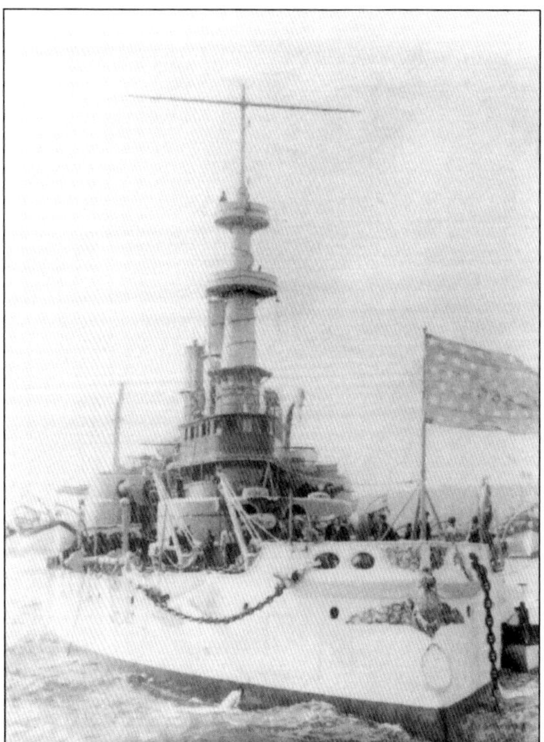

Since 1849, US Navy vessels have been named after the Commonwealth of Massachusetts, one of the 13 original colonies and the birthplace of the Navy. The second vessel to bear the name fought in the Civil War, and the third was broken up before she was completed in 1884. The fourth, shown here, was built as a battleship and was commissioned on June 10, 1896. (Author's collection.)

With the outbreak of the Spanish-American War, the *Massachusetts* left Norfolk, Virginia, in May 1898 to participate in the blockade of Cuba. Later, her gunners fired on Cuban shore batteries and assisted in attacking several enemy vessels. After the war, she served in the North Atlantic Squadron until she was decommissioned in 1906. (Author's collection.)

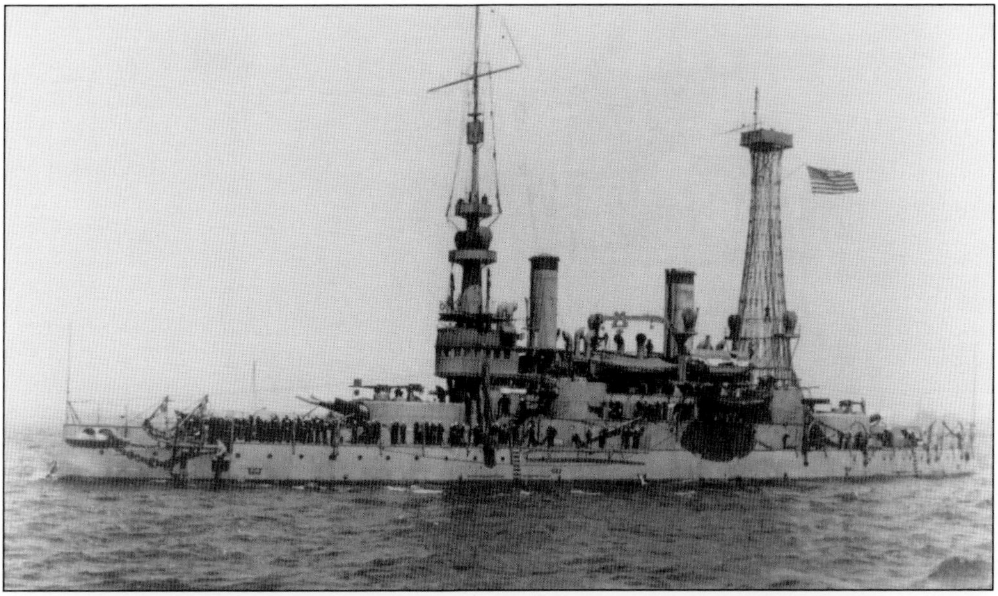

After several modifications, including a cage mast near her stern, she was put back into service in 1910. The *Massachusetts* was used for many years as a training ship for midshipmen from the Naval Academy, including future World War II Admiral of the Fleet Chester W. Nimitz. Soon after World War I, she was decommissioned and sunk off Pensacola, Florida.

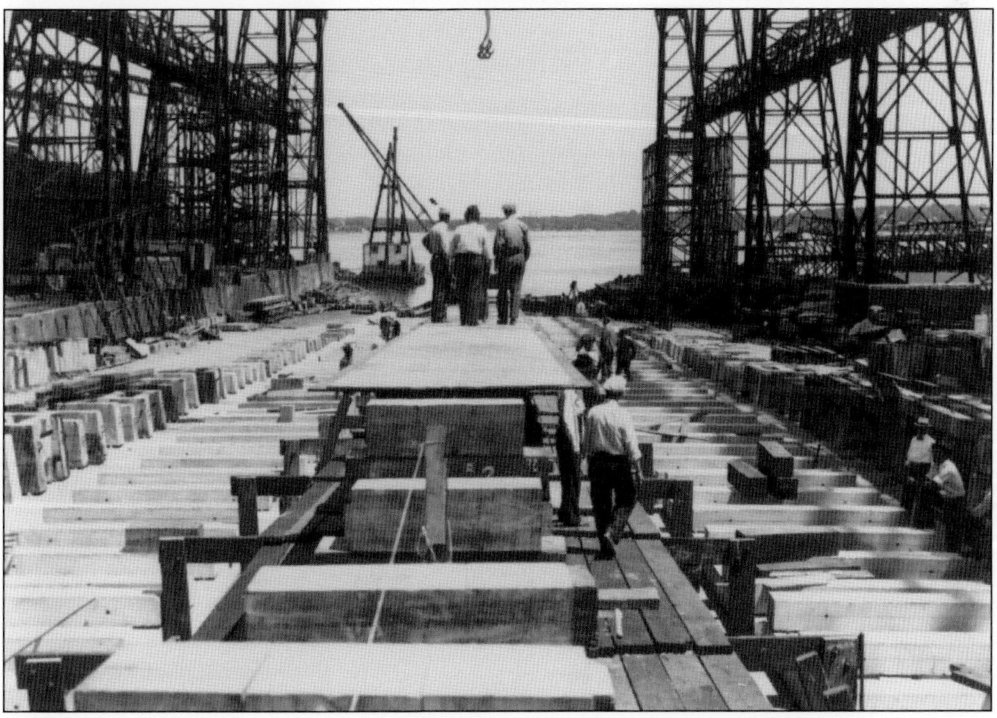

In 1938, the contract for building the fifth USS *Massachusetts* was awarded to the Bethlehem Steel Company in Quincy, Massachusetts. Situated along the banks of the Fore River, the yard employed around 7,000 workers and had been at its present location since 1901. Dwarfed by massive scaffolding, workers "walk her keel" on July 20, 1939.

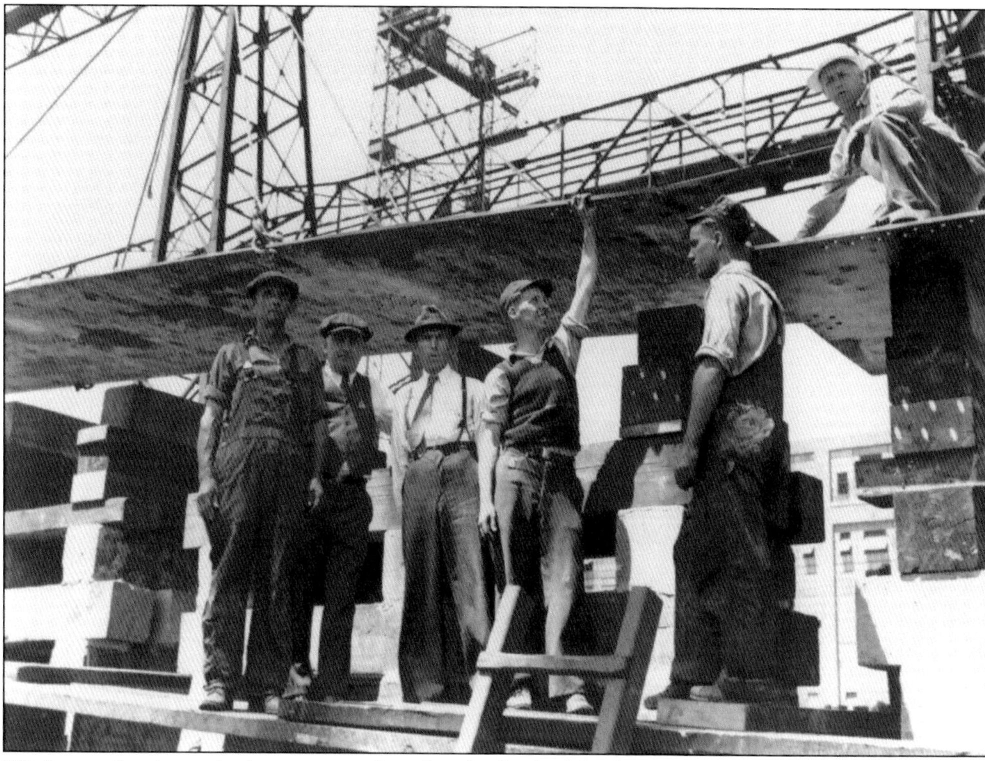

With war clouds on the horizon, workers lay the keel of the future USS *Massachusetts*. As a local newspaper noted, the laying of a ship's keel was not a historic event in the City of Quincy, because the yard was one of the most active in the country. The ship was of the South Dakota class of battleships, and her sisters were the *South Dakota*, *Indiana*, and *Alabama*.

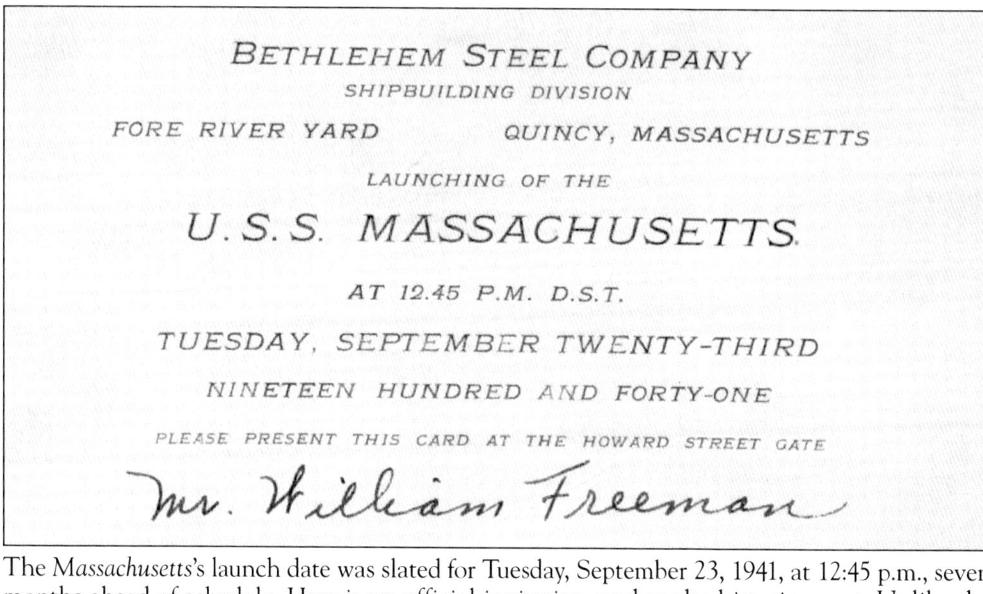

BETHLEHEM STEEL COMPANY
SHIPBUILDING DIVISION
FORE RIVER YARD QUINCY, MASSACHUSETTS
LAUNCHING OF THE
U.S.S. MASSACHUSETTS
AT 12.45 P.M. D.S.T.
TUESDAY, SEPTEMBER TWENTY-THIRD
NINETEEN HUNDRED AND FORTY-ONE
PLEASE PRESENT THIS CARD AT THE HOWARD STREET GATE
Mr. William Freeman

The *Massachusetts*'s launch date was slated for Tuesday, September 23, 1941, at 12:45 p.m., seven months ahead of schedule. Here is an official invitation card to the historic event. Unlike the laying of her keel, the launching of the *Massachusetts* was a proud accomplishment for both the workers and the Navy.

The battleship's massive hull is seen here prior to launching. The wooden cradle, called a poppet, helps slide the vessel into the water. The black chains are used to slow her down and act as a brake after her launching. She was built with a 36-foot draft and a standard displacement of 35,000 tons.

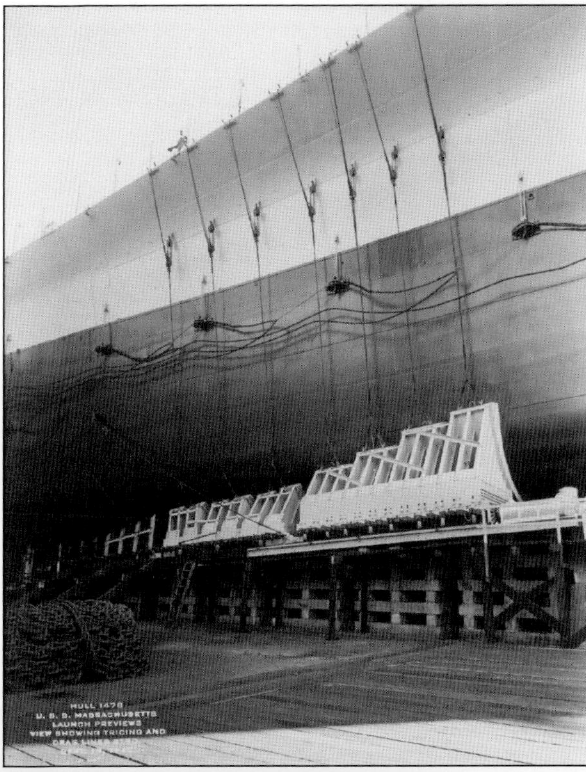

This view of the portside aft shows how her steel plates are riveted together, piece by piece. Ships of the South Dakota class were designed to travel at a top speed of 25 knots, giving them the ability to steam with aircraft carriers, cruisers, and destroyers. Each of her four propellers weighed 25 tons.

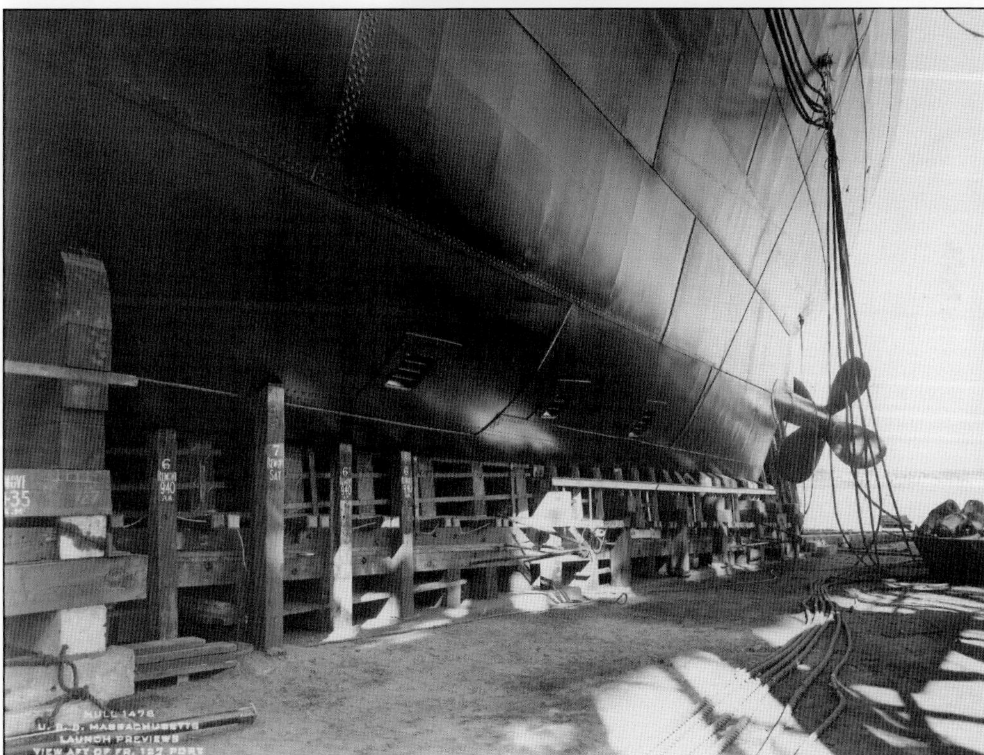

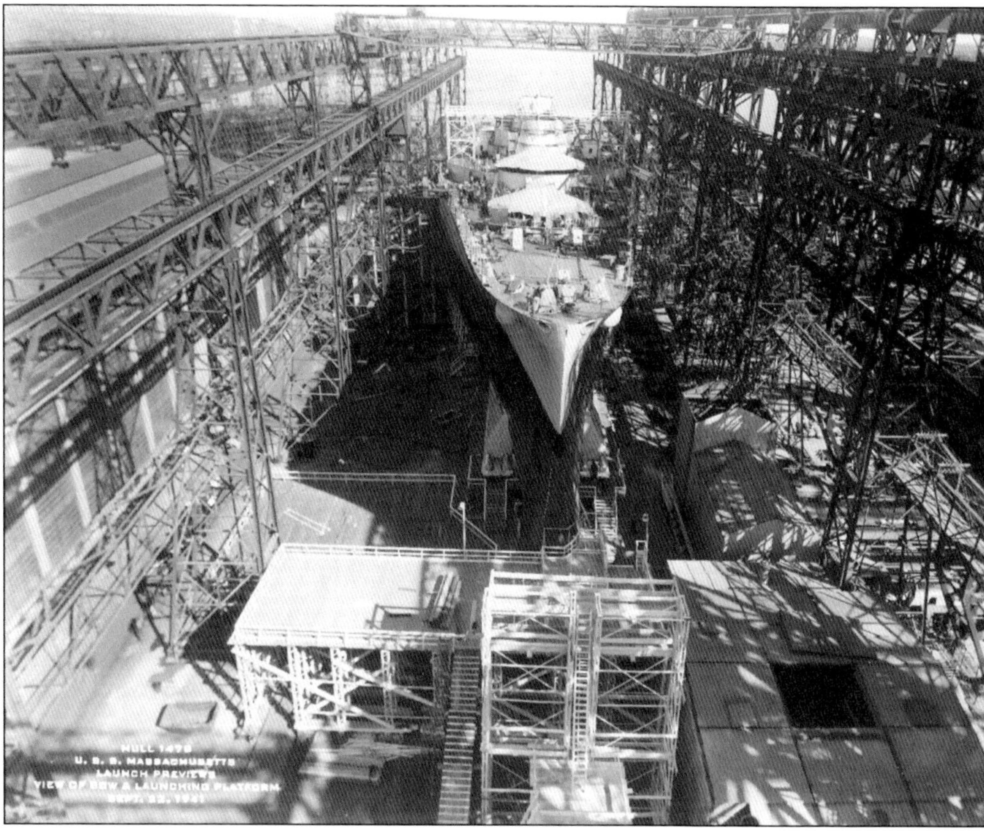

Seen here on September 22, 1941, hull number 1478 would wait one more day until she officially received her name at the time-honored christening ceremony. Just in front of the bow can be seen the launch platform from which Mrs. Charles Francis Adams would christen her. Adams's husband was the former secretary of the Navy and a member of Quincy's most famous family.

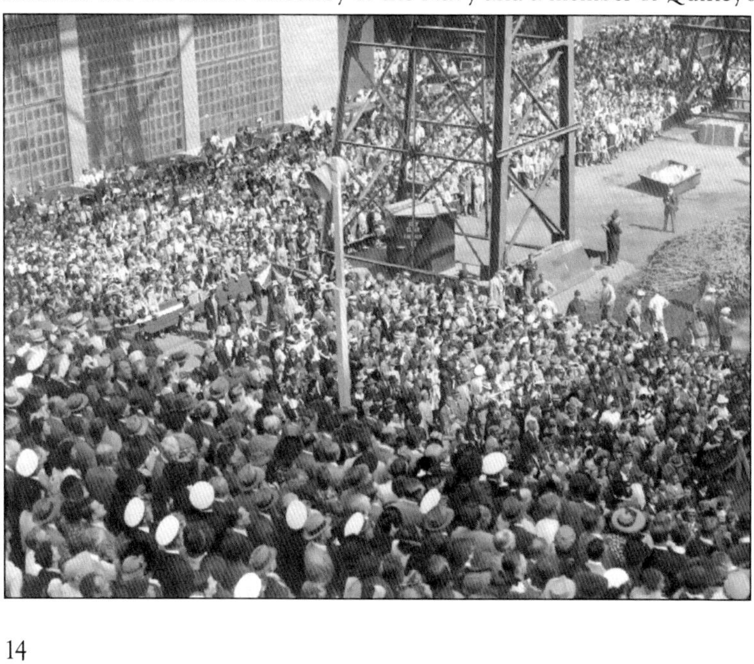

Clear skies prevailed for the launch on September 23, 1941. A crowd of 7,500 came out to see the launching of a ship named for their home state. In attendance were many naval officials, such as Secretary of the Navy Frank Knox and the commander in chief of the Atlantic Fleet, Adm. Ernest J. King.

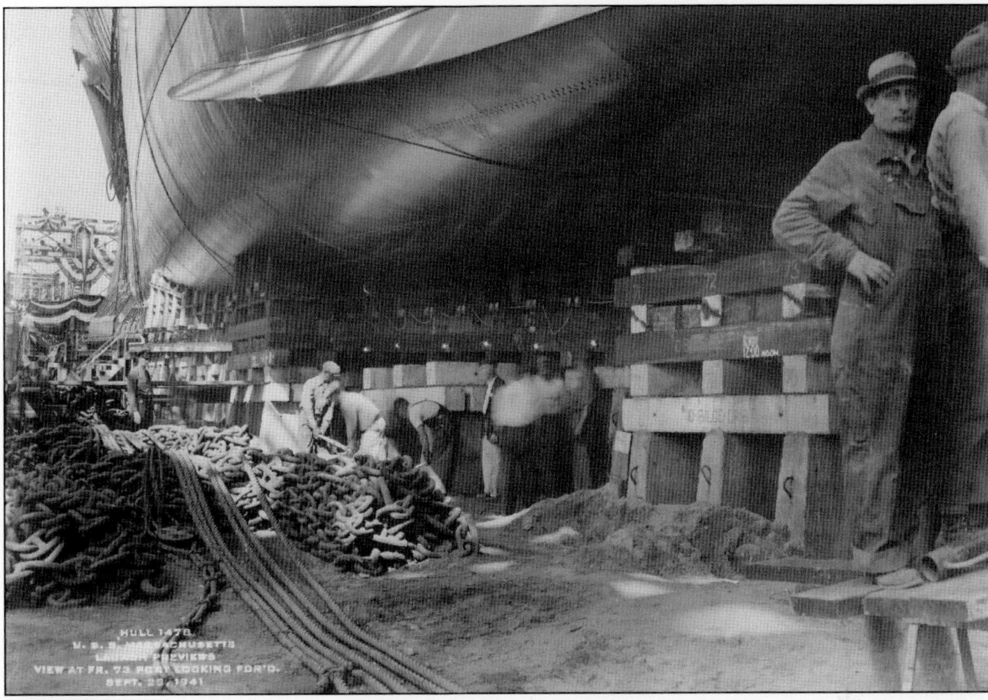

As a police officer looks on in the distance at left, yard workers make the final preparations before the 12:45 p.m. launching. City and state politicians attended as well, including Gov. Leverett Saltonstall. Following a Navy tradition, schoolchildren throughout the state raised money for the purchase of silverware for the ship.

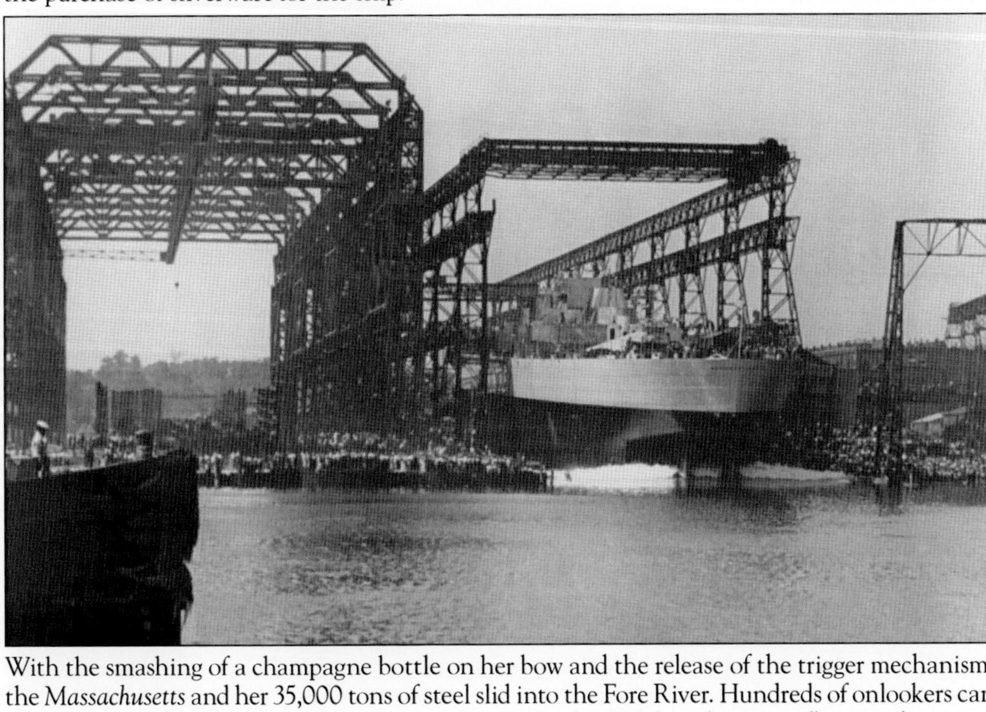

With the smashing of a champagne bottle on her bow and the release of the trigger mechanism, the *Massachusetts* and her 35,000 tons of steel slid into the Fore River. Hundreds of onlookers can be seen lining the waterfront. In a matter of seconds, the 680-foot ship was afloat on the river.

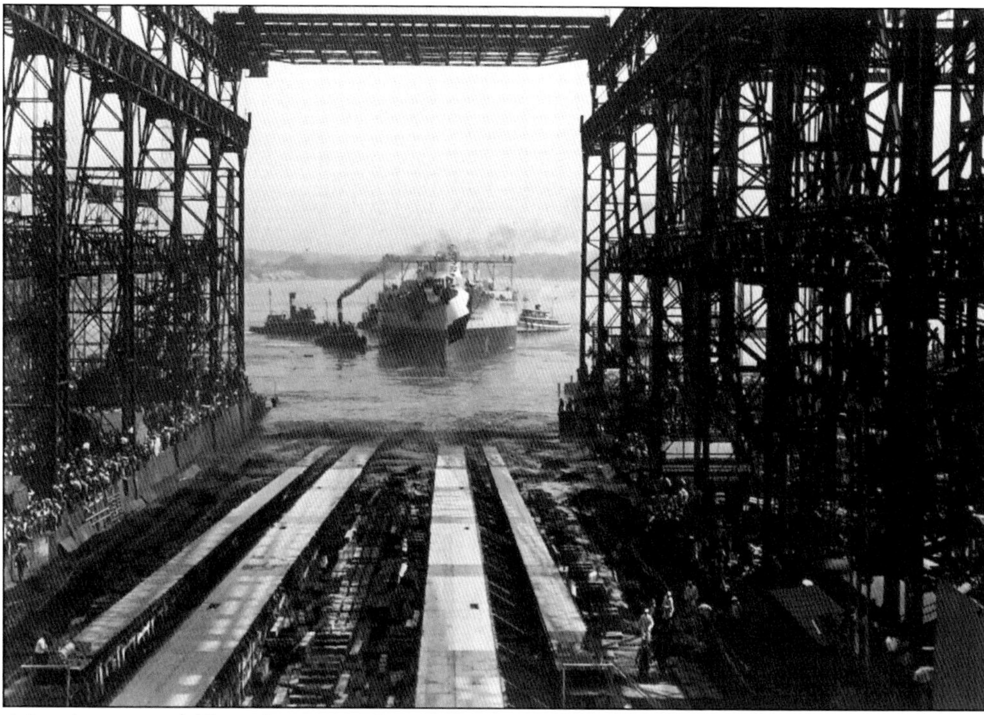

After the successful launching into the Fore River, tugs moved in to assist the *Massachusetts*. She was moved to another area of the shipyard, where workers continued to turn her into a warship. When she was completely finished, her weight had jumped from 35,000 tons to 41,000 tons.

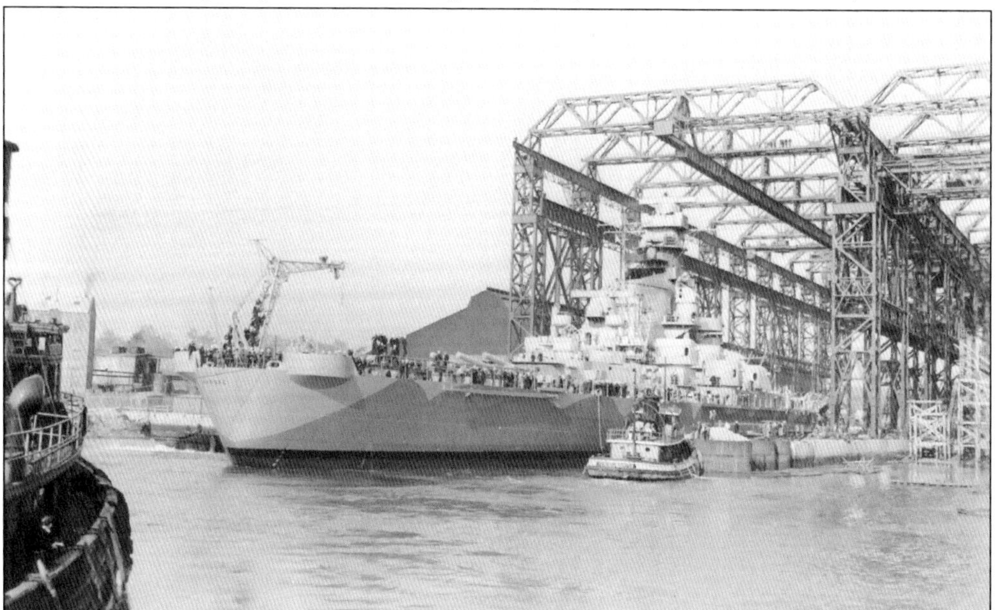

Built at a cost of $80 million, the *Massachusetts* was the Navy's newest battleship. Launched at a time of peace, she was commissioned with the world at war. On May 12, 1942, tugs eased her out of her slip so she could sail to Boston for her commissioning. The crane rising above her stern was used to retrieve her scout planes after they made a successful water landing.

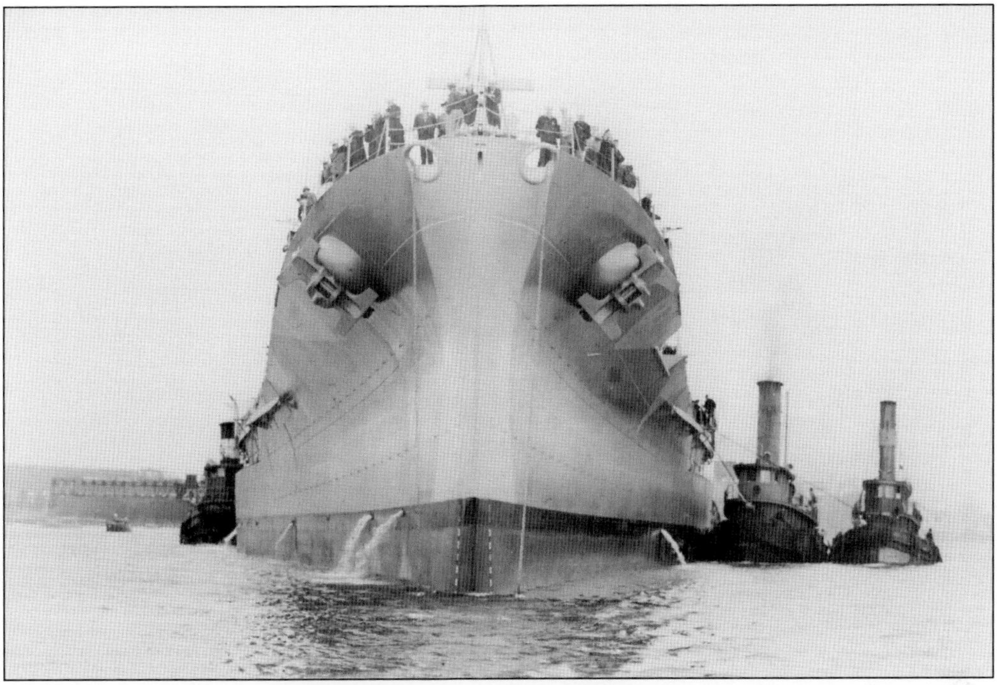

While the *Massachusetts* was being built, most of her officers and enlisted personnel reported to her in Quincy. That way, they had a chance to familiarize themselves with the newest technology in the fleet. Several shipyard workers figured they would be drafted soon enough, so they enlisted in the Navy and were assigned to the *Massachusetts*.

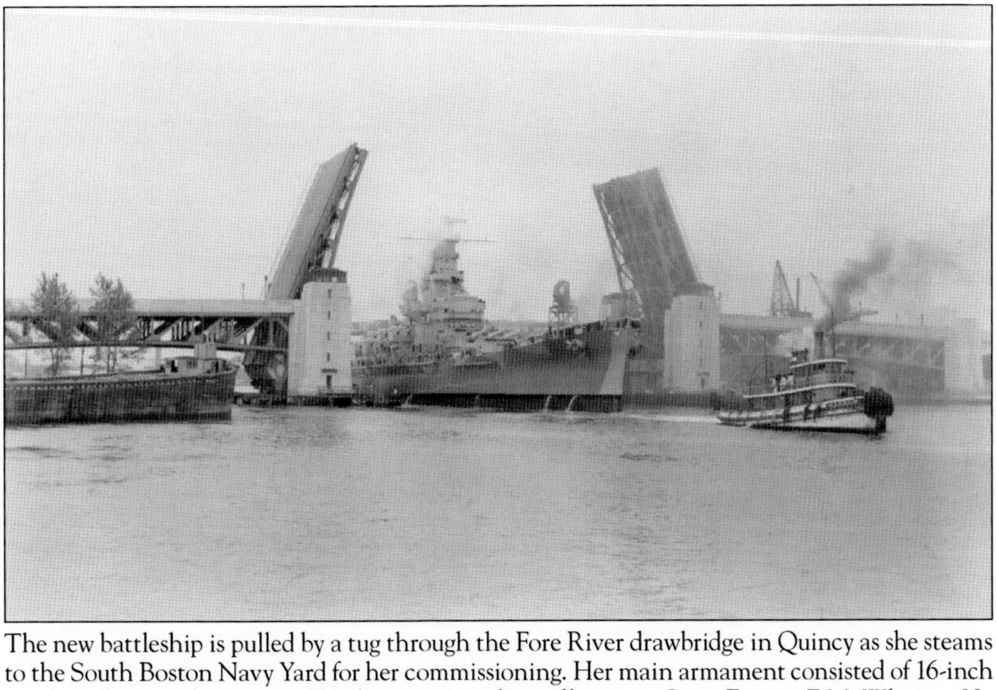

The new battleship is pulled by a tug through the Fore River drawbridge in Quincy as she steams to the South Boston Navy Yard for her commissioning. Her main armament consisted of 16-inch gun barrels in triple mounts. Her first commanding officer was Capt. Francis E.M. Whiting. He was assisted by a crew of over 2,000 sailors and Marines.

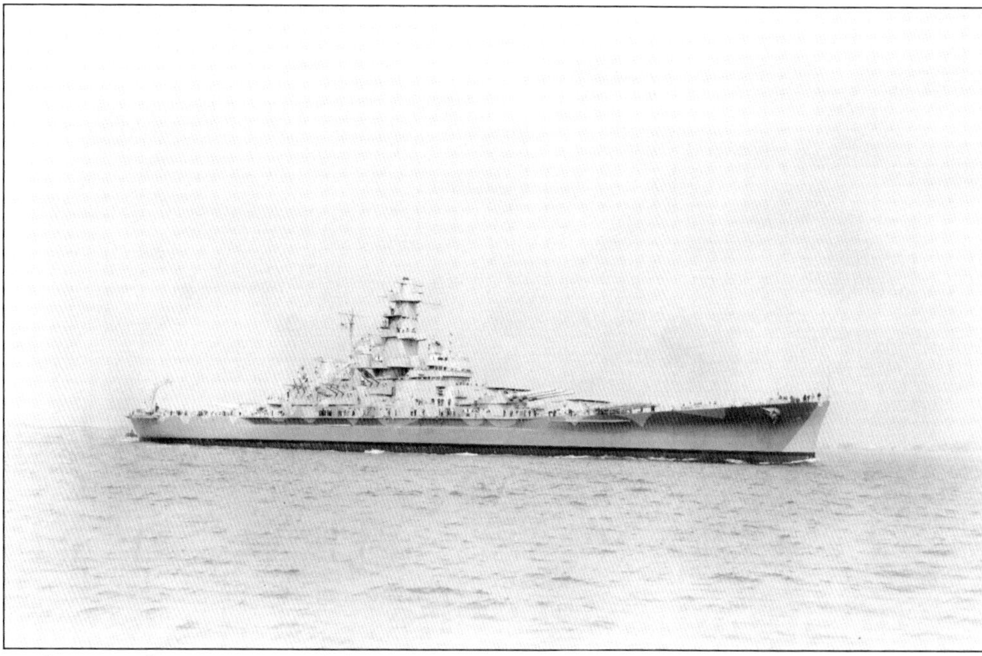

As the *Massachusetts* approached the inner harbor, tugs had to open the submarine nets, as U-boats were operating off the East Coast. By 11:30 a.m., she was docked at the Navy Yard in South Boston, where the commandant of the First Naval District, Rear Adm. W. Tarrant, accepted the ship for the Navy from the general manager of the Fore River Shipyard.

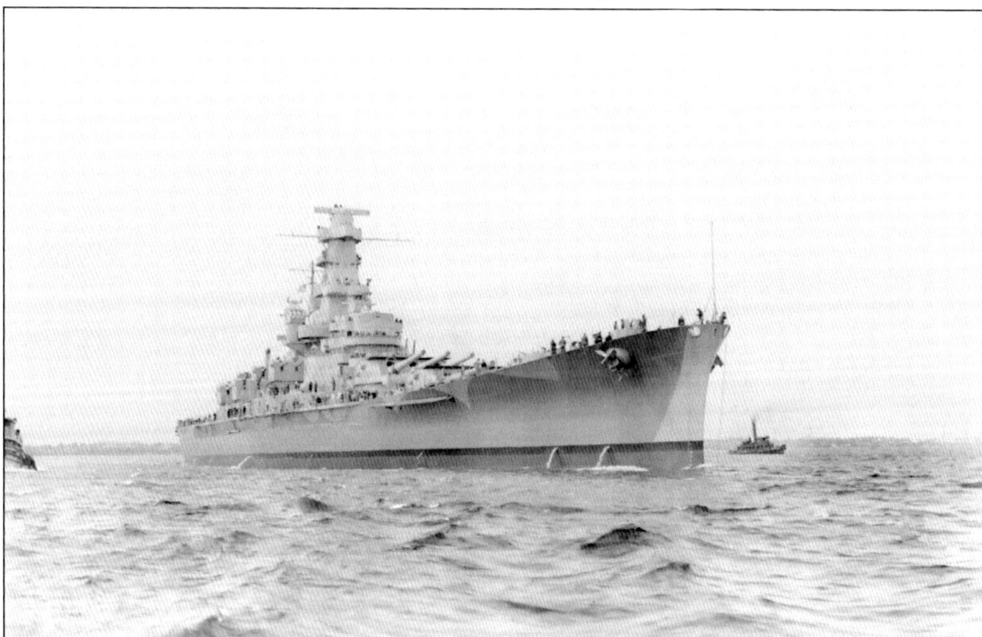

A brief commissioning ceremony commenced, and speeches were made by former secretary of the Navy Charles Francis Adams and the governor of Massachusetts, Leverett E. Saltonstall. The event was carried out without publicity, and there were no official guests or witnesses. The next day Secretary of the Navy Frank Knox visited the ship and addressed the crew.

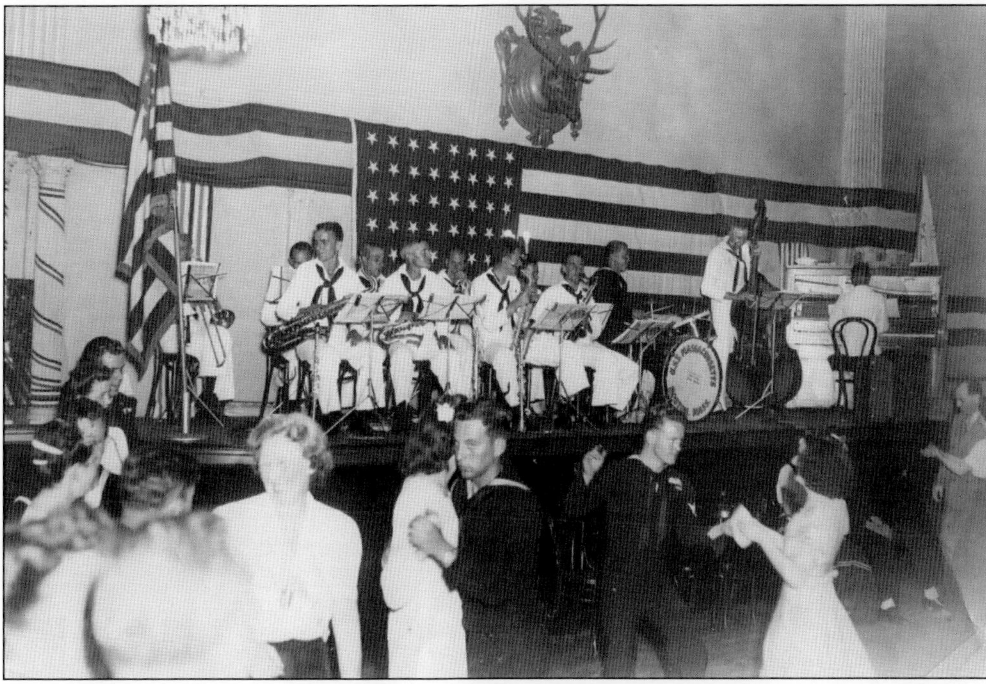

The ship's crew was a mixture of "old salts" and teenagers, with the majority never having been to sea before. Somehow, this group would have to be turned into a cohesive unit that would operate like a machine during times of life and death. Ship's dances were one way to build camaraderie and reduce stress.

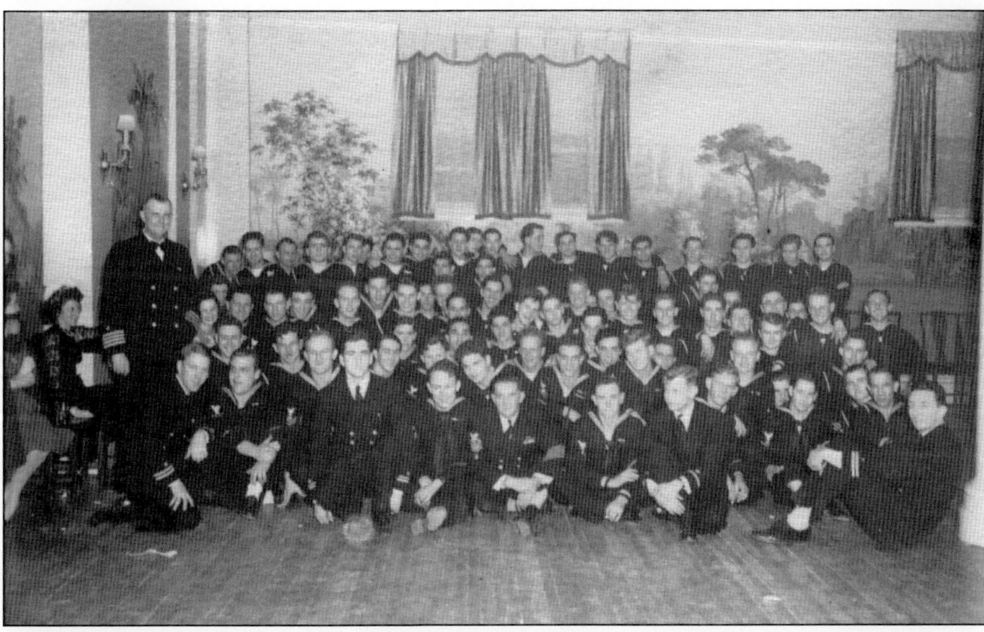

The 6th Division poses for a group photograph at the Beaconsfield Hotel in September 1942. The three-story, 200-room hotel was located at 1731 Beacon Street in Brookline, just a short distance from Boston College. The lavish residential hotel was built in 1902 by Henry M. Whitney, who also owned and operated the hotel in its early years.

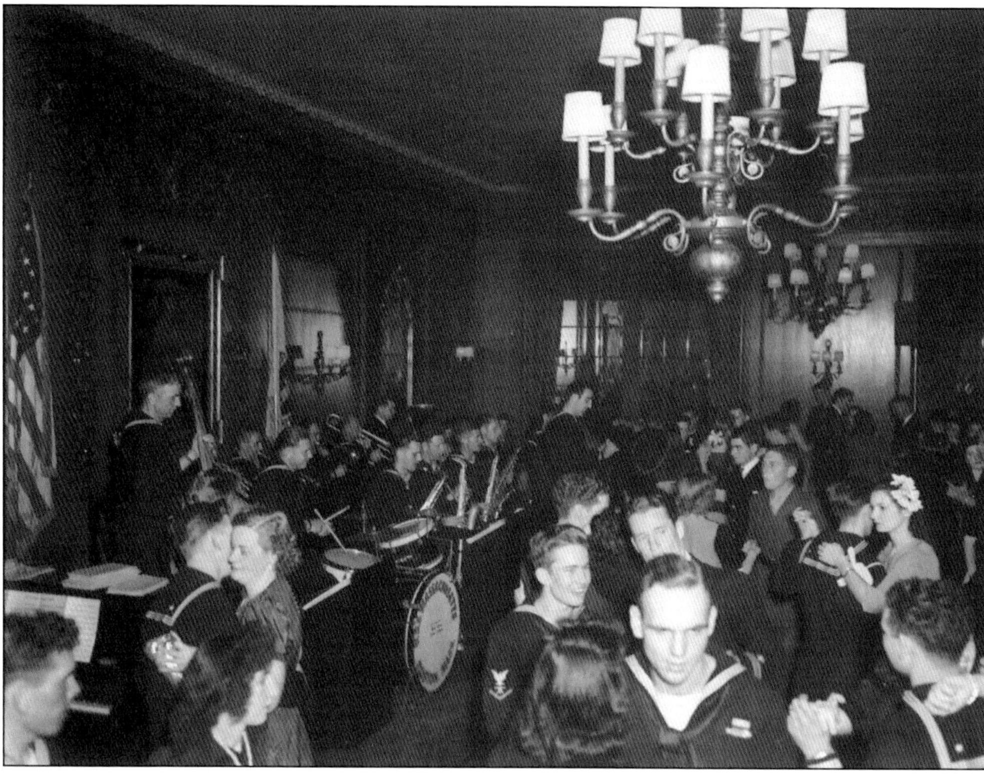

Sailors and their dates enjoyed one last dance at the Copley Hotel in Boston during October 1942. Soon, both ship and crew would sail to the war zone and an unknown fate. For months, the crew had drilled and trained for every eventuality, and they would soon be put to the ultimate test.

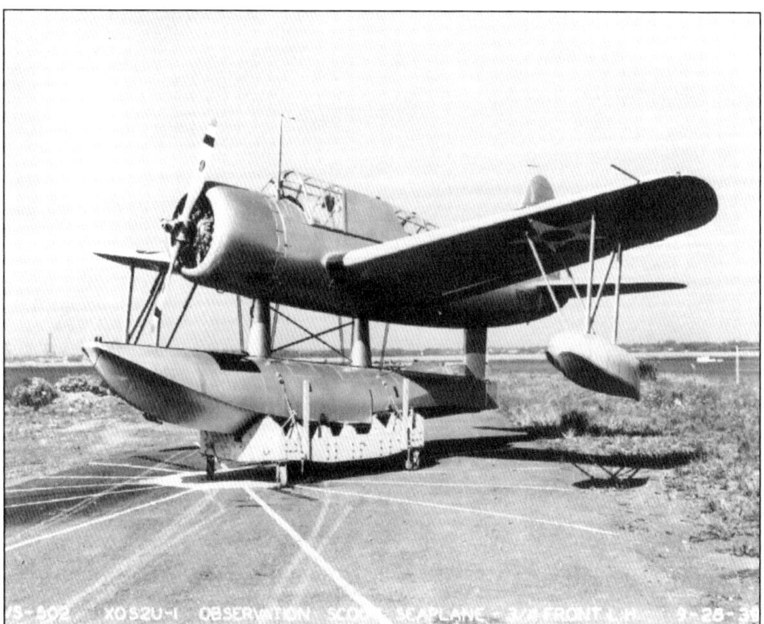

The *Massachusetts* could carry between two and three Vought OS2U Kingfisher observation floatplanes. The large central float, along with the port and starboard wing floats, provided the aircraft's buoyancy. These planes were launched from catapults from the stern of Big Mamie and were recovered by crane. The Kingfisher crew included a pilot and a radioman.

This aft-facing photograph offers an excellent view of Big Mamie's port Kingfisher floatplane. The Kingfisher was used for various tasks, such as searching in advance of the ship for the enemy fleet. When the battleship opened up with her 16-inch guns, the Kingfisher could radio adjustments to the gunners. It was also used to rescue downed pilots who had parachuted into the ocean.

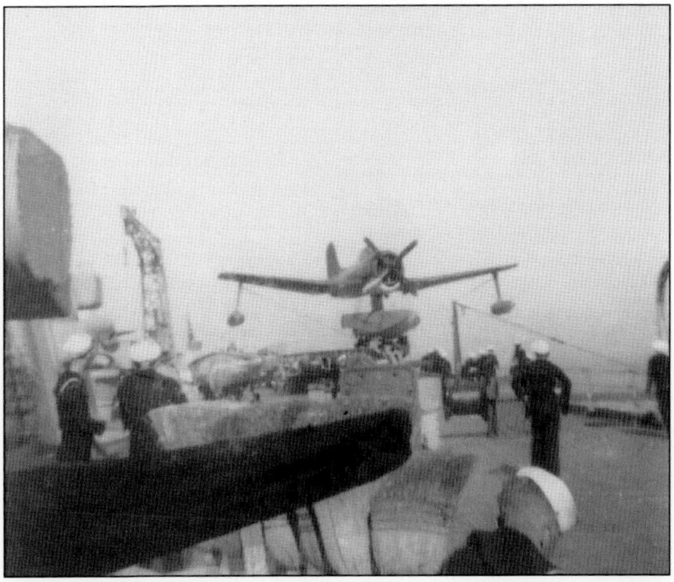

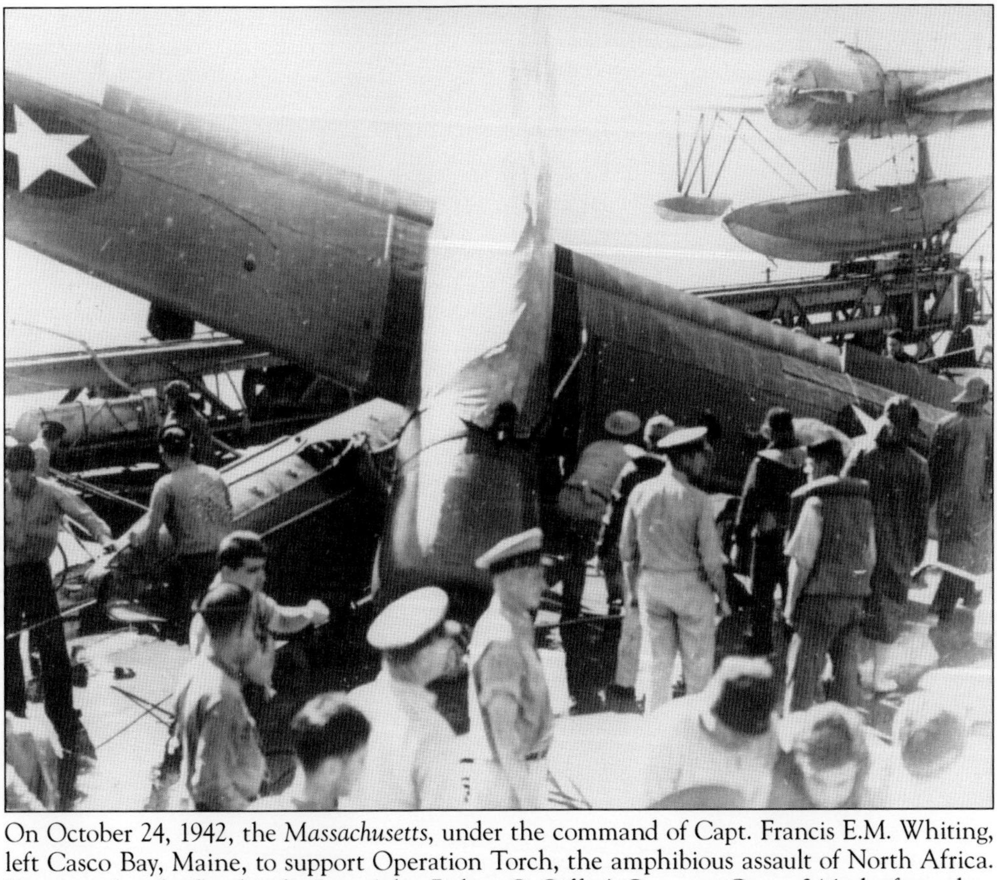

On October 24, 1942, the *Massachusetts*, under the command of Capt. Francis E.M. Whiting, left Casco Bay, Maine, to support Operation Torch, the amphibious assault of North Africa. Designated as the flagship for Rear Adm. Robert C. Giffen's Covering Group 34.1, she formed up with the Western Naval Task Force four days later. During the crossing, she encountered heavy weather, which damaged one of her planes.

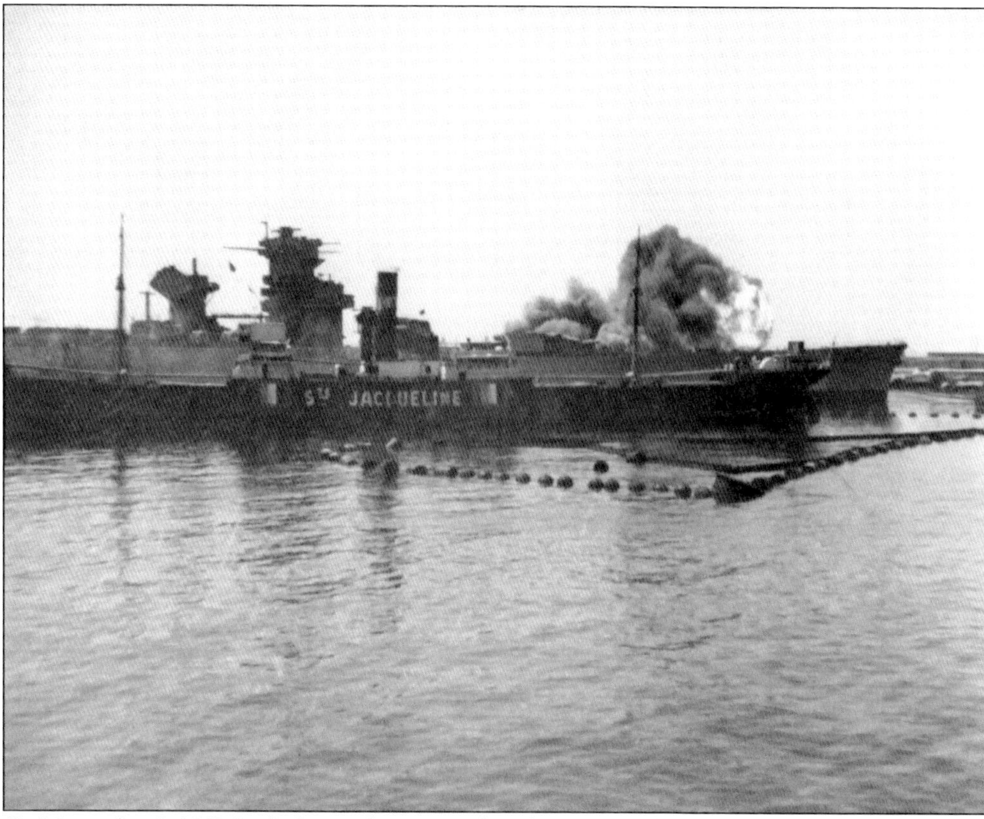

On November 8, 1942, both ship and crew got their first taste of battle. Off the city of Casablanca, the *Massachusetts* was ready to fight any of the Vichy French ships that dared to challenge the invasion. She came under enemy attack for the first time when the battleship *Jean Bart* opened fire on her at 7:02 a.m.

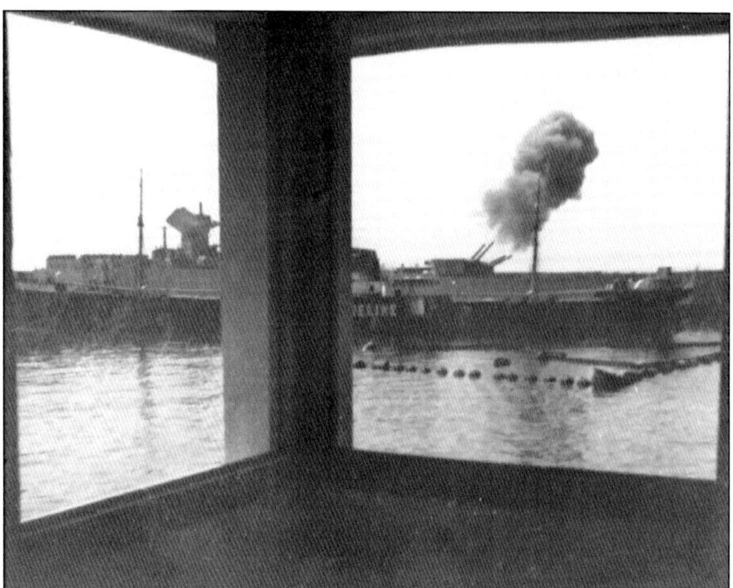

Fire and smoke belch from the forward turret of the *Jean Bart* as she takes the *Massachusetts* under fire. At 7:04 a.m., Big Mamie's 16-inch guns fired in anger for the first time. It is believed that the shells that left her guns on that November morning were the first 16-inch shells to be fired at the enemy in World War II.

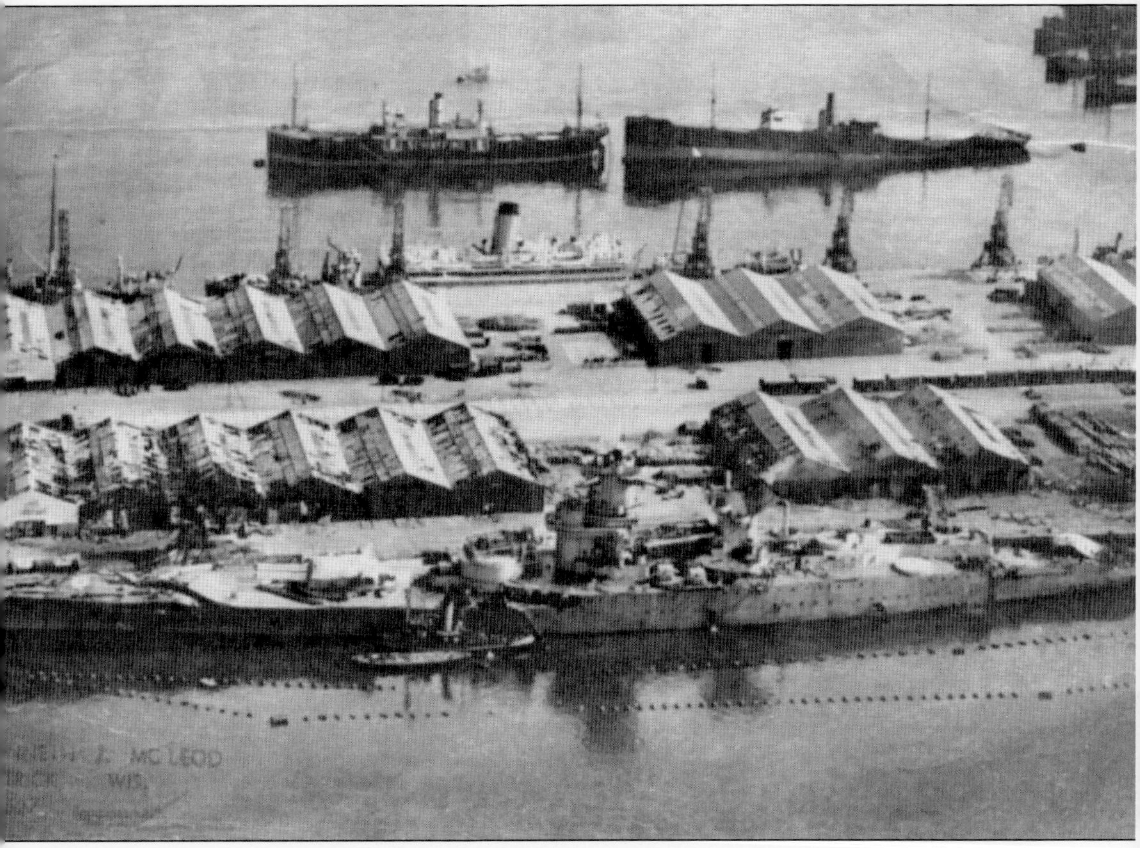

Although she had the help of French fishing trawlers spotting for her, the *Jean Bart's* shells missed the *Massachusetts* by 600 yards. This photograph, taken after the battle was over, shows the destructive firepower of Big Mamie's 16-inch guns. The *Jean Bart* is heavily damaged from bow to stern, and many surrounding buildings have been damaged.

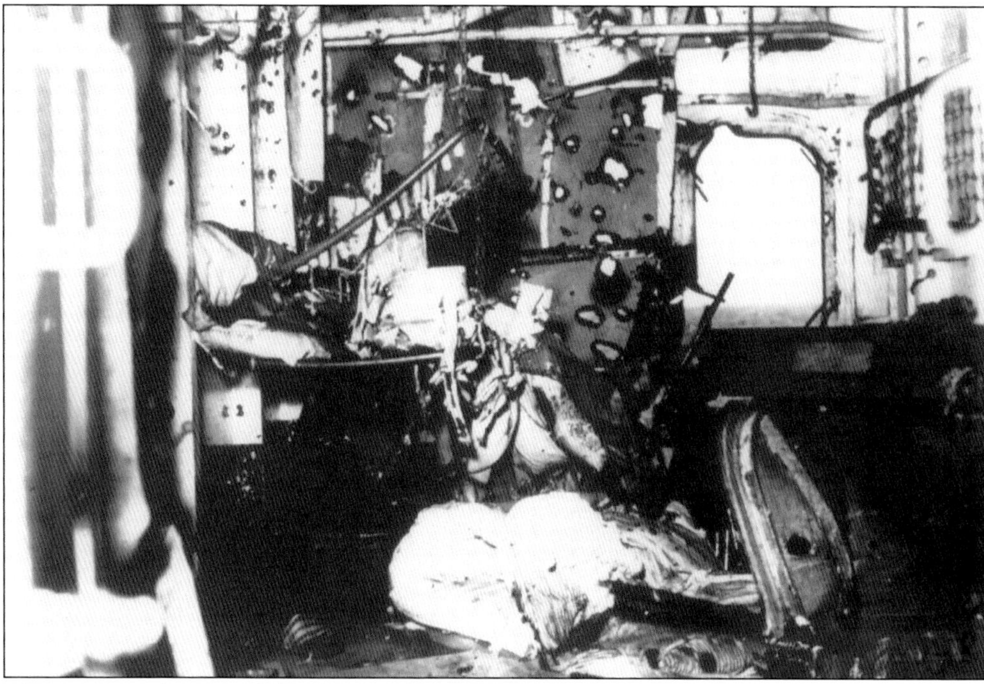

This is an inside view of the damage done to the *Jean Bart* by the shells of the *Massachusetts*. Big Mamie's gunners scored five hits and put the enemy vessel out of action within 16 minutes. Damage included a hole in the hull beneath the waterline, a wrecked after control station, and a jammed forward turret.

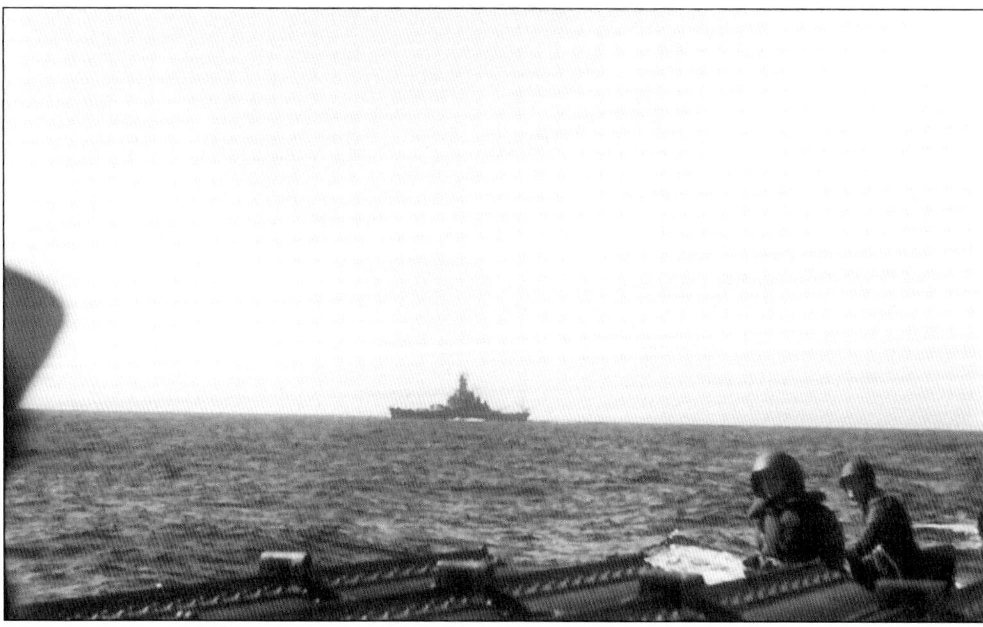

This photograph, taken from the destroyer *Mayrant* (DD-402), shows the *Massachusetts* in the distance on that historic morning. Shortly after 10:00 a.m., four torpedoes from an enemy submarine were fired at Mighty Mamie from under 1,000 yards. It was a close call, as the fourth torpedo streaked past her starboard side a mere 15 feet away.

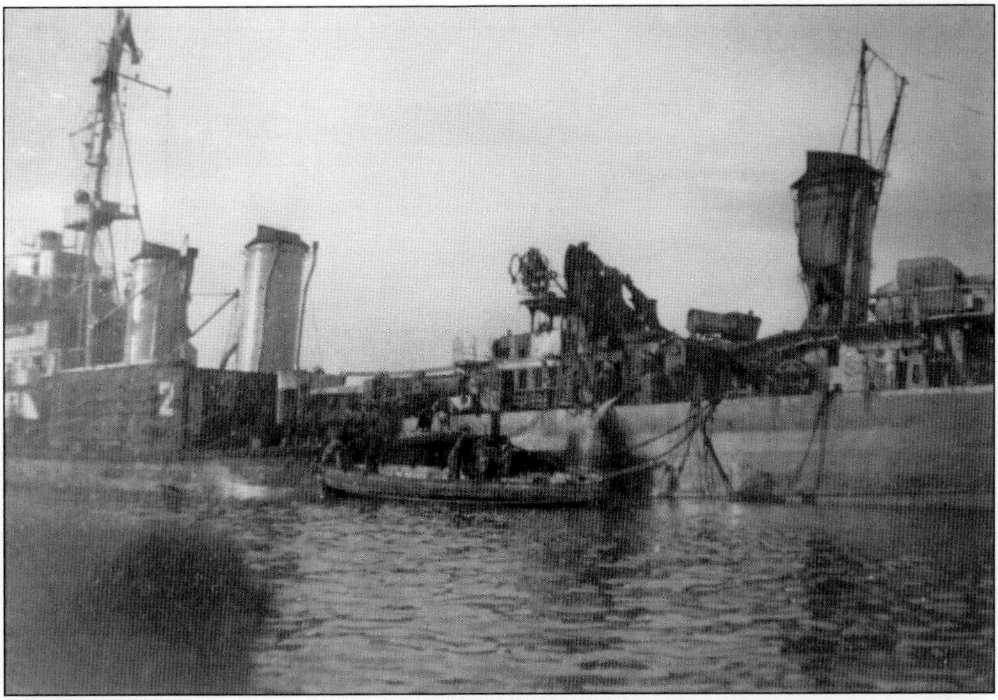

Big Mamie was credited with the destruction of the *Jean Bart* and the sinking of two destroyers. She also silenced shore batteries and inflicted significant damage on ships like the one pictured here. The Vichy French forces surrendered on November 11, and the next day, the *Massachusetts* set sail for the States.

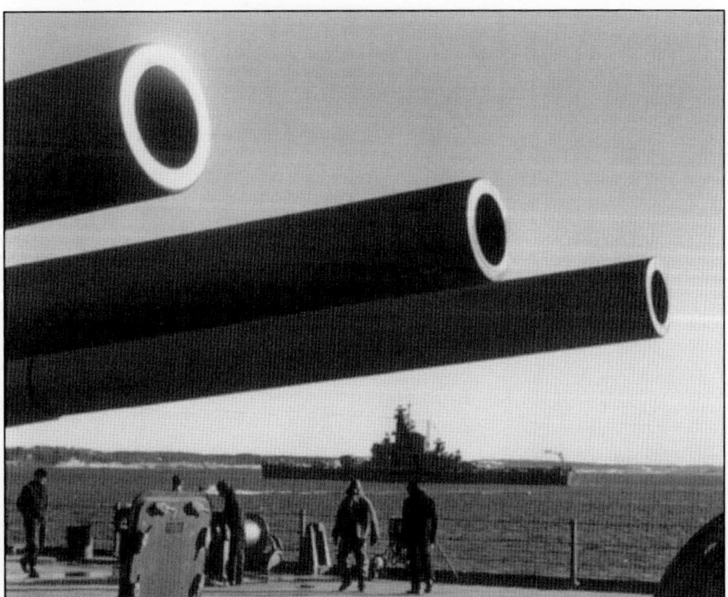

The *Massachusetts* made stops at Norfolk and Boston before heading to Portland, Maine. For the next several months, the crew constantly trained to improve its fighting efficiency. A sailor aboard one of her sister ships, the USS *Alabama* (BB-60), took this photograph of the *Massachusetts* moored in Casco Bay, Maine, in January 1943. (Author's collection.)

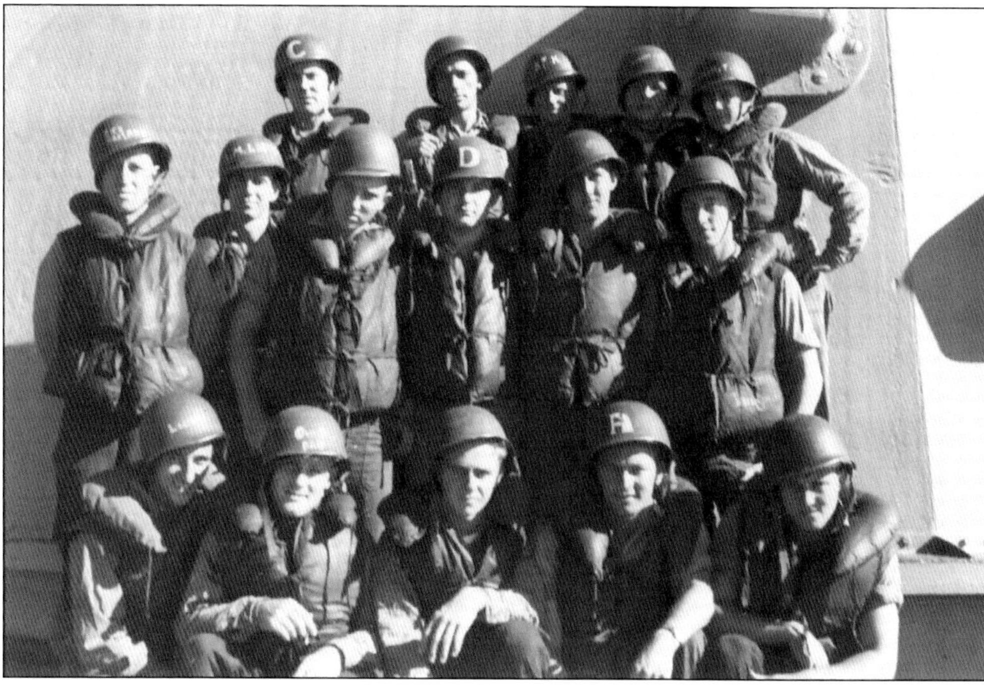

On February 6, 1943, the battle-tested *Massachusetts*, now under the command of Capt. Robert O. Glover, left Portland for service in the Pacific theater. Sailing as part of the fast carrier task forces, she helped attack the Japanese in the Solomon and Gilbert Islands. Here, one of her 40-millimeter gun crews poses wearing their general quarters steel helmets and life jackets.

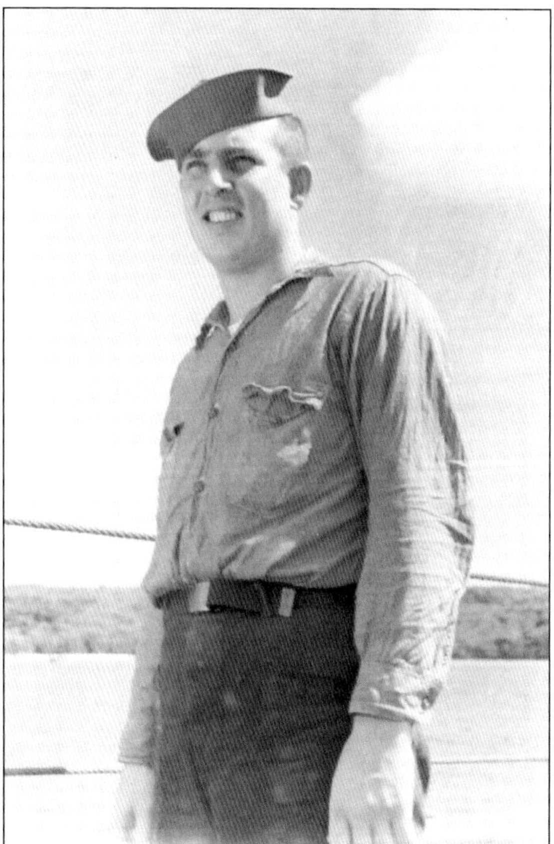

Donald Beer, born and raised in Ohio, enlisted in the Navy at the age of 21 on October 26, 1941. After completing boot camp, he was assigned to the *Massachusetts* while she was being built in Quincy. He served aboard Big Mamie until his discharge from the Navy in September 1945. (Courtesy of Joe Hesson.)

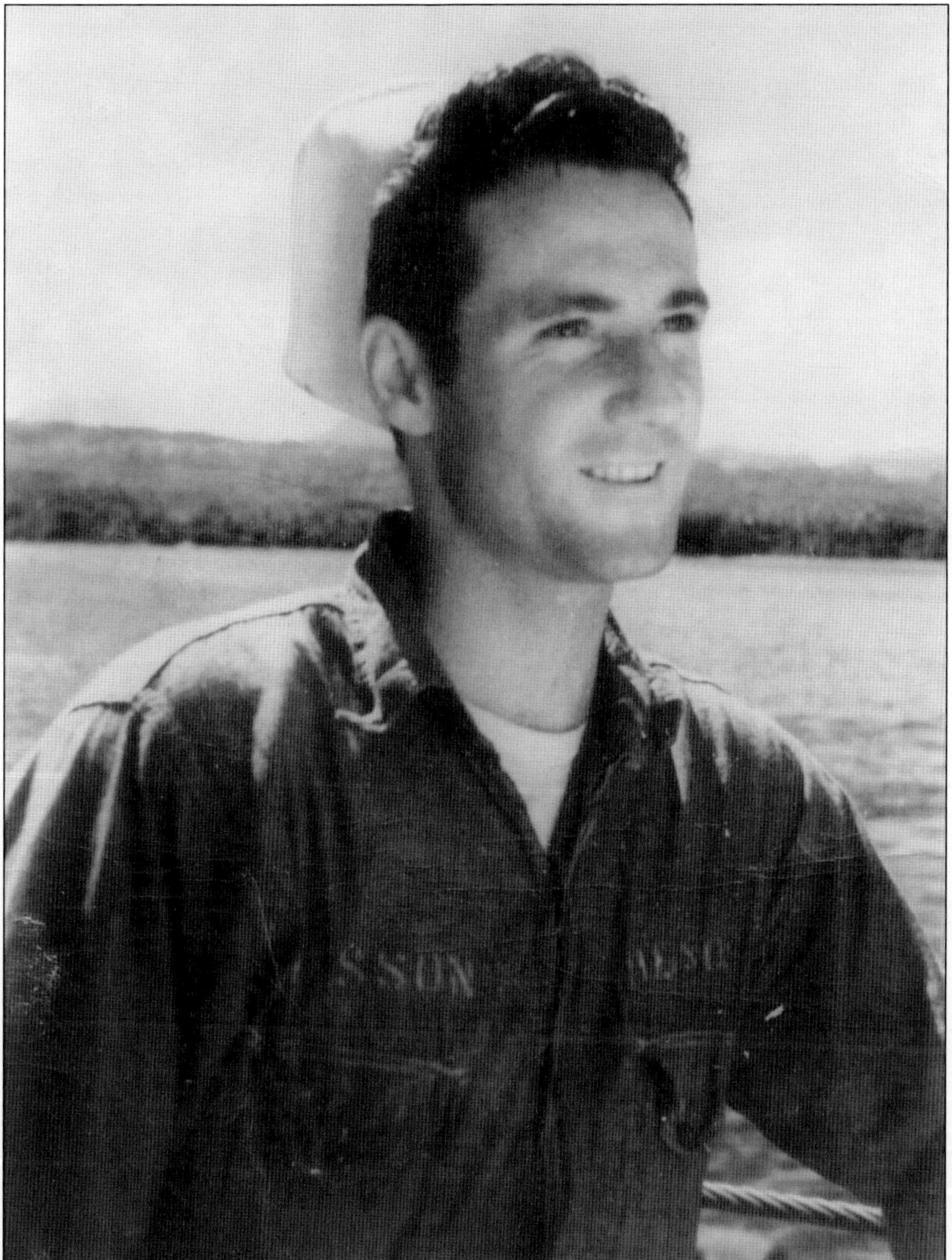

After hearing of the destruction at Pearl Harbor, James Hesson immediately enlisted in the Navy. An original plank owner, he spent his entire naval service on the *Massachusetts*. A member of the 6th Division, he was a gunner's mate for one of the 5-inch, 38-caliber guns. Often recounted over the years is Hesson's at-bat against future hall of fame pitcher Bob Feller in an inter-ship ballgame between Big Mamie and the "Bama," the nickname of one of her sister ships, the USS *Alabama* (BB-60). Rapid Robert threw three pitches, too fast to be seen, for strikes, but Hesson always maintained that the last one sounded low and away. (Courtesy of Joe Hesson.)

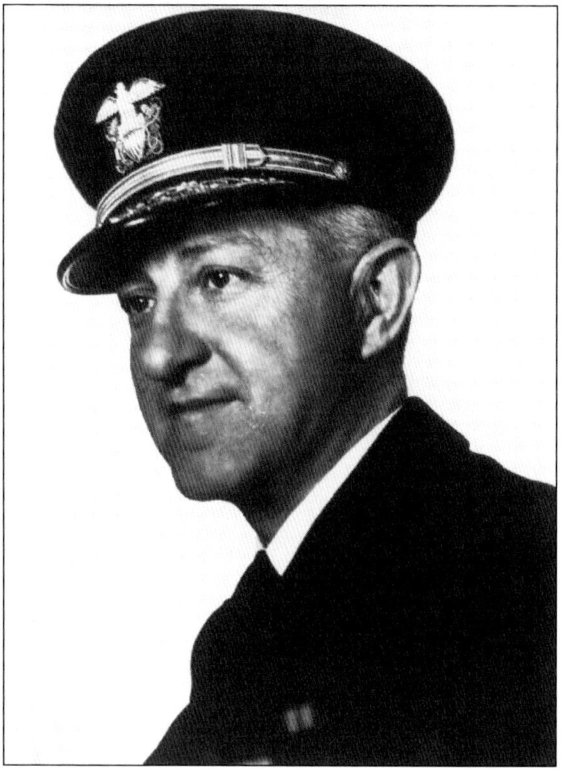

Capt. Theodore D. Ruddock, Big Mamie's third commanding officer, took over on September 27, 1943. A 1913 Naval Academy graduate, he rose steadily through the ranks and became an expert on ordnance. In 1944, he was promoted to commander of Battle Division 4. He would eventually retire from the Navy in 1951 with the rank of vice admiral.

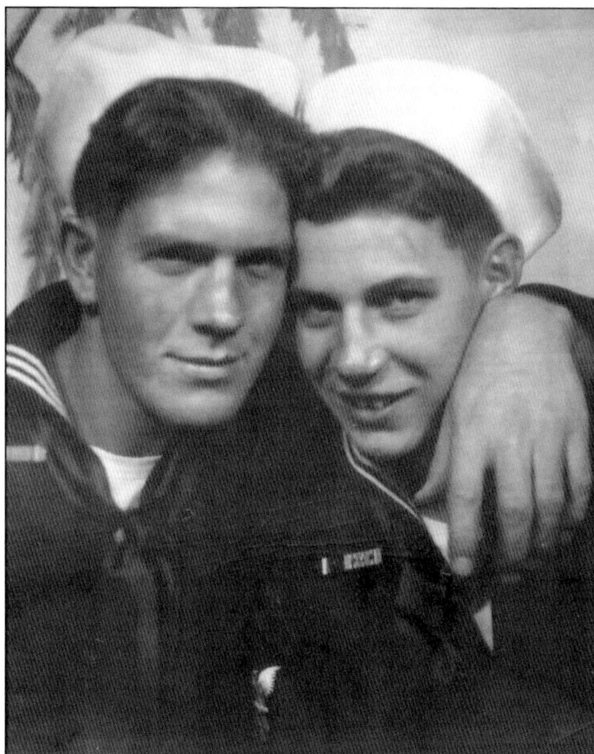

Thomas Howard (left) and Harry Jacobsen met in boot camp and became good friends at the Farragut Naval Training Station in Idaho, which at the time was the second-largest naval training station in the country. They reported aboard ship in 1943, and both served as water tenders. Their duties included standing watches in the fire room when underway, and maintaining, repairing, and overhauling the boiler system. They remain great friends to this day. (Courtesy of Thomas Howard.)

"Mighty Massy"

The Ship

Keel Laid . . . . 20 July 1939
Launching . . . . 23 Sept. 1941
Sponsor . . . Mrs. Charles Francis Adams
Commissioned . . . . 12 May 1942
Built . . Fore River Shipyard, Quincy, Mass.
Cost $76,885,750
Flagship of ComBatDiv Eight
— Rear Admiral Glenn Benson Davis

Captains

1. Capt. Francis E. M. Whiting, U.S.N.
2. Capt. Robert Ogden Glover, U.S.N.
3. Capt. Theodore D. Ruddock, U.S.N.
4. Capt. William W. Warlick, U.S.N.

Anniversary Committee

Capt. William W. Warlick, Commanding Officer.
Comdr. James A. McNally, Executive Officer.
Lieut. Samuel W. Densmore, Ath. and Rec. Off.
Chaplain William Leo McBlain.
Chaplain William P. Anderson.
Ensign Jonathan J. Crowder.
Ensign Llewellyn Harkness.
ChCarp. Herbert E. Ackerman.
APC Harold M. Boatright.
Rinebarger, C. H. CBgmstr.
Riding, J. P., EM3c.
Christy, J. V., Sea1c.

The Log

8 November 1942 . . . Casablanca

5 — 15 April 1943 . . . . ?
27 June — 25 July 1943 . . . . ?
30 August — 5 Sept. 1943 . . . . . . ?
19 November 1943 . . . . ?
20 — 25 November 1943 . . . . ?
25 — 26 November 1943 . . . . ?
8 December 1943 . . . . ?
29 January 1944 . . . . ?
30 January 1944 . . . . ?
31 January 1944 . . . . ?
16 — 17 February 1944 . . . . ?
22 February 1944 . . . . ?
22 March — 5 April 1944 . . . . ?
13 — 22 April 1944 . . . . ?
29 — 30 April 1944 . . . . ?
1 May 1944 . . . . ?

The Day

Sports

Tug of War; Rope Climbing; Carry-All; Five Legged Race; Pie Eating; Caterpillar; Dressing; Chinning the Egg; Medicine Ball Heave; Swimming; Wheelbarrow; Obstacle Race; Egg Race; Indian Wrestle.

Entertainment

Master of Ceremonies Matigzeck, J. F., Spec. 3c
Massachusetts Music Masters Norton, H. L. Chief Musician
Specialties: Siders, Meyers, Letourneau, Mittleton, Harms, Ippolito, Lamar, Remolino, Riggs, Cichocki, Hillion, Perry, DeLaney, Kenny, McMahon, Emerick, Carducci, Stone, Lore.
Ship's Quartet: Fosha, Perry, Springer, Hausman.

Boxing

"Tally-Hoers"		"Ack-Ackers"
Mauler Niedosik (170)	vs.	Snake Hips Smith (170)
Bird Legs Moton (120)	vs.	Slippery Meuse (120)
Killer Kowitz (175)	vs.	Slasher Haas (175)
Block Buster Batts (200)	vs.	Bad News Riding (200)
Pop Myers (150)	vs.	Slugger Williams (150)

Alternates: Letourneau (160), Nearing (150), Perry (120).
Judges: Ens. L. C. Philips, Ens. J. J. Crowder.
Seconds: Freese, Downing, Moreno, Caulkins.
Coach: Breitenbach, C. G., CGM.

Ship's Hymn

HAIL MASSACHUSETTS, GREAT THINE HONOR BE
SAIL ON TO VICTORY, MANNED BY MEN WHO MUST BE FREE
THE PROUDEST OF FINE SHIPS THAT EVER SAILED OVER THE SEA
WE KNOW THAT WHATEVER COMES YOU WILL BE THERE
TO TAKE US ON TO VICTORY.
STAUNCH MEN SAIL IN YOU, MEN WHO MAKE YOUR CREW
WE PUT OUR FAITH IN YOU, BRAVE MEN WITH A JOB TO DO
AS ONE MAN PLEDGE ALL THE CREW, OUR TASK SURELY WILL BE DONE
WE WILL STAND TOGETHER, FIGHT TOGETHER, WIN TOGETHER
'TIL THIS WAR IS WON.

Lyrics: Comdr. J. A. McNally
Music: Companero, E., Mus. 1-c

After shelling the island of Ponape on May 1, 1944, the *Massachusetts* headed to the Puget Sound Naval Yard in Bremerton, Washington, for an overhaul. While en route, she turned two years old on May 12. Her crew went to great lengths to commemorate the special day, as can be seen from this page of her birthday pamphlet. On July 15, she headed back to the war zone.

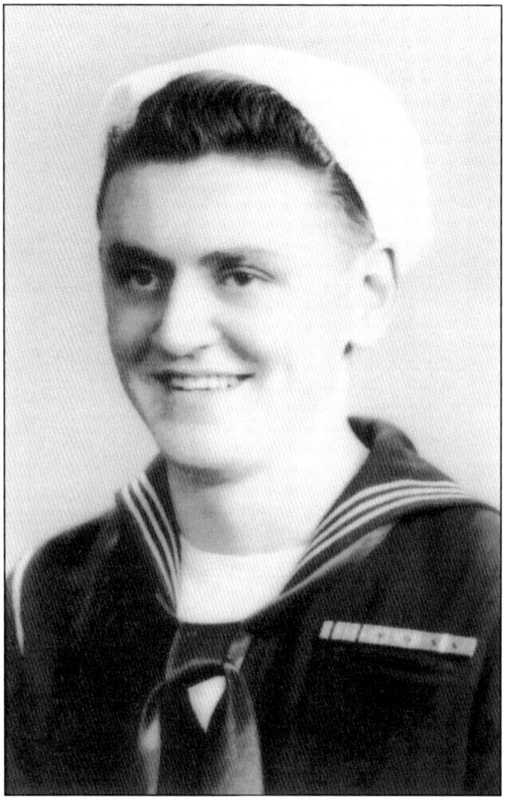

After learning it took two years to qualify as a Navy pilot, Bud Ruville enlisted on August 19, 1943. Since he was not yet 18 years of age, both of his parents had to sign his enlistment papers. After graduating from boot camp and serving three months of KP duty, he was sent to San Francisco, where he boarded a troop ship and left for Hawaii. (Courtesy of Tom Martin.)

Ruville reported aboard the *Massachusetts* in the Pacific at Eniwetok as she was returning to the combat zone after being overhauled in Washington State. Ruville, a signalman, was aboard Big Mamie until the end of the war. (Courtesy of Tom Martin.)

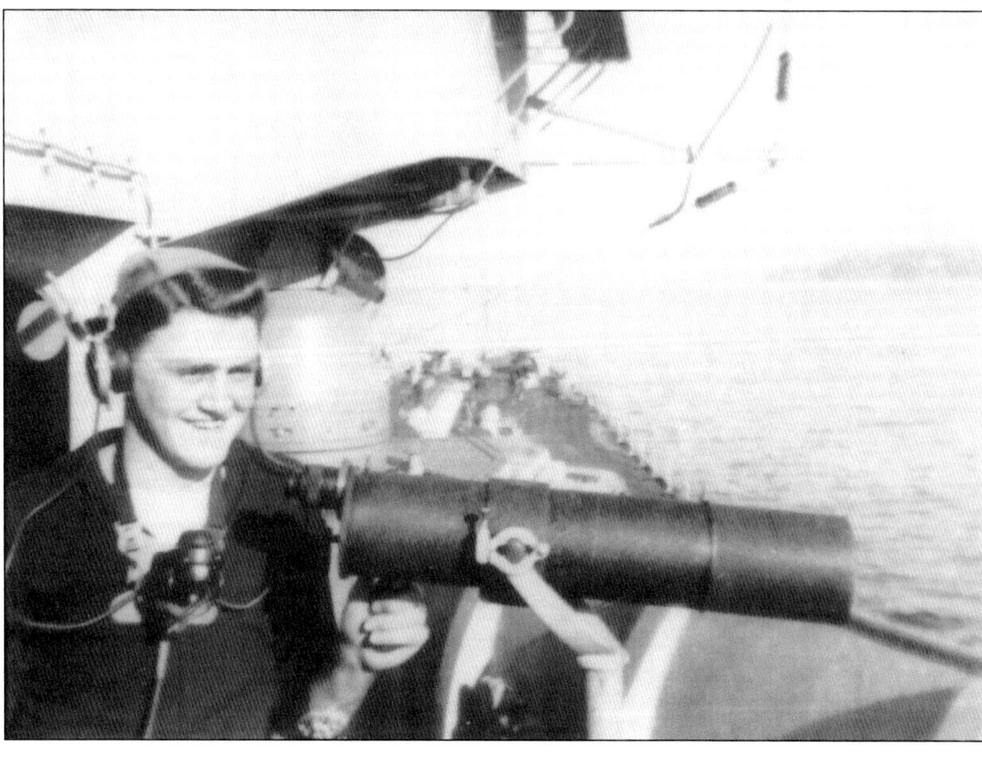

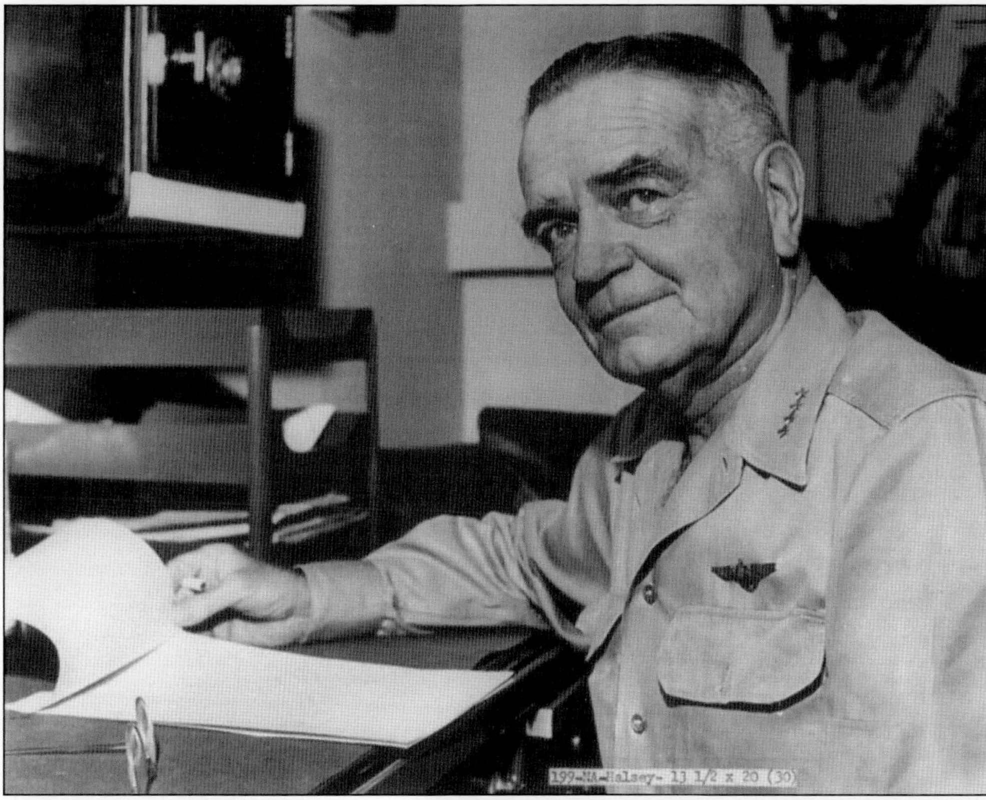

In late October 1944, Big Mamie found herself at one of the largest naval engagements in the history of the world, and one of the most decisive of the Pacific War, the Battle of Leyte Gulf. Under the overall command of Third Fleet's admiral, "Bull" Halsey, on the battleship *New Jersey*, the Americans attacked a large Japanese force off Cape Engano in the northern Philippines. Planes from the carriers the *Massachusetts* was escorting sank four enemy flattops.

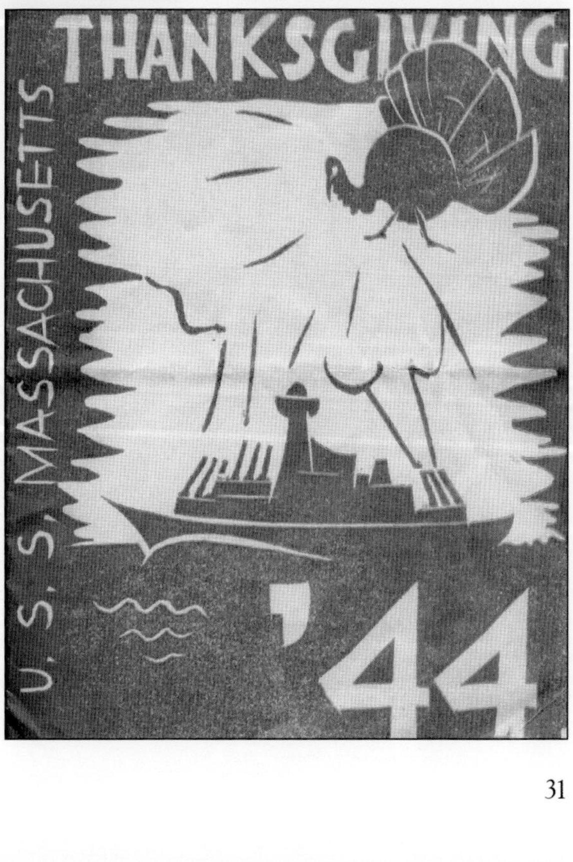

After the Battle of Leyte Gulf, the *Massachusetts* protected carrier task forces as they attacked enemy airfields throughout the Philippines. While heading to the advanced Navy base on Ulithi Atoll, the crew celebrated another Thanksgiving at war, grateful to still be alive. Almost 2,000 of their fellow Navy men had been killed at the Battle of Leyte Gulf.

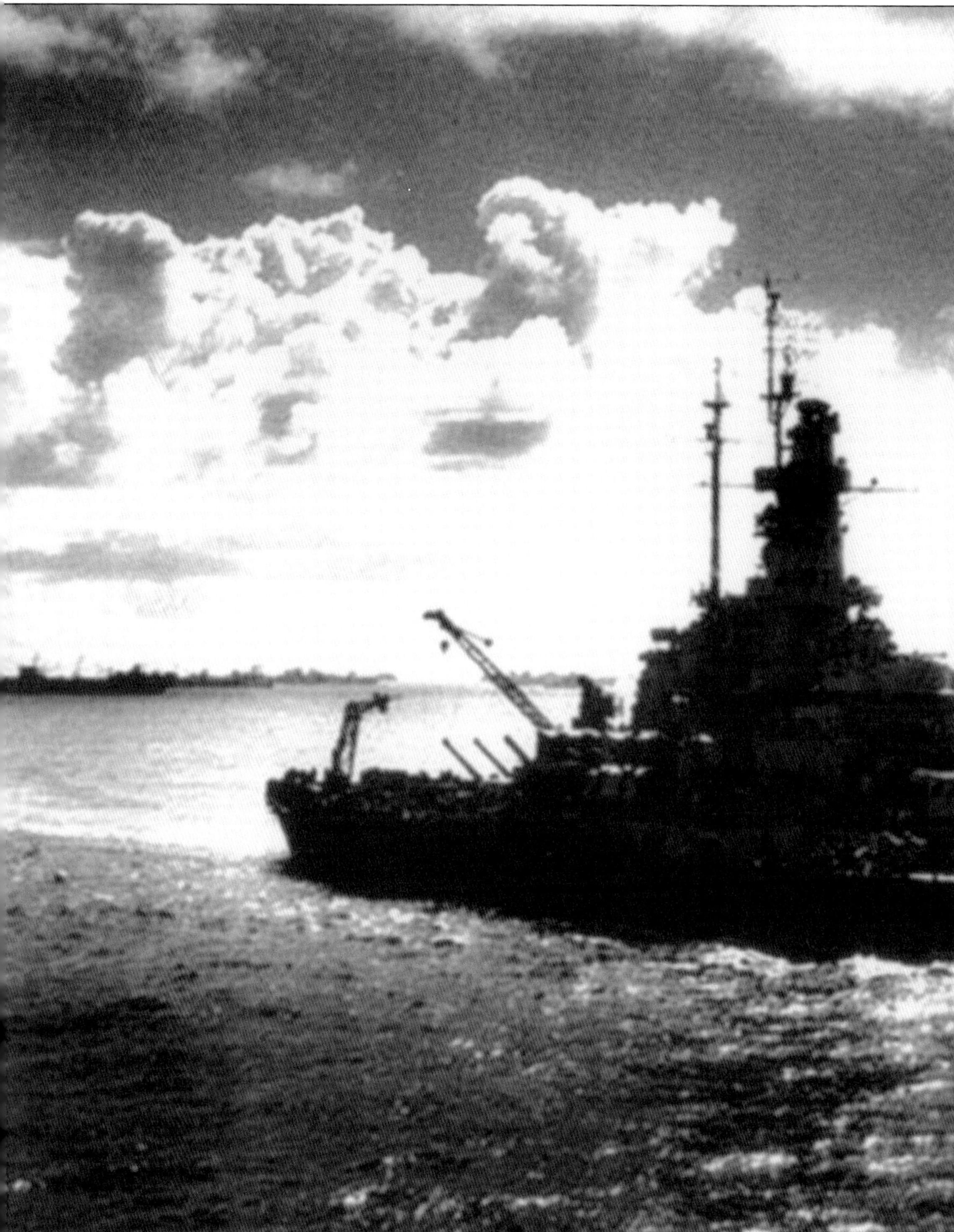

Big Mamie arrived at Ulithi Anchorage on November 24, 1944, during a break in operations in the Philippines. In the middle of December, she sailed through a typhoon with winds of over 120

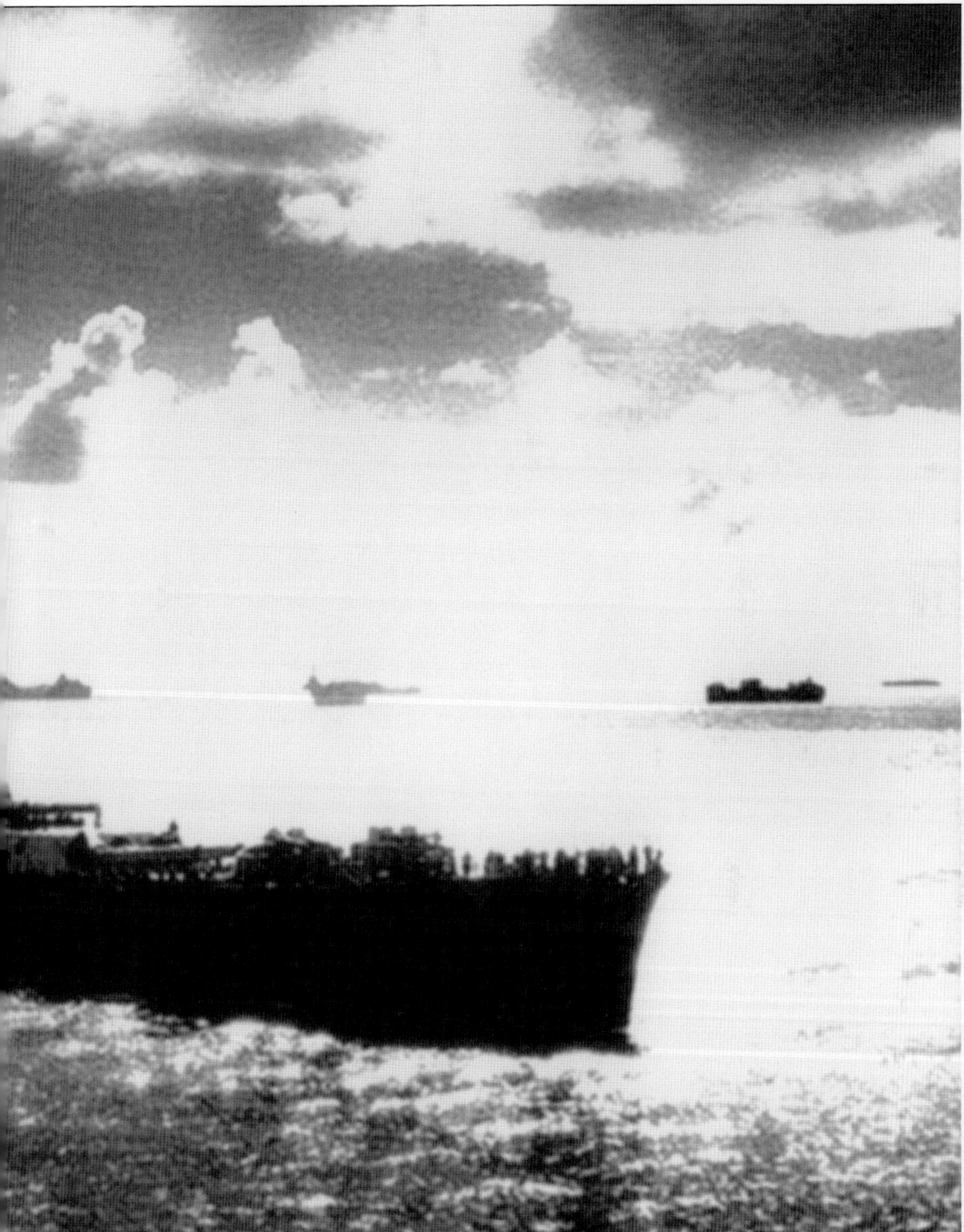

knots. Although the battleship sustained minor damage, three destroyers capsized with the loss of almost 800 sailors. (Author's collection.)

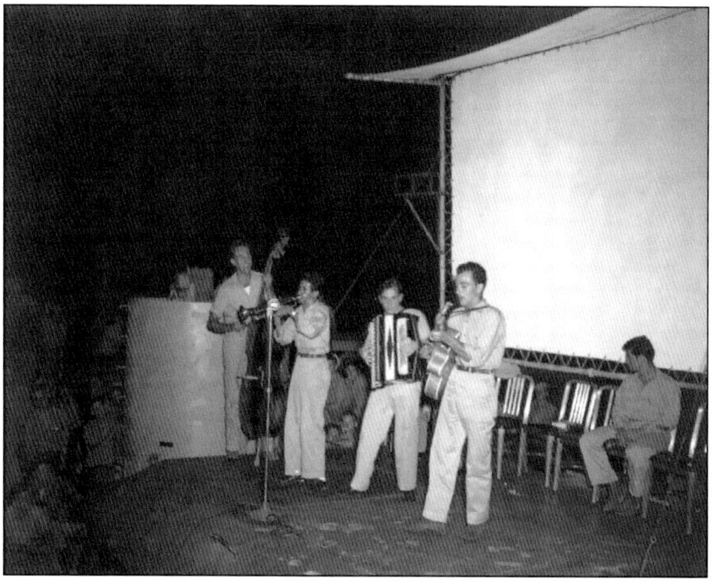

To help relieve the stress of combat and improve morale, the crew was treated to concerts, movies, and variety shows on the fantail. The mushroom ventilator shaft behind turret No. 3 served as the stage. At right in this photograph is the makeshift movie screen. Front-row seating is occupied by the captain and officers.

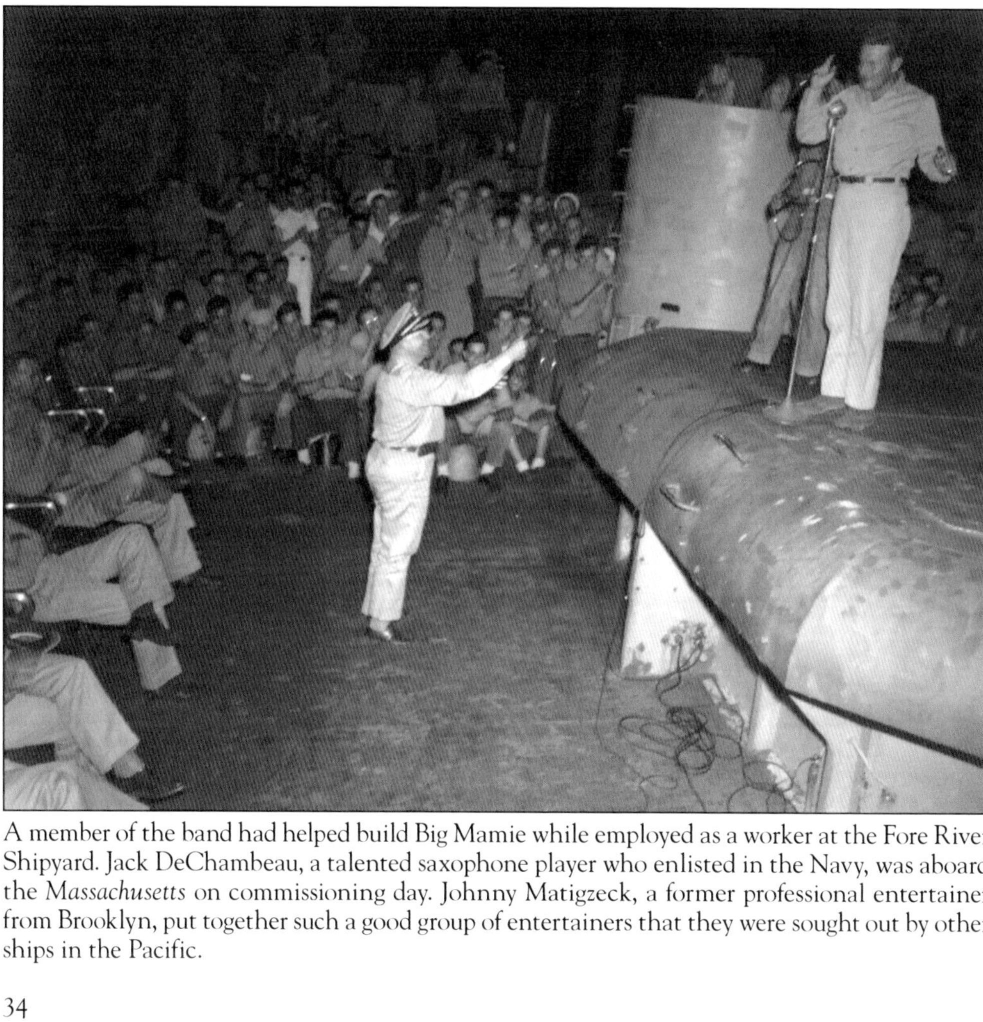

A member of the band had helped build Big Mamie while employed as a worker at the Fore River Shipyard. Jack DeChambeau, a talented saxophone player who enlisted in the Navy, was aboard the *Massachusetts* on commissioning day. Johnny Matigzeck, a former professional entertainer from Brooklyn, put together such a good group of entertainers that they were sought out by other ships in the Pacific.

Parker Burk enlisted on March 8, 1942, in Boston. He held the rate of seaman, second class when the *Massachusetts* was commissioned that May. He spent the entire war aboard BB-59 until he was transferred shortly after the Japanese surrendered. (Courtesy of Joe Hesson.)

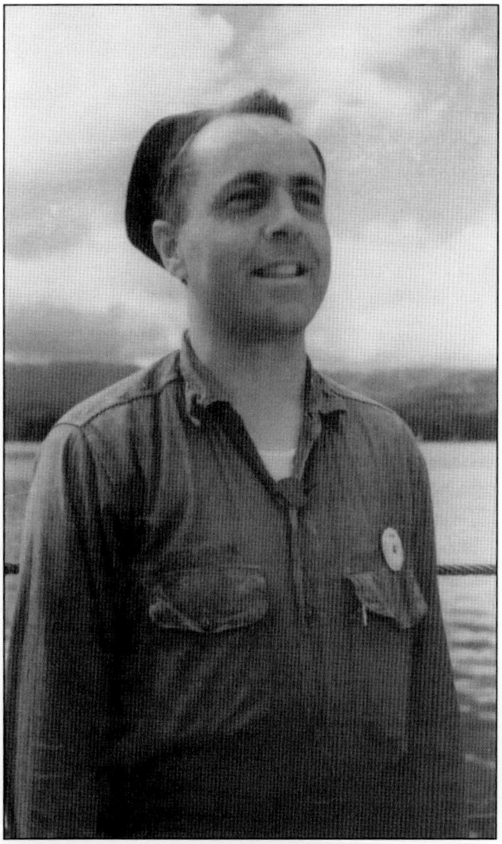

A priest conducts mass in the enlisted men's mess. Religious services, both Catholic and nondenominational, were held every Sunday. The Navy made it a point to meet the spiritual needs of its sailors. The chaplain's office produced the weekly *Bay Stater,* the official ship's newsletter, which included columns on the background of the crew, along with jokes and cartoons.

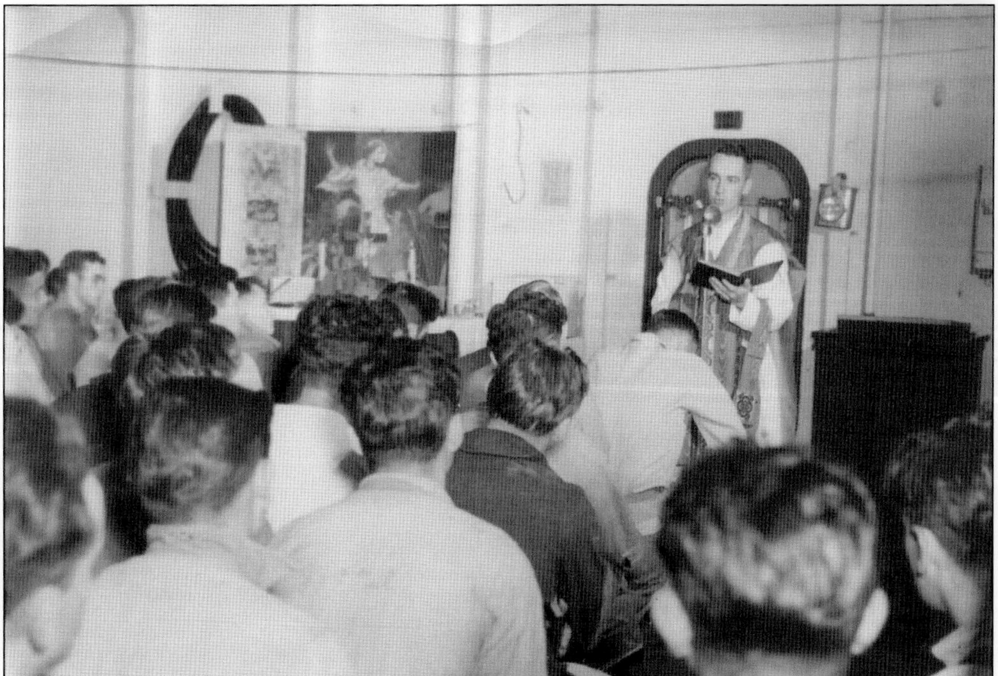

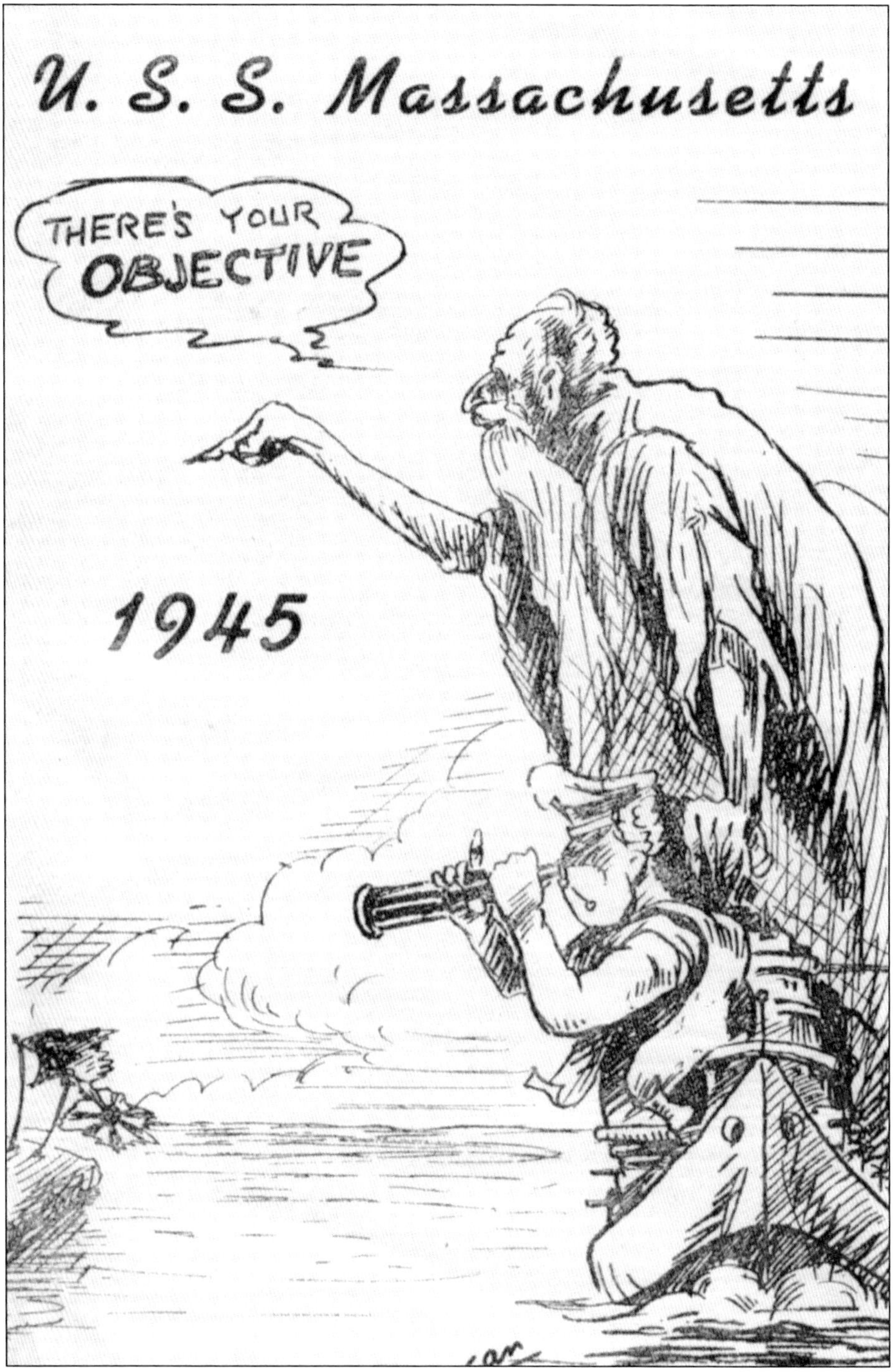

The New Year's Day Dinner of 1945 consisted of "Roast Young Tom Turkey" and all the fixings, along with pumpkin pie for dessert. Steaming with Task Force 38, Big Mamie smashed Japanese airpower in the Philippines and Formosa. In the middle of the month, the task force operated on the South China Sea and launched air strikes on shipping and airfields from Indo-China to Hong Kong.

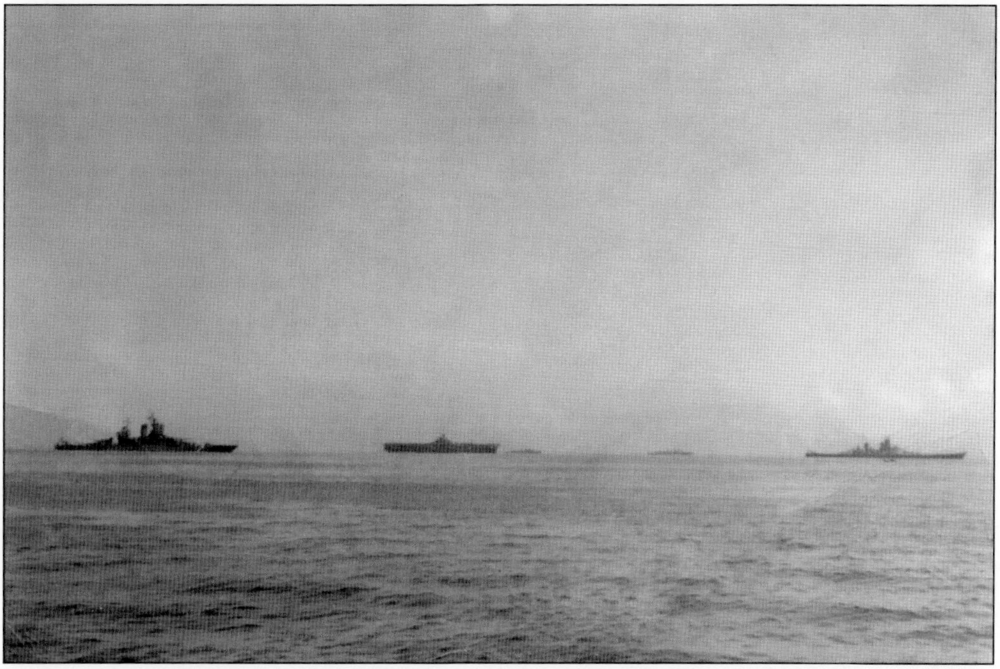

February was a very busy month for both ship and crew. Big Mamie's gunners fired salvo after salvo on Iwo Jima before the invasion began and protected the carriers by shooting down kamikazes before they crashed into the flattops. In addition, she sailed with a task force in the middle of the month for the first raid on Tokyo by carrier-based planes. (Author's collection.)

In late March, her big guns opened up on Okinawa prior to the invasion, and she continued to provide air cover against the daily kamikaze attacks. On May 2, 1945, Capt. William W. Warlick addressed the crew and presented citations to sailors. The three crew members on the right are, from left to right, ARM S.J. Krajeski, Lt. Alfred Cenedello Jr., and Lt. George A. Robinson.

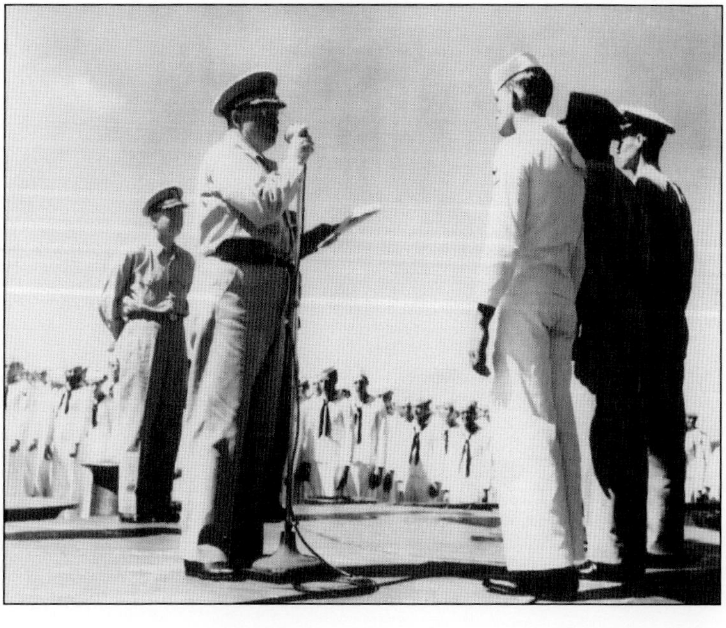

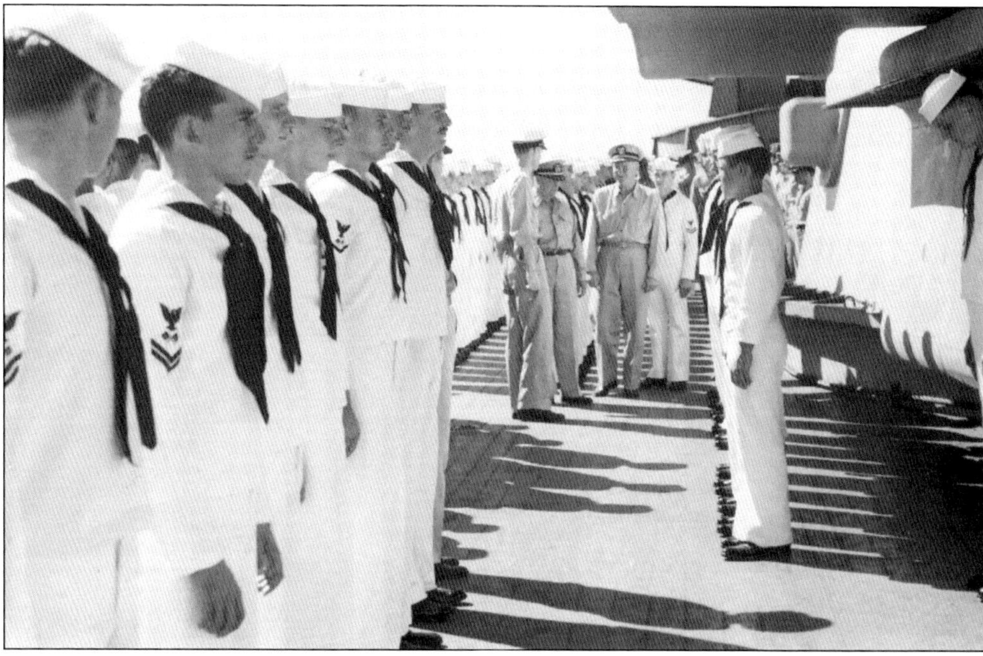

Capt. John R. Redman, the fifth commanding officer of Big Mamie, is seen here making his first inspection of ship and crew. Captain Redman was a Naval Academy graduate and served as the communications officer on the staff of the commander in chief, United States Pacific Fleet, Adm. Chester Nimitz, from October 1942 to March 1945.

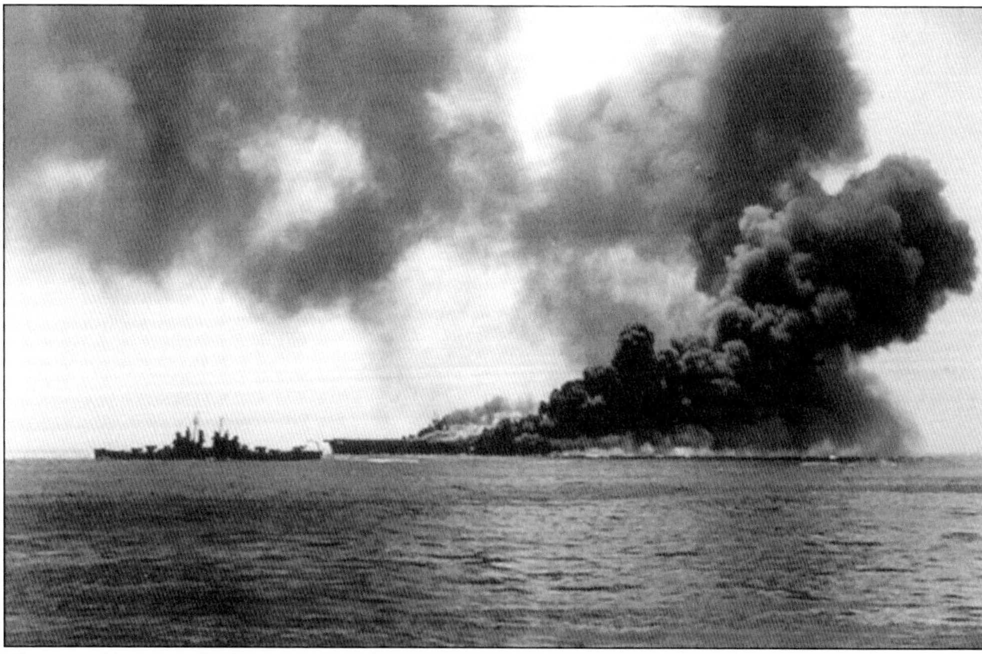

The naval battle off Okinawa proved to be the most costly naval campaign of the entire war. On the morning of May 11, 1945, the carrier USS *Bunker Hill* (CV-17) was hit by two kamikazes, with the loss of almost 400 of her crew. By the end of the operation, the Navy had lost over 30 vessels, almost 5,000 sailors had died, and over 4,000 men had been wounded. (Author's collection.)

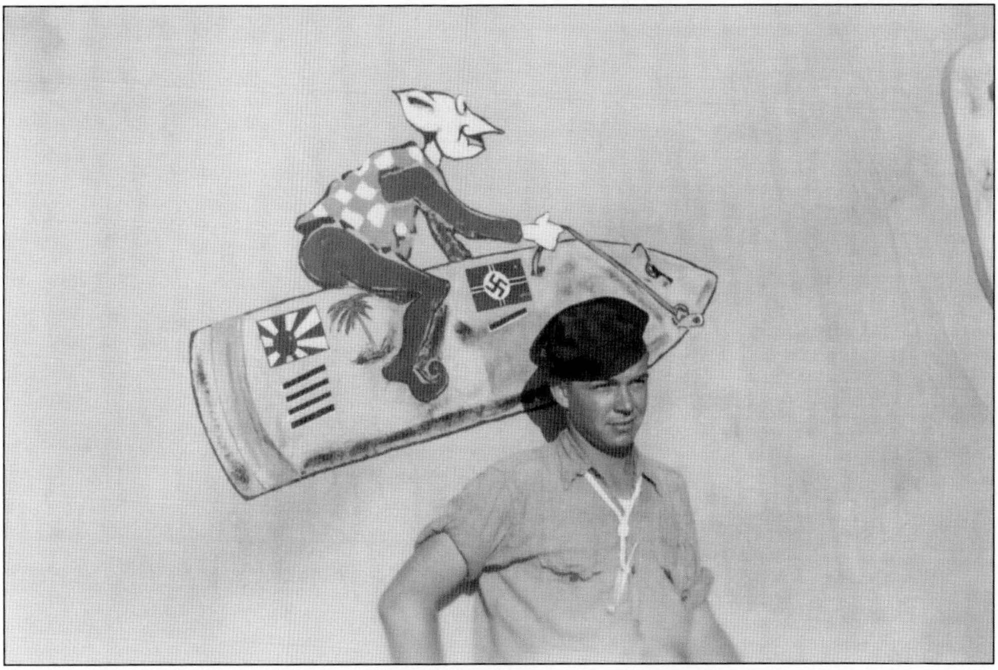

Boatswain's Mate Kenneth McLeod is pictured under the "goblin" on turret No. 1. On June 5, 1945, Big Mamie steamed through another typhoon that damaged 36 ships, but she suffered only minor damage. Although Big Mamie was scheduled to return to the States for another yearly overhaul, the Navy decided to keep her in the war until the Japanese finally gave up. On July 1, she steamed with Halsey's Third Fleet as carrier planes attacked Tokyo again.

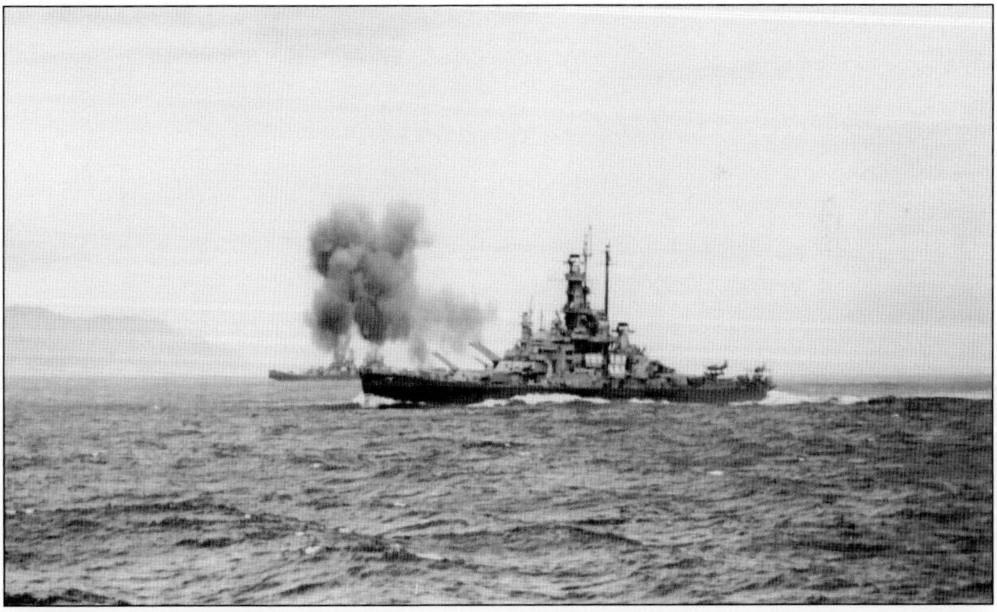

On July 14, the *South Dakota* (BB-57) fired the initial salvo of the first naval gunfire bombardment of the Japanese home islands. A photographer aboard the ship captured the *Indiana* (BB-58) firing a salvo at the Kaimaishi plant of the Japan Iron Company, 250 miles north of Tokyo. The superstructure of the *Massachusetts* is visible beyond the *Indiana*'s bridge. (Author's collection.)

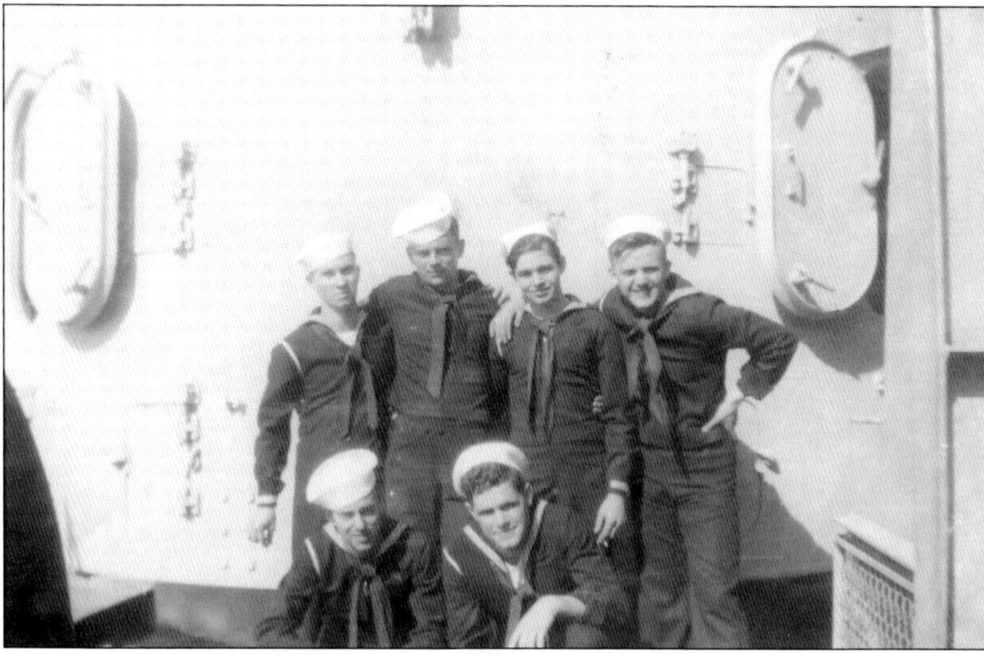

On July 29, the *Massachusetts* conducted a midnight bombardment of Hamamatsu, an industrial and railroad center. After destroying a factory that made aircraft propellers, Admiral Halsey sent a message to Big Mamie and fellow battleships, stating that their new nickname was the "Hamamatsu Hammer Club." On August 9, as the second atomic bomb was dropped on Nagasaki, Big Mamie returned to blast Honshu. It was here that, it is believed, the last 16-inch shell was fired in World War II. This photograph of unidentified sailors was taken in the last week of the war.

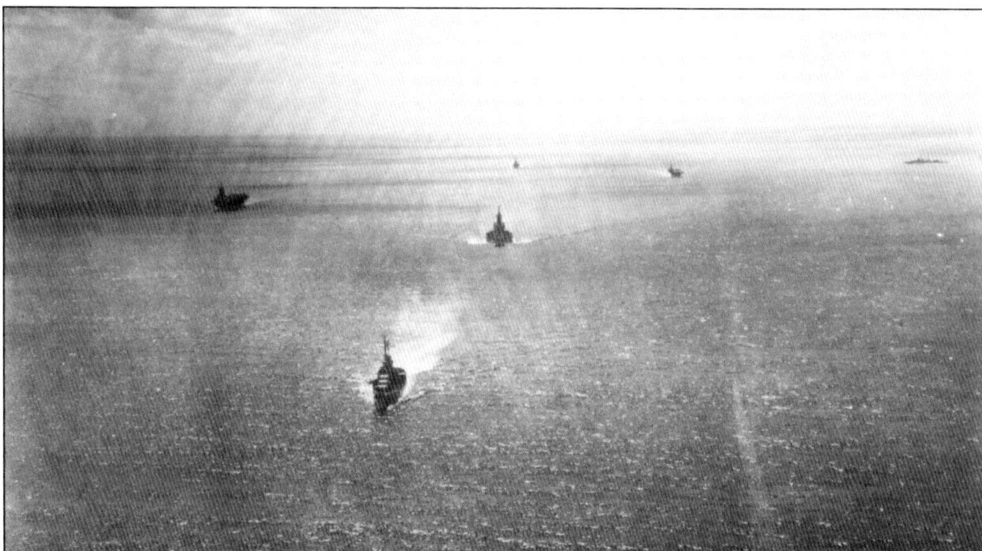

Soon after the Japanese officially surrendered in September 1945, Big Mamie steamed home. During the war, she logged over 225,000 nautical miles, sank or damaged five ships, shot down at least 18 Japanese planes, and her Kingfisher pilots saved the lives of seven aviators. Never losing a man, she received 11 Battle Stars, and it is believed that she fired both the first and last 16-inch shells in World War II.

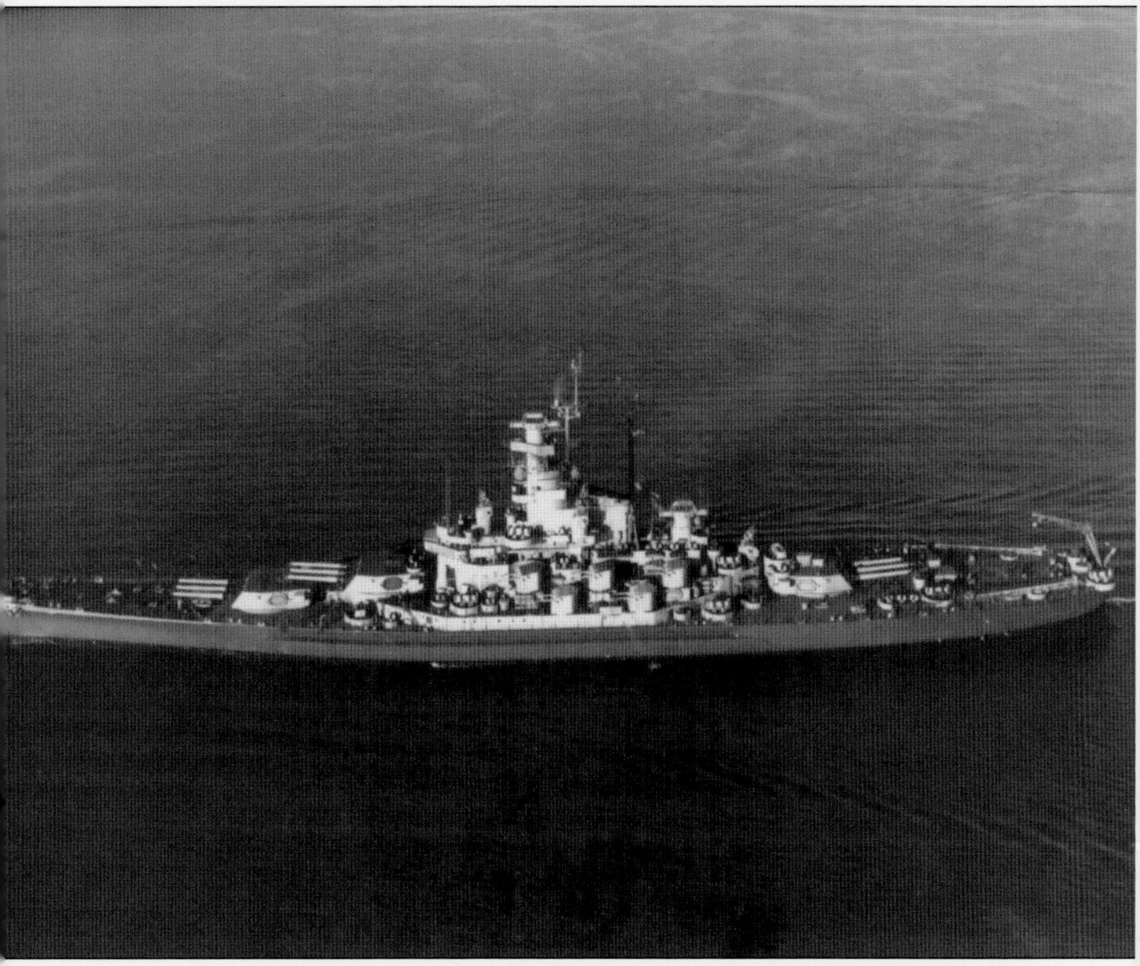

Big Mamie arrived at the Bremerton Navy Yard in Washington on September 13, 1945, where she was overhauled. On January 22, she conducted her post-refit trials in Puget Sound, and on the 28th, she steamed south for operations off California. On April 4, she left San Francisco and headed to Norfolk, Virginia, by way of the Panama Canal. (Courtesy of the US Naval Institute.)

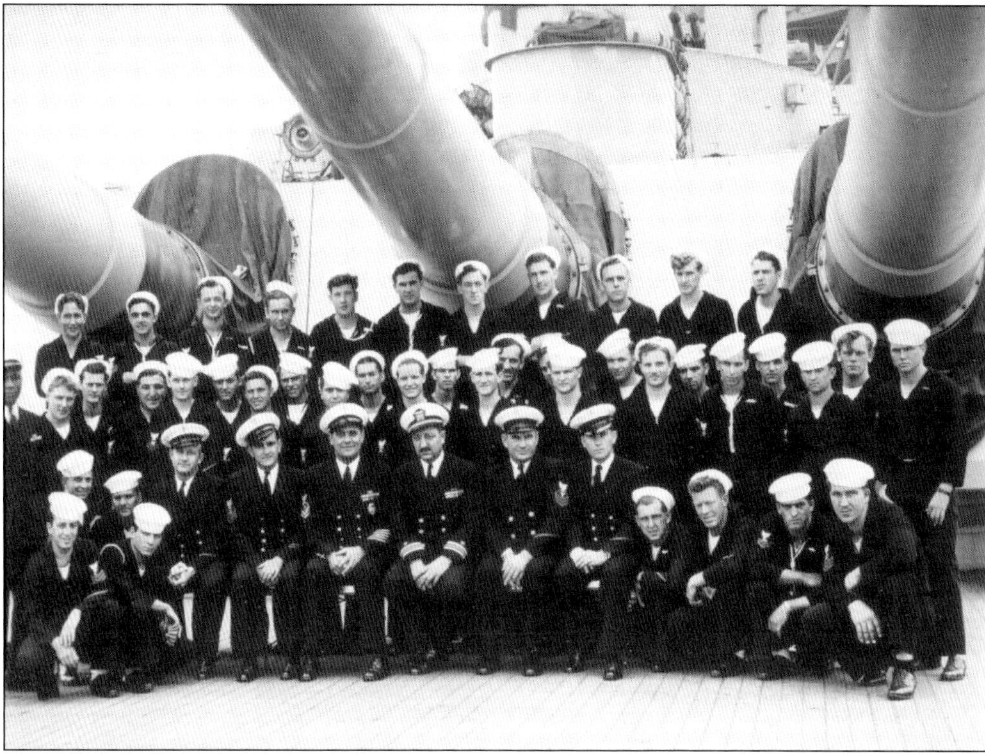

Arriving on April 22, her sailors manned the rails to render honors to Pres. Harry S. Truman, who was aboard the new aircraft carrier *Franklin D. Roosevelt* (CVB-42). Some of the sailors who had stood tall during her commissioning in May 1942 were still aboard, and in May 1946, they posed for one last photograph.

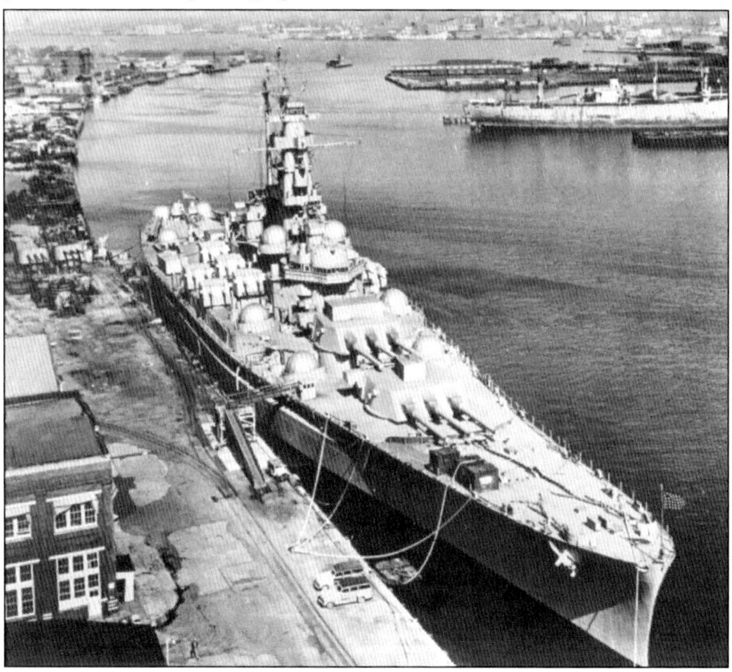

With a massive demobilization of the Navy, the *Massachusetts* began her mothballing at the St. Helen's Annex of the Norfolk Navy Yard. Several large steel "cocoons" were placed over her 40-millimeter gun mounts, making them airtight. On March 27, 1947, Big Mamie was decommissioned and entered the Atlantic Reserve Fleet in Norfolk, where she would wait to serve her country again.

Two

BATTLESHIP COVE

For the next 18 years, Big Mamie sat idle in Norfolk. On June 1, 1962, old and technically obsolete, she was struck from the Naval Register and was prepared for scrapping. When former crew members learned in early 1963 that Big Mamie was going to be destroyed, they began the fight to save her. Their first stop was the Massachusetts State House and a meeting with Gov. Endicott Peabody. If the governor promised financial support from the state, he could request the ship as a donation from the Navy.

Although Governor Peabody refused to provide state funding, Big Mamie's boys would not be deterred. On February 10, 1964, the nonprofit USS *Massachusetts* Memorial Committee Inc. was created with the specific task of raising the funds to save Big Mamie and find her a new home.

What had started with the battleship's sailors soon became an "all-hands" effort, as ordinary citizens, civic groups, leading Bostonians, politicians, and schoolchildren fought to save the battleship named for their home state. Refusing to give up the ship paid off, as the Navy donated the *Massachusetts* to the Memorial Committee in 1965.

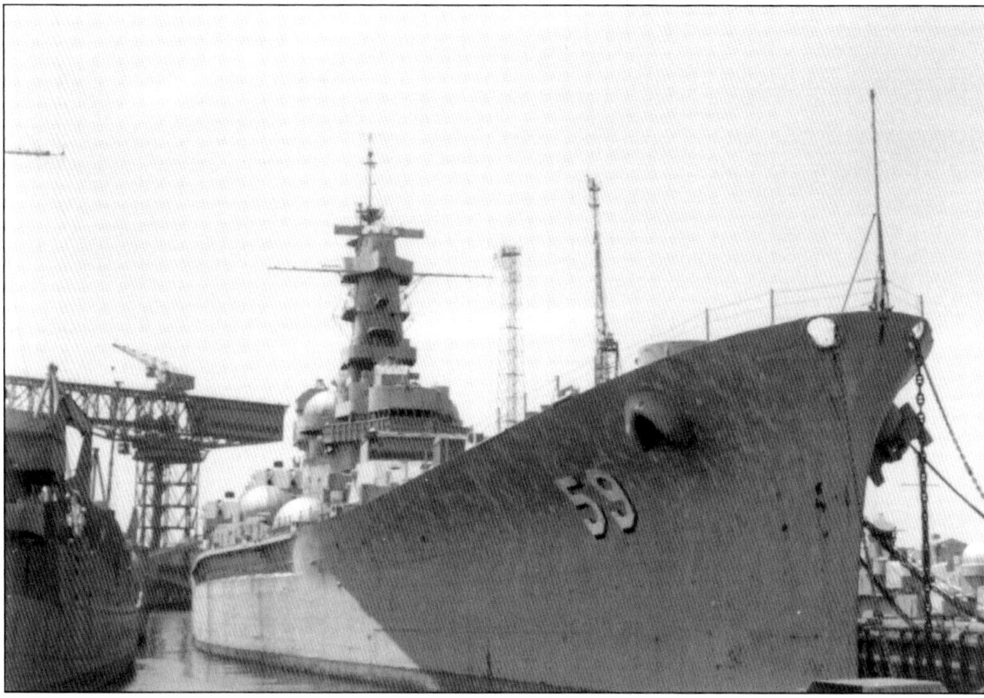

Big Mamie patiently waited to fight for America again, but her services were never needed. At one time, battleships had been queens of the seas, but they had subsequently been replaced by the aircraft carrier. When former crew members living in Massachusetts heard that their ship was going to the scrap yard, they came up with an alternate idea: Big Mamie should be brought back to the Bay State to serve as the official memorial for the commonwealth's citizens killed in World War II. (Author's collection.)

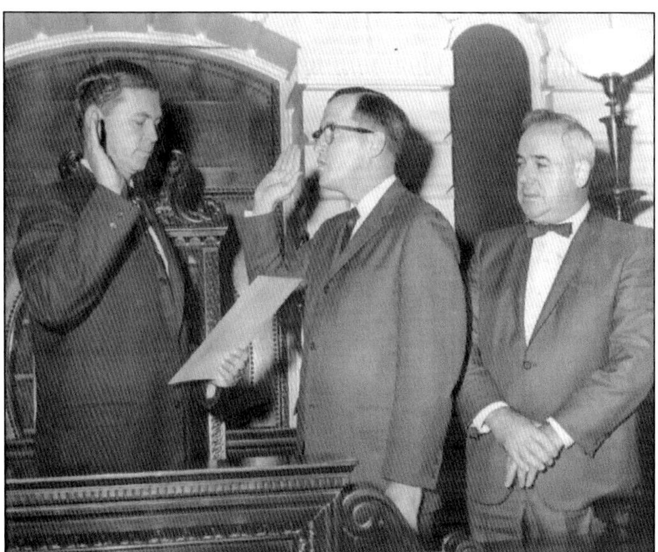

The governors of Texas and North Carolina created state commissions in order to save battleships named for their respective states from the scrap yard. When the governor of Massachusetts was asked by former crew members to do the same, his answer was "no." Gov. Endicott Peabody (left) stated that Boston already had the USS *Constitution* as a museum ship. The governor had ironically been an officer on the submarine *Lionfish*, destined to be preserved at Battleship Cove. (Author's collection.)

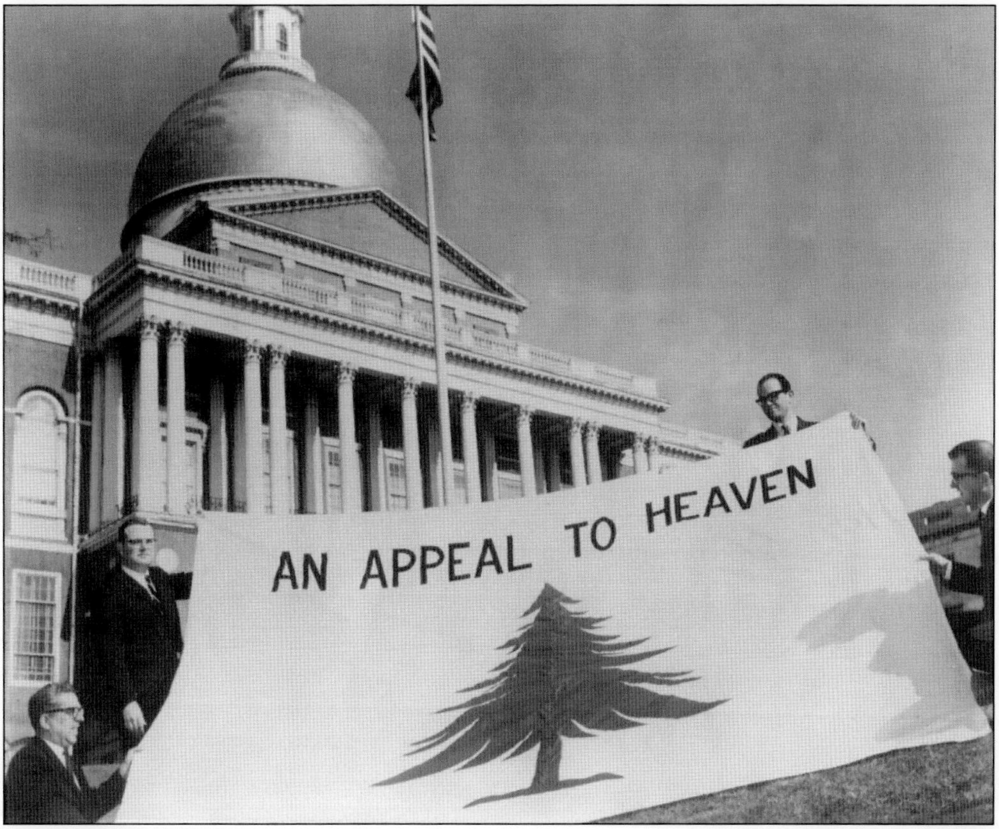

Determined to save their ship, former crew members formed the nonprofit USS *Massachusetts* Memorial Committee on February 10, 1964, with the sole purpose of raising the revenue needed to turn Big Mamie into a memorial and museum. Shown here are, from left to right, former shipmates Edward Palmer, Jack Cassidy, Martin Alder, and an unidentified former sailor. They are displaying the "pine tree flag," the first fighting flag of the Massachusetts Navy, outside the state house. Although no state money would be used to save the ship, both the governor and other elected officials provided assistance to the project in many ways.

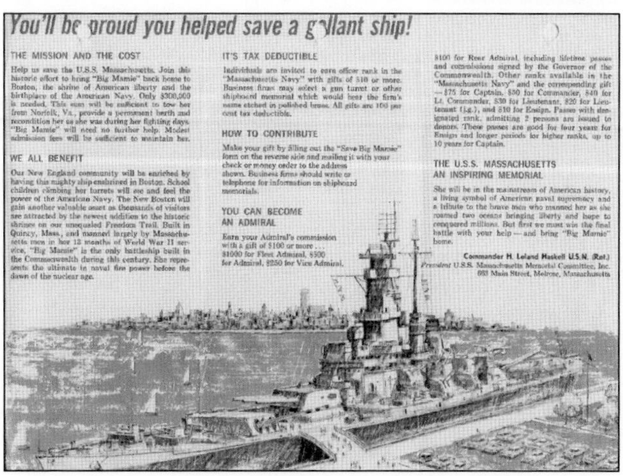

You'll be proud you helped save a gallant ship!

THE MISSION AND THE COST

Help us save the U.S.S. Massachusetts. Join this historic effort to bring "Big Mamie" back home to Boston, the shrine of American liberty and the birthplace of the American Navy. Only $300,000 is needed. This sum will be sufficient to tow her from Norfolk, Va., provide a permanent berth and recondition her as she was during her fighting days. "Big Mamie" will need no further help. Modest admission fees will be sufficient to maintain her.

WE ALL BENEFIT

Our New England community will be enriched by having this mighty ship enshrined in Boston. School children climbing her turrets will see and feel the power of the American Navy. The New Boston will gain another valuable asset as thousands of visitors are attracted by the newest addition to the historic shrines on our unequaled Freedom Trail. Built in Quincy, Mass., and manned largely by Massachusetts men in her 12 months of World War II service, "Big Mamie" is the only battleship built in the Commonwealth during this century. She represents the ultimate in naval fire power before the dawn of the nuclear age.

IT'S TAX DEDUCTIBLE

Individuals are invited to earn officer rank in the "Massachusetts Navy" with gifts of $10 or more. Business firms may select a gun turret or other shipboard memorial which would bear the firm's name etched in polished brass. All gifts are 100 per cent tax deductible.

HOW TO CONTRIBUTE

Make your gift by filling out the "Save Big Mamie" form on the reverse side and mailing it with your check or money order to the address shown. Business firms should write or telephone for information on shipboard memorials.

YOU CAN BECOME AN ADMIRAL

Earn your Admiral's commission with a gift of $100 or more . . . $1000 for Fleet Admiral, $500 for Admiral, $250 for Vice Admiral, $100 for Rear Admiral, including lifetime passes and commissions signed by the Governor of the Commonwealth. Other ranks available in the "Massachusetts Navy" and the corresponding gift —$75 for Captain, $50 for Commander, $40 for Lt. Commander, $30 for Lieutenant, $20 for Lieutenant (j.g.), and $10 for Ensign. Passes with designated rank, admitting 2 persons are issued to donors. These passes are good for four years for Ensign and longer periods for higher ranks, up to 10 years for Captain.

THE U.S.S. MASSACHUSETTS AN INSPIRING MEMORIAL

She will be in the mainstream of American history, a living symbol of American naval supremacy and a tribute to the brave men who manned her as she roamed two oceans bringing liberty and hope to conquered millions. But first we must win the final battle with your help — and bring "Big Mamie" home.

Commander H. Leland Haskell U.S.N. (Ret.)
President U.S.S. Massachusetts Memorial Committee, Inc.
693 Main Street, Melrose, Massachusetts

Along with the money needed to save the ship, the association needed a berth big enough to accommodate a huge battleship. As such, the city of Boston was the clear choice, with Piers No. 1 and No. 2 at the mouth of the Fort Point Channel. For numerous reasons, Charlestown, Pier No. 4 in South Boston, Castle Island Terminal, and East Boston were ruled out. The Hutchenson Company of Boston printed stationery and brochures, like the one shown here, free of charge.

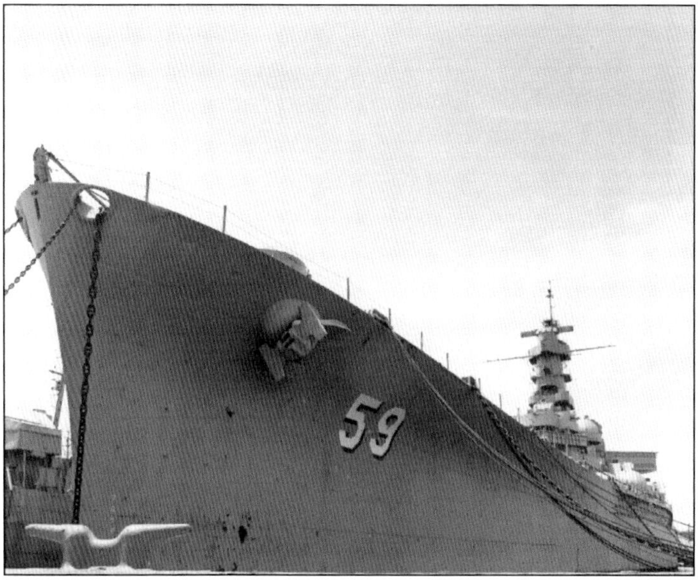

The committee set a goal of raising $250,000, which would include the towing of the old war horse from Virginia to Massachusetts. Through the selling of "honorary" Massachusetts Navy ranks and commissions, advertising, school drives, and tremendous hard work and dedication, the citizens of the Bay Sate, along with Big Mamie's sailors, saved the veteran battleship from the scrap pile.

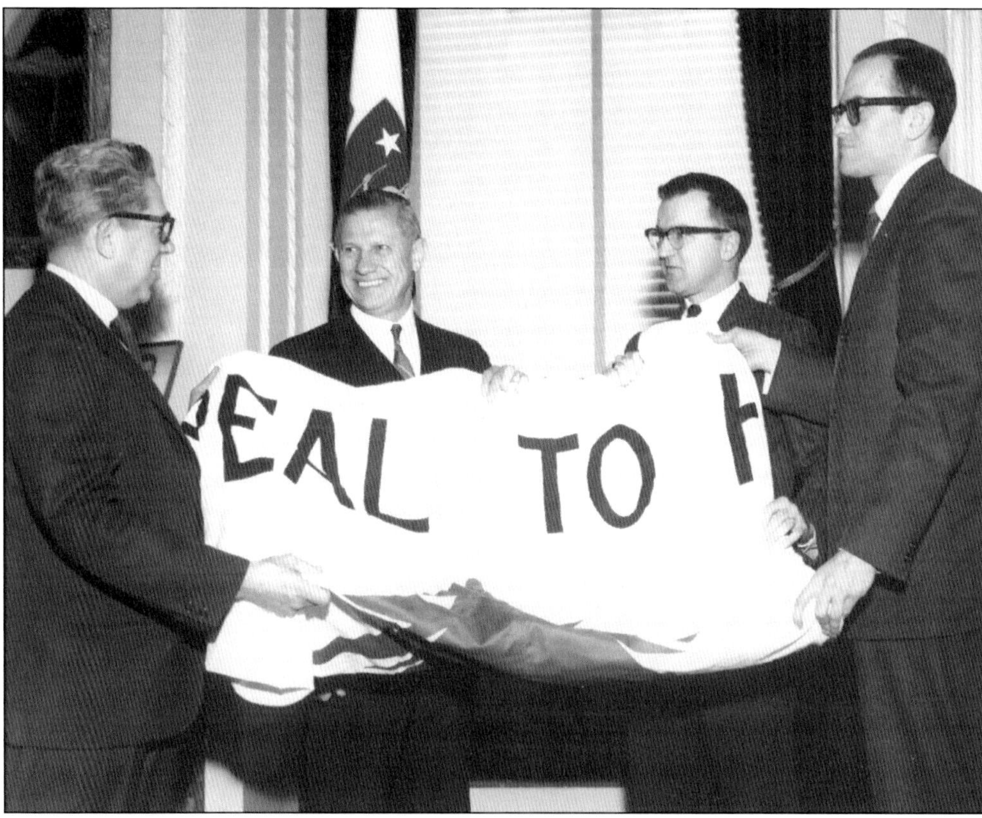

In June 1964, the Navy informed Ed Palmer (left) to expect the official donation of Big Mamie to the memorial committee by the next month. However, the committee had been unable to locate a berth for the steel behemoth, including the most coveted port of Boston. Although Fall River had already been ruled out, Palmer telephoned that city's mayor, who became quite interested in "a million dollar tourist attraction." The "Spindle City" would be the new home of the *Massachusetts*.

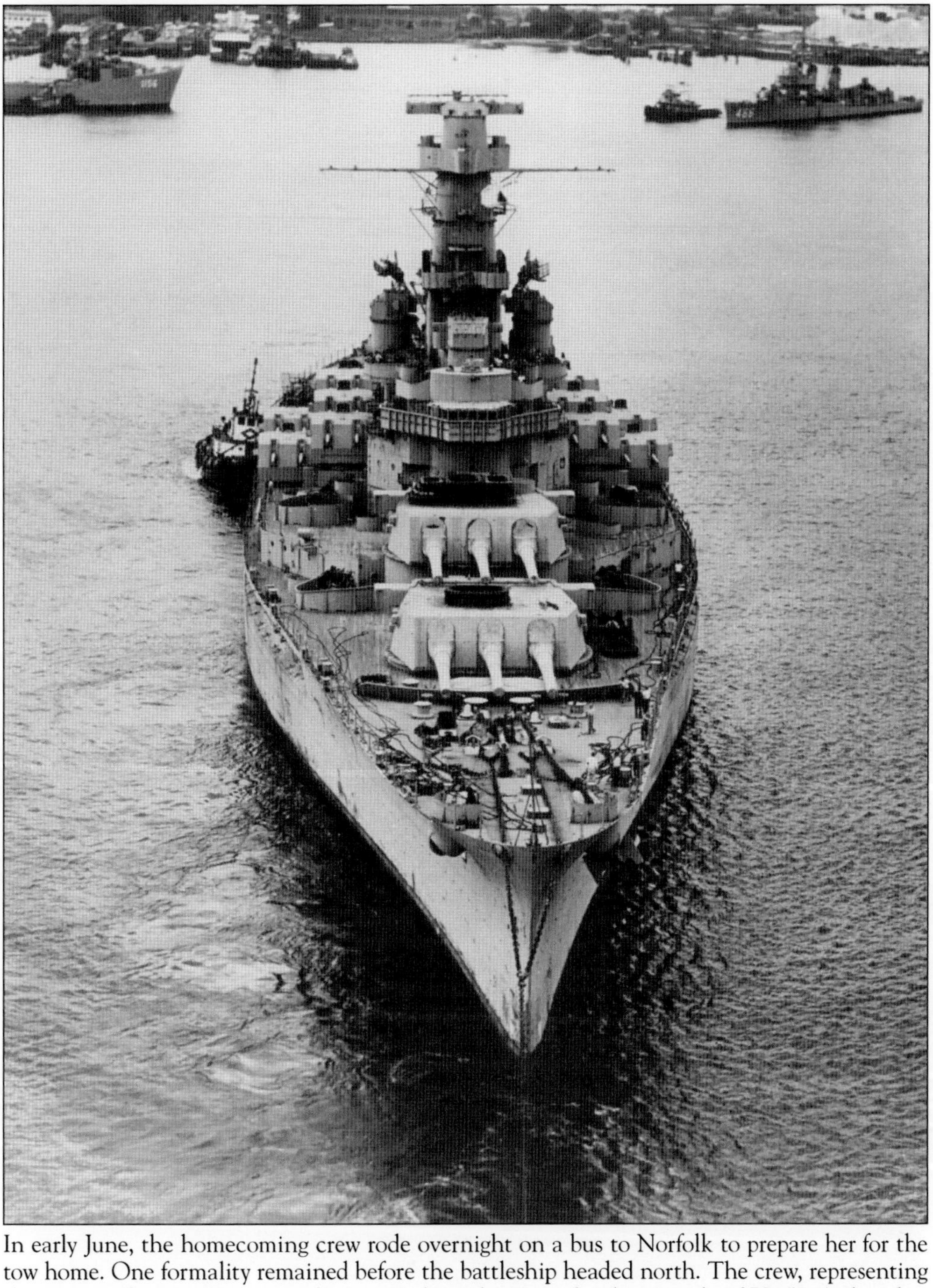

In early June, the homecoming crew rode overnight on a bus to Norfolk to prepare her for the tow home. One formality remained before the battleship headed north. The crew, representing the memorial committee, signed a receipt from the Navy for the custody of BB-59. At last, her lines were parted, and four tugs, including the new ocean tug *Margaret Moran,* moved her away from the pier and down the channel to the Atlantic. In the background of this photograph, a tugboat tows the Fletcher-class destroyer USS *Waller* (DD-466). The huge cranes in Portsmouth removed more than 100 feet of Big Mamie's masts so the ship could pass underneath the Mount Hope and Braga Bridges.

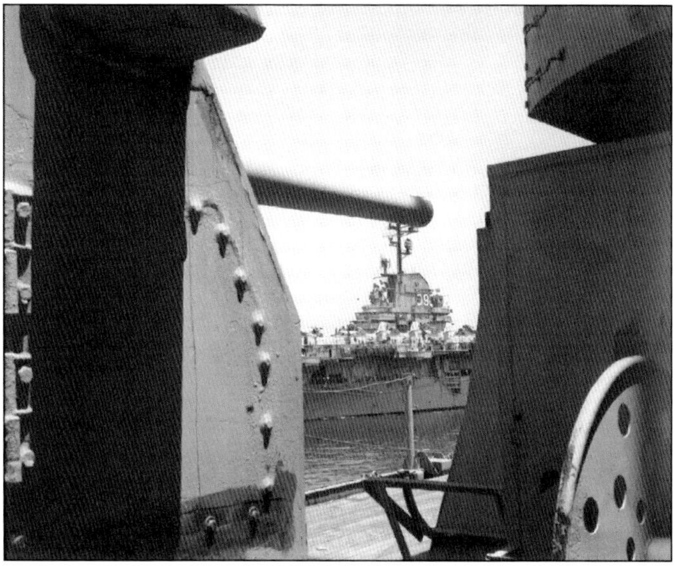

The old battleship passes the aircraft carrier USS *Lake Champlain* (CV-39) as the latter heads in to Norfolk. It was aircraft carriers that made battleships like Big Mamie obsolete. Soon after this photograph was taken, the *Lake Champlain* embarked Naval Academy midshipmen for a summer cruise to Halifax, Nova Scotia, and Kingston, Jamaica, where she represented the United States at the island's celebration of its independence on August 3.

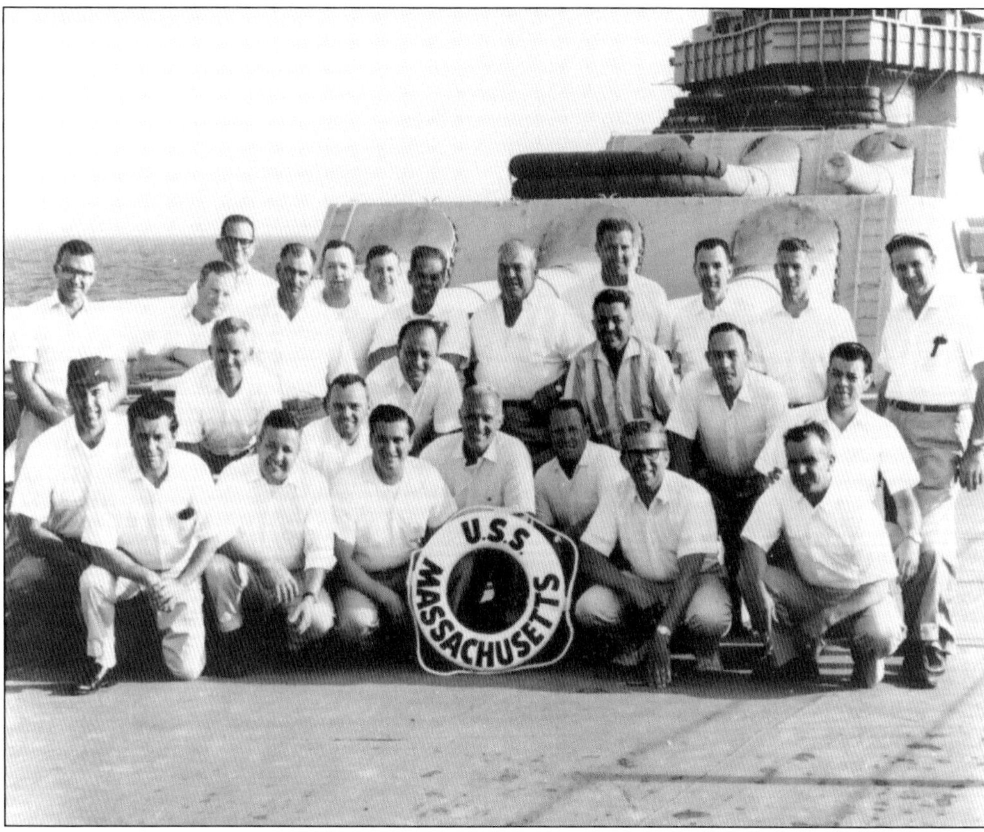

Accompanying Big Mamie on her homecoming to Fall River were 26 men, including 11 former crewmen. The trip took five days, including two in which the vessel was shrouded in fog. Her crew spent the time chipping and scrapping her old paint and then adding a new coat for her arrival in Fall River.

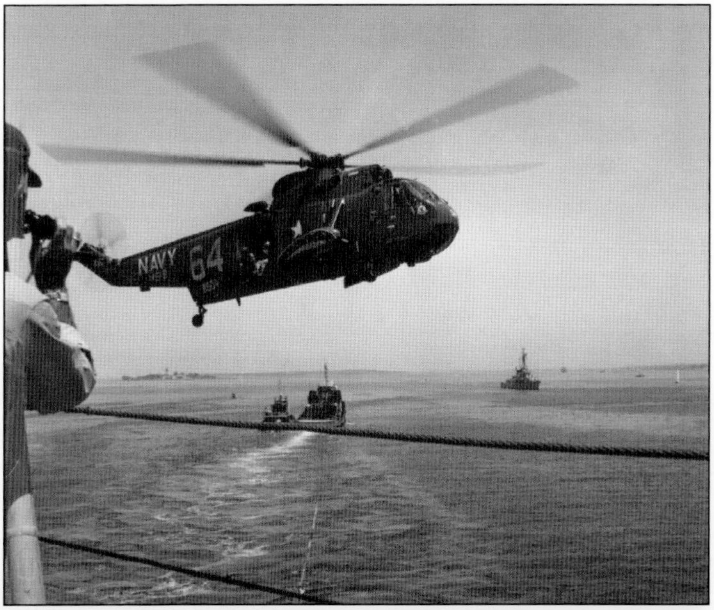

A US Navy helicopter hovers off of Big Mamie as she makes her way up Narragansett Bay to Fall River on June 12, 1965. The helicopter carried official US Navy photographers, as this was an excellent public relations event for the Navy. In addition, Gov. John H. Volpe rode in the helicopter and circled over the battleship a few times before later being transferred to the destroyer USS *Glennon* (DD-840).

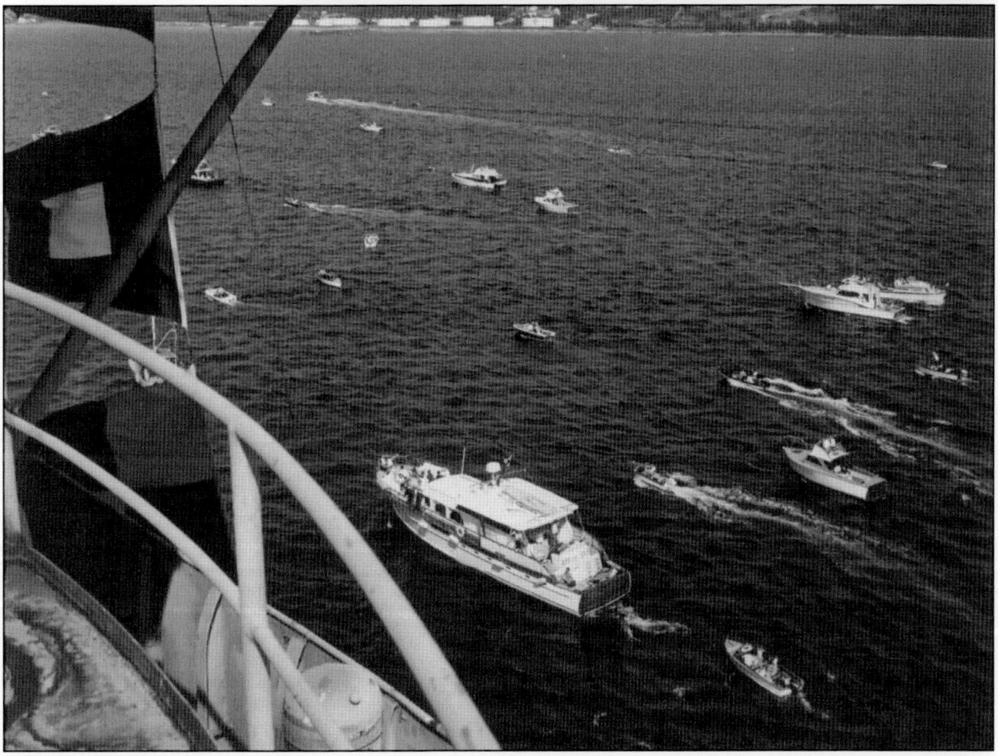

An armada of pleasure craft accompanied the *Massachusetts*, and the vessels loudly blasted their horns in welcome. Big Mamie displayed a large banner that read, "Thank you Schoolchildren of Massachusetts," in appreciation and recognition of the thousands of children who donated over $53,000. Boston Public Schools raised almost $5,000. The vessel's future home of Fall River raised the second-highest total, almost $3,000. Just down the coast, the children of the City of New Bedford gave $2,644.

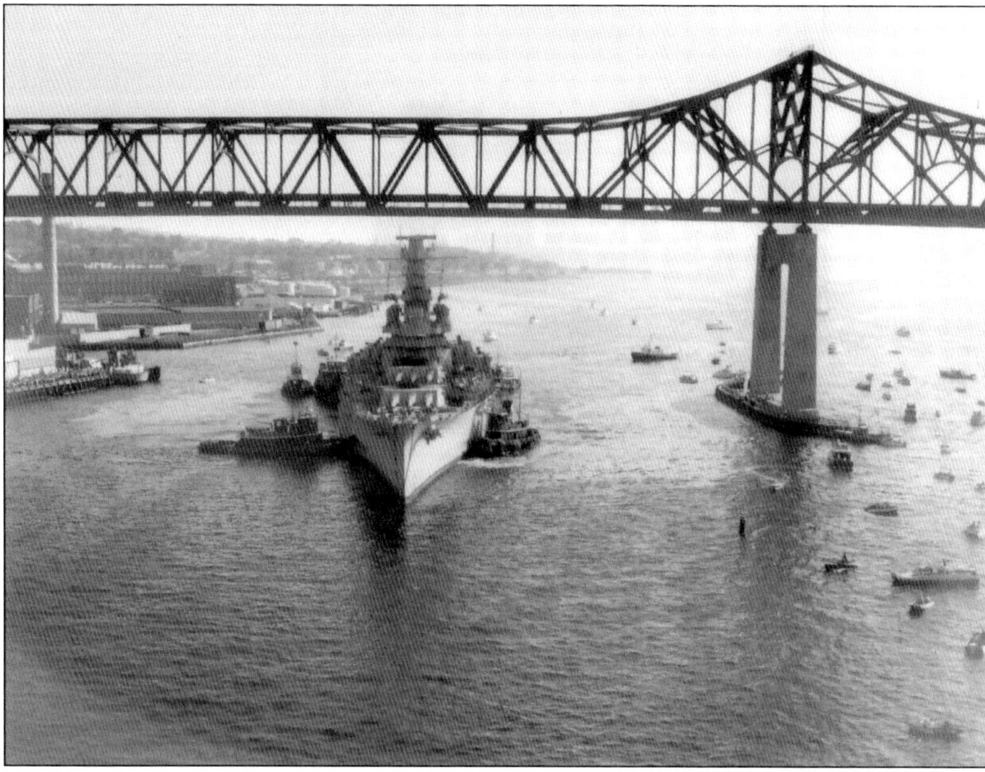

More than half a million people lined the shores of Narragansett Bay and the Taunton River to cheer the arrival of the old battleship. Across New England, she was on the front pages of newspapers and was given heavy radio and television coverage. The Navy took the families of Big Mamie's homecoming crew on a destroyer so they could meet the battleship upon her arrival. (Author's collection.)

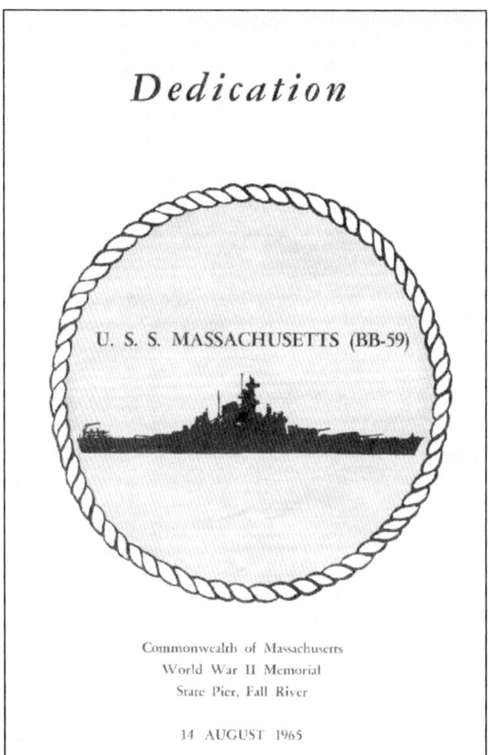

Dedication

U. S. S. MASSACHUSETTS (BB-59)

Commonwealth of Massachusetts
World War II Memorial
State Pier, Fall River

14 AUGUST 1965

On Saturday, August 14, 1965, a ceremony was held to dedicate the *Massachusetts* as the official World War II memorial of the commonwealth. The program included speeches from Secretary of the Navy Paul Nitze, Gov. John Volpe, and other elected officials. The US Naval Band from Boston performed, and a flyover was conducted by planes from Quonset Naval Air Station.

The platform is set up on the fantail of Big Mamie during the dedication on August 14. Hundreds witnessed the historic event, some even watching by boat, as seen at upper right. The ship had already been open for a week, although visitors could only walk on the main deck. The price of admission was $1.

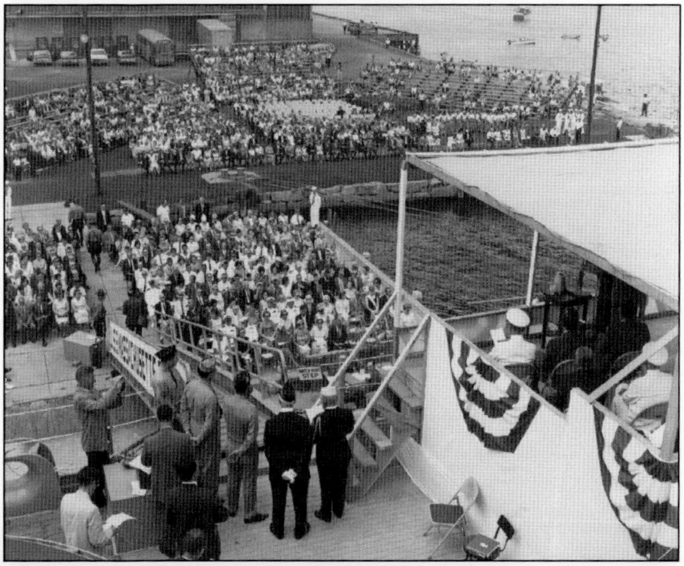

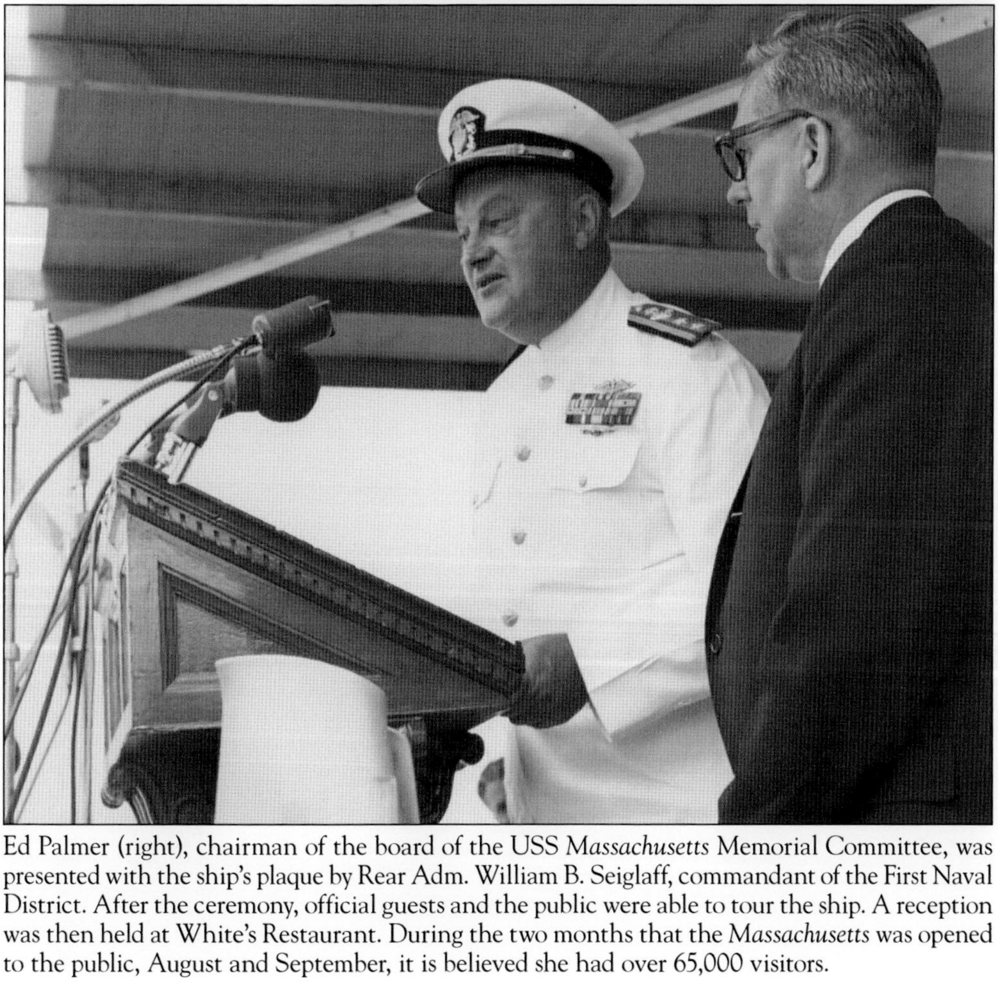

Ed Palmer (right), chairman of the board of the USS *Massachusetts* Memorial Committee, was presented with the ship's plaque by Rear Adm. William B. Seiglaff, commandant of the First Naval District. After the ceremony, official guests and the public were able to tour the ship. A reception was then held at White's Restaurant. During the two months that the *Massachusetts* was opened to the public, August and September, it is believed she had over 65,000 visitors.

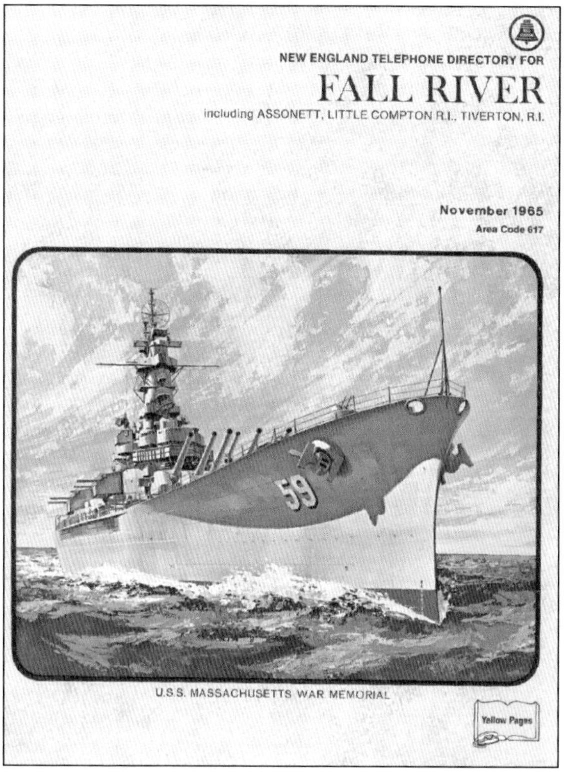

Big Mamie graces the November 1965 phone book for the Fall River area. She appeared on the covers of all New England Telephone Company directories for all of the cities and towns in Massachusetts during 1965–1967. This promotion was arranged by Ed Palmer, an employee of the telephone company's public relations department in Boston. Bringing the battleship into the homes of area residents was a great way to market the new tourist attraction.

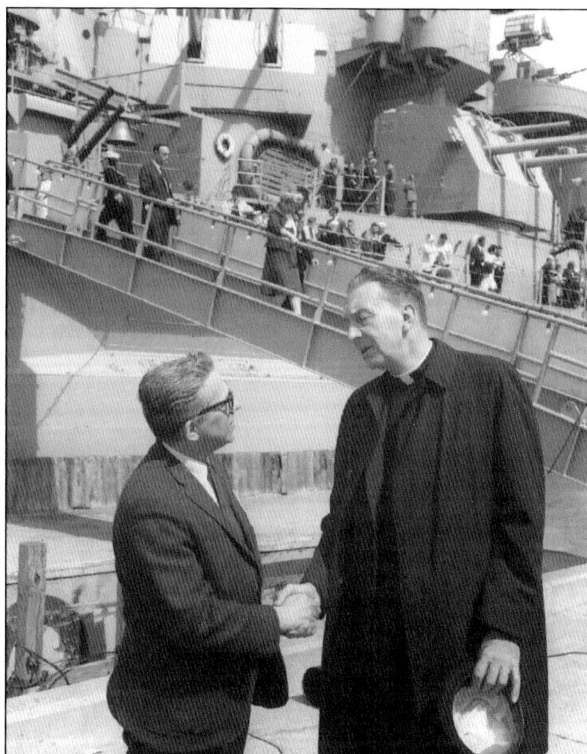

Former shipmates Ed Palmer (left) and Father Joe Moody converse during their reunion in 1966. Father Joe was born in New York in 1904 and was ordained to the priesthood in 1929. While traveling in Europe in the late 1930s, he saw Adolf Hitler speak at Nuremberg. In 1941, he was appointed to the Chaplain Corps and assigned to Big Mamie until he was transferred to the *Yorktown* in 1944. He passed away a month before his 90th birthday, in 1994.

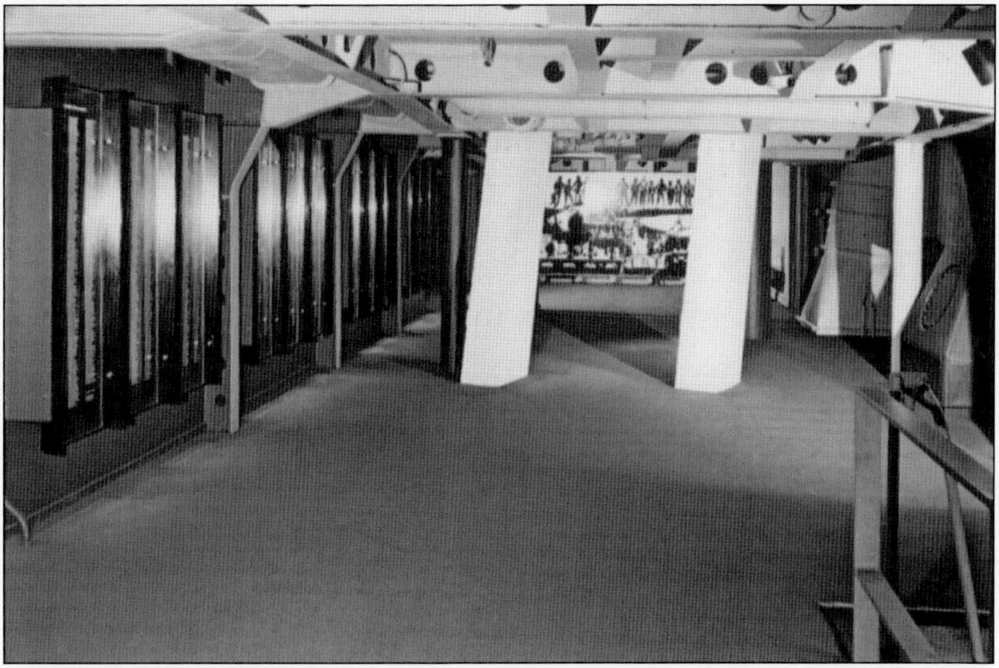

In 1966, Gov. John Volpe formed a committee of three men to plan and build a suitable memorial to the more than 13,000 citizens of the state who died in service to their country in World War II. In the summer of 1968, the memorial was completed on the main deck of Big Mamie, within the superstructure, aft of the wardroom. Visitors can read over 13,000 names, listed by county and service, and be reminded of the cost of freedom. (Author's collection.)

In late 1967, volunteers began an ambitious project of acquiring and completely restoring an original Kingfisher for display aboard the *Massachusetts*. While over a thousand had been built, only two were known to be in existence, one aboard the museum ship *Alabama*, and the other housed at the Smithsonian Institution in a junked condition. The Smithsonian agreed to loan the aircraft, and it was transported by truck to the Naval Air Station, Quonset Point, Rhode Island.

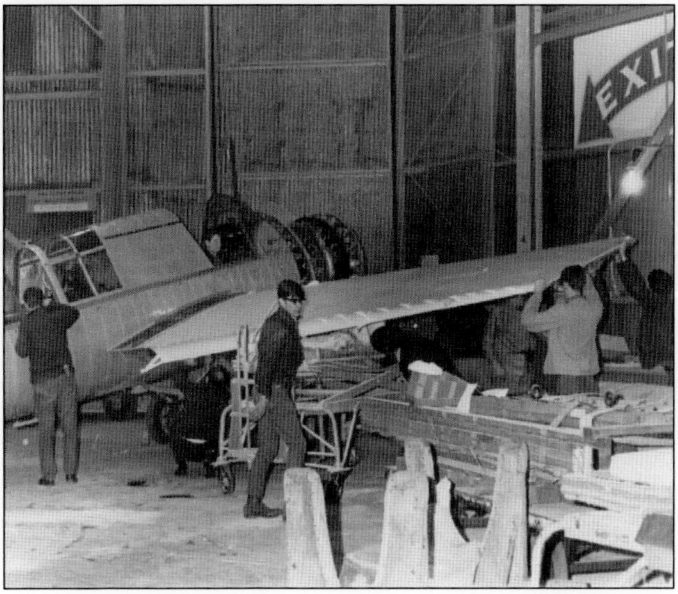

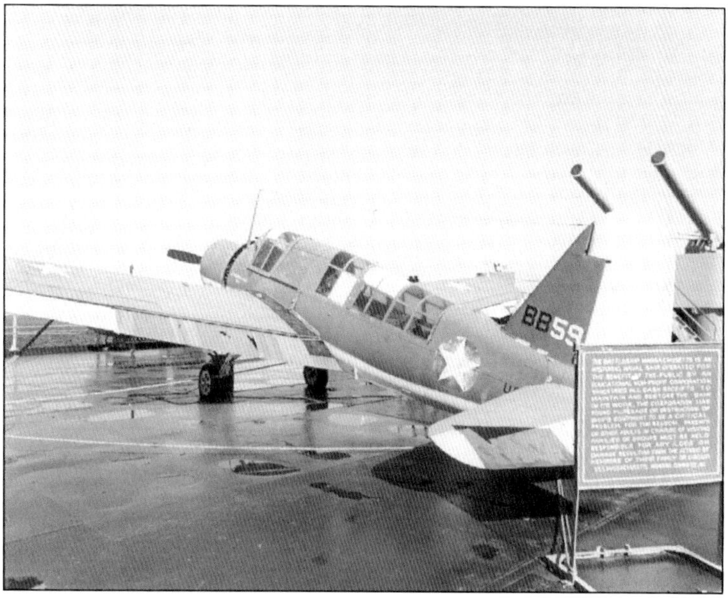

The director of the project was Capt. John J. O'Neil, a weekend warrior from the Naval Air Station, Weymouth, Massachusetts. Captain O'Neil was supported by Explorer Scouts, sponsored by the Naval Air Rework Facility, NAS Quonset Point, and the Davisville, Rhode Island, Seabee Base. In addition, the Scouts were advised by civilian employees of NAS Quonset Point.

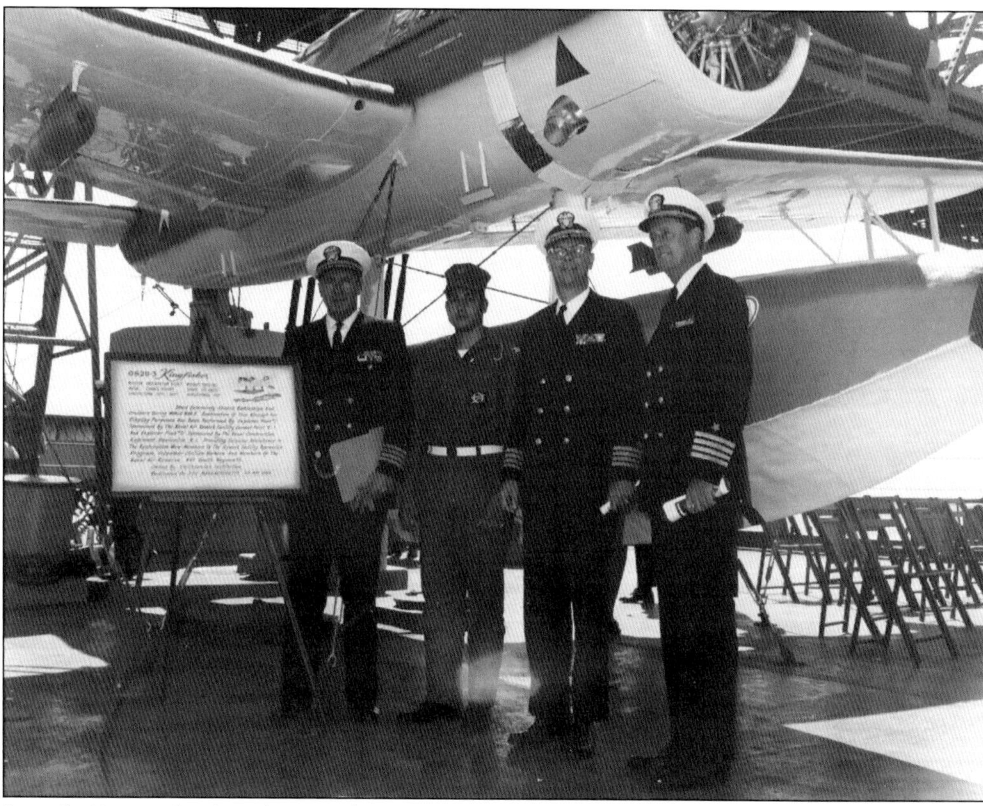

It took 18 months, but the Smithsonian Kingfisher was completely restored, including the operational engine. The museum had an official dedication ceremony on May 26, 1969, attended by active Navy personnel, local politicians, and a representative from Gov. Francis Sargent's office. The Kingfisher was proudly displayed on the fantail of the *Massachusetts* until the Smithsonian's loan of the aircraft expired 11 years later.

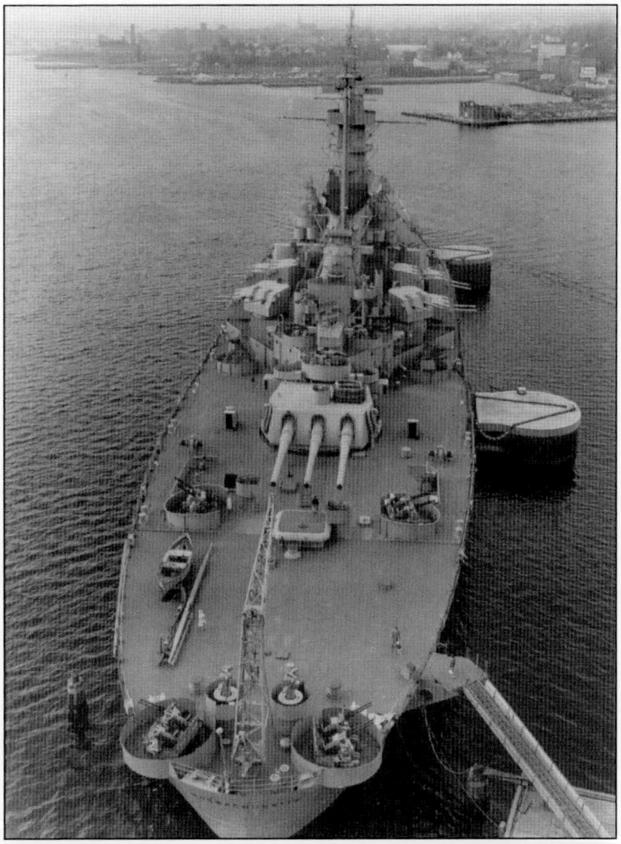

Over the next three years, attendance soared to over 200,000 people per year, with over 265,000 visitors in 1966 alone. In 1969, the *Massachusetts* was moved to a deepwater mooring so that she was at a right angle to the Braga Bridge, thereby truly creating Battleship Cove. The Fall River waterfront can be seen at upper right.

A customer looks over the souvenirs in the gift shop in this 1970 photograph. The shop sold an array of gifts, such as models, hats, T-shirts, postcards, and coffee mugs. In 1984, a new ship's store was built and opened to the public. Located at the front of the museum, it also served as the ticket booth.

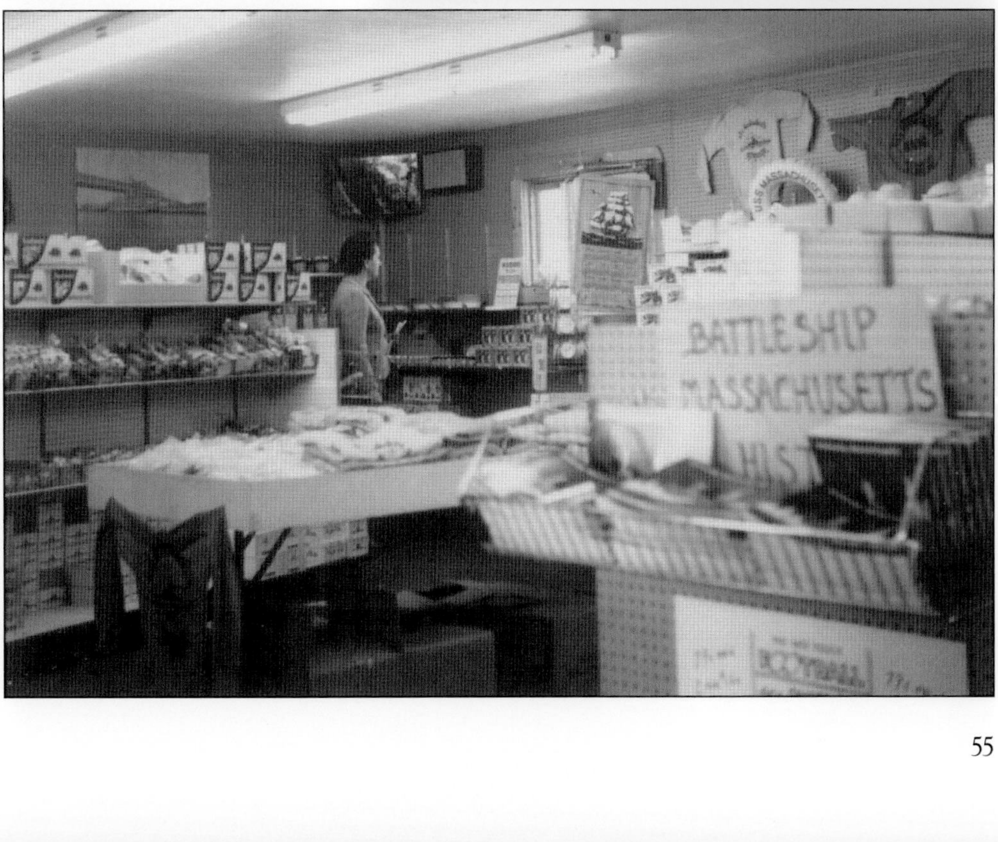

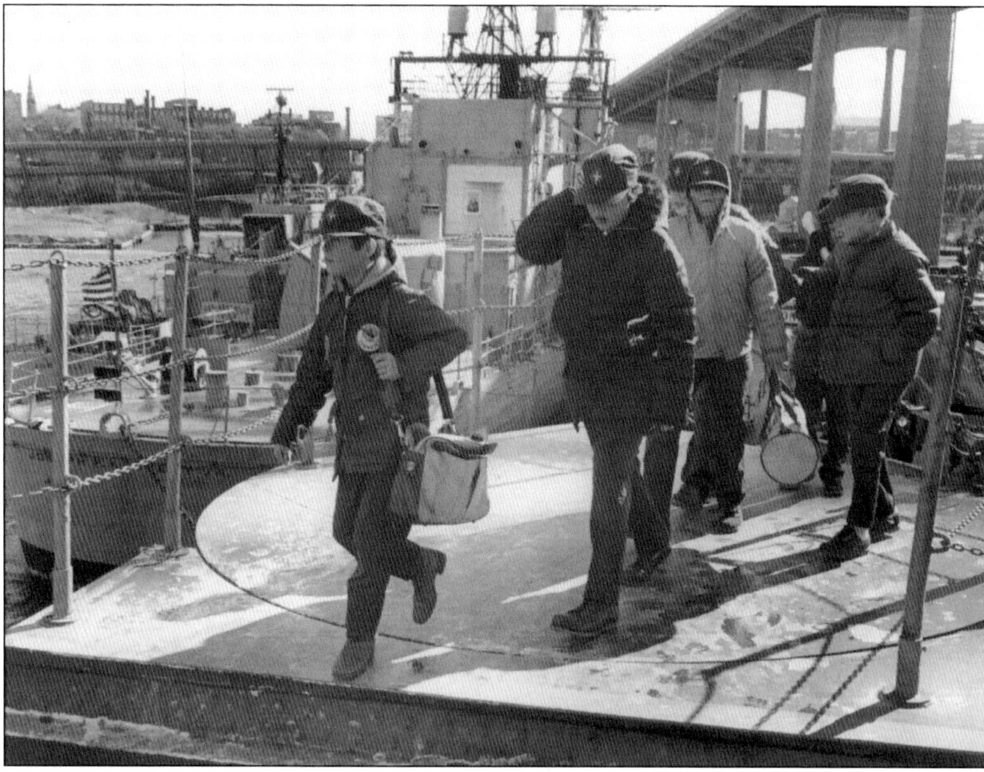

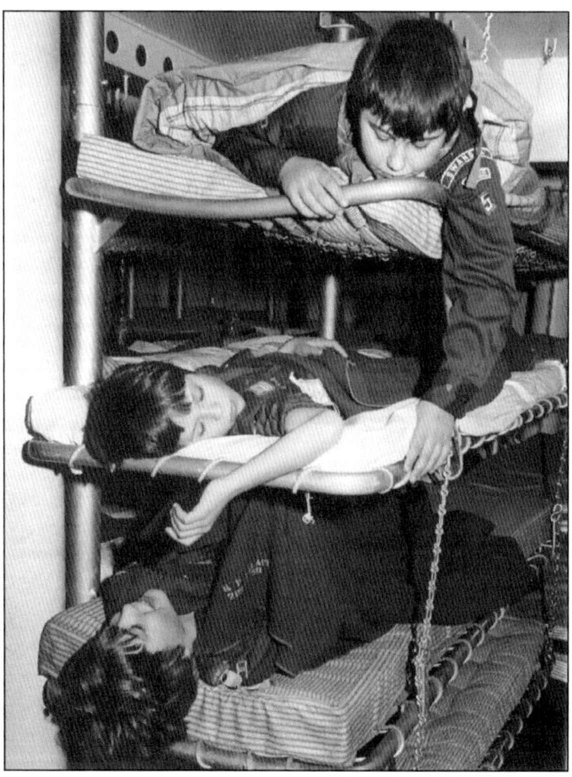

In 1972, an Overnight Youth Group Camping Program was started, with fewer than 100 children and their chaperones sleeping on the deck of the battleship wardroom. The program took off and officially became known as Nautical Nights. It became so well known that it was quickly copied by other museum ships and attractions, like Boston's Museum of Science.

The program is open to youth groups, including Boy Scout and Girl Scout troops. Some nights are reserved for families. The program offers exploration of the ship, sleeping in the same racks the crew used, learning about life aboard ship, and talking with veterans. In addition, dinner and breakfast are served in the wardroom. Nautical Nights has become the museum's most profitable special program.

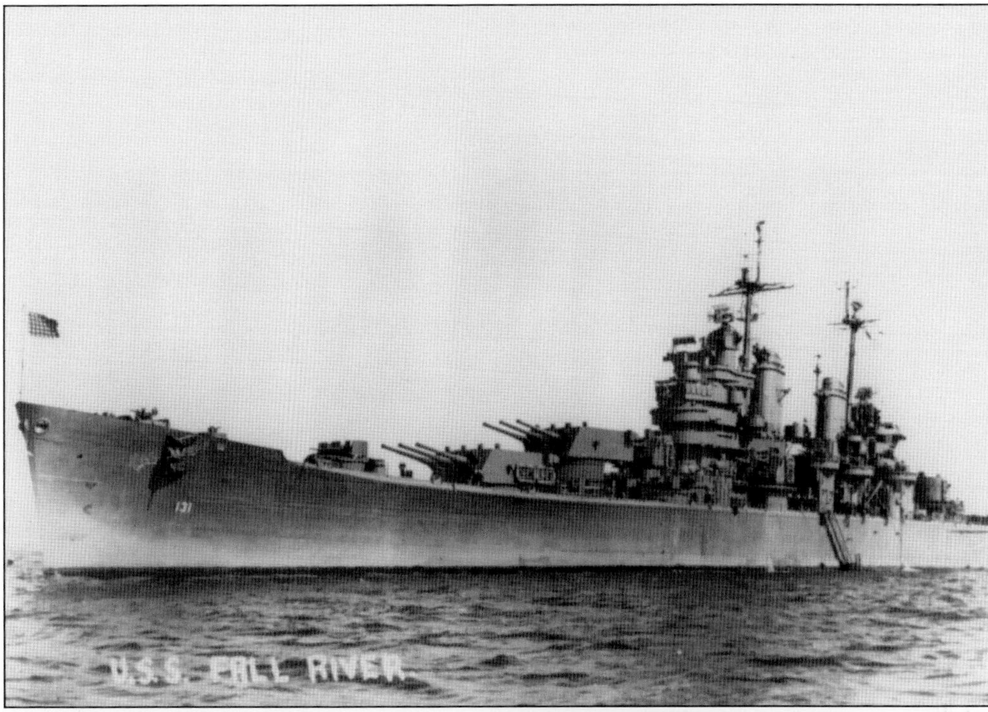

The 674-foot-long heavy cruiser USS *Fall River* (CA-131) was built by the New York Shipbuilding Corporation in Camden, New Jersey, and commissioned on July 1, 1945. From May 21 to September 14, 1946, she was involved in Operation Crossroads, the testing of atomic weapons in the Marshall Islands. Placed in the reserve fleet in 1947, she was scrapped in 1972.

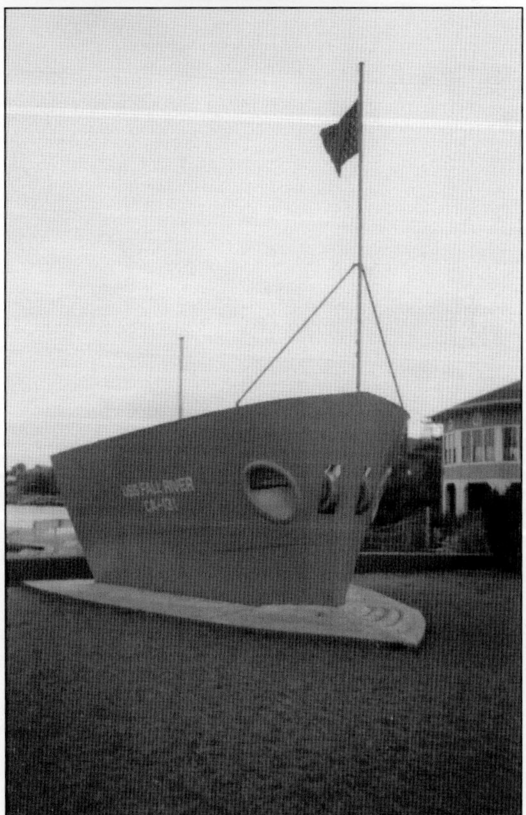

Through the use of a grant in 1974, Battleship Cove was able to obtain the tip of *Fall River's* bow. It was subsequently placed at the museum entrance. Over the years, the Fall River Shipmates Association has held many reunions at Battleship Cove. (Author's collection.)

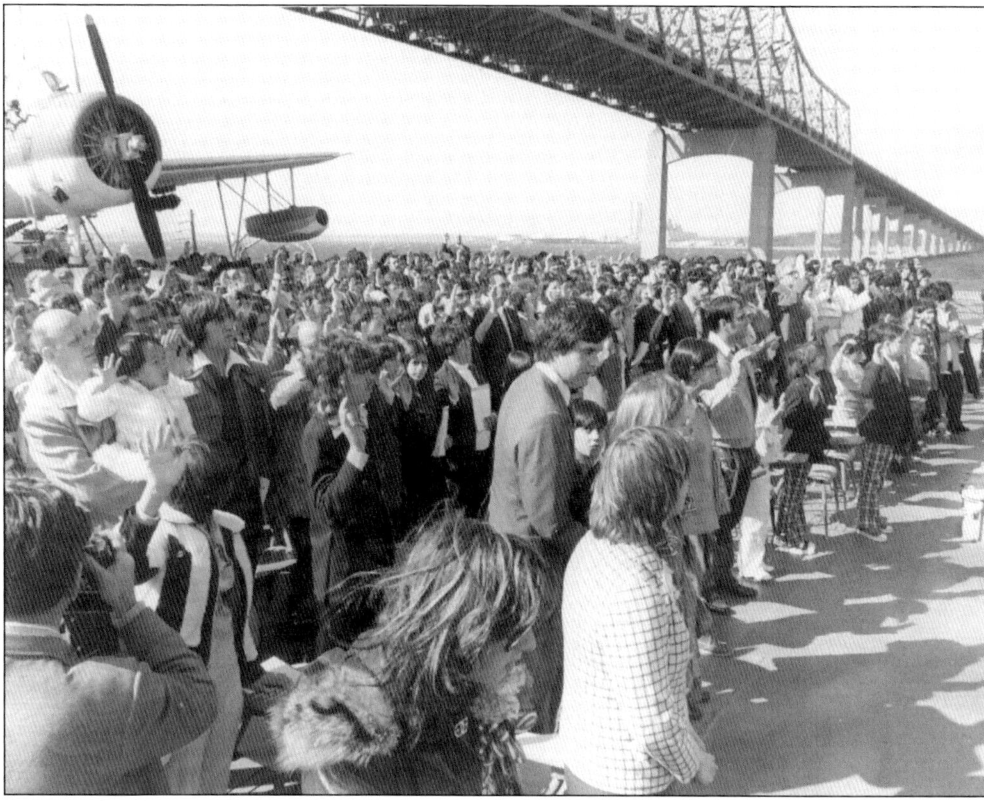

In 1976, development extended beyond the museum ships to the waterfront, with the conceptual planning of the Fall River Heritage State Park. In addition, the ships received $68,000 in maritime preservation grants. On the stern of the *Massachusetts*, 269 new immigrants became citizens of the United States on October 15, 1976.

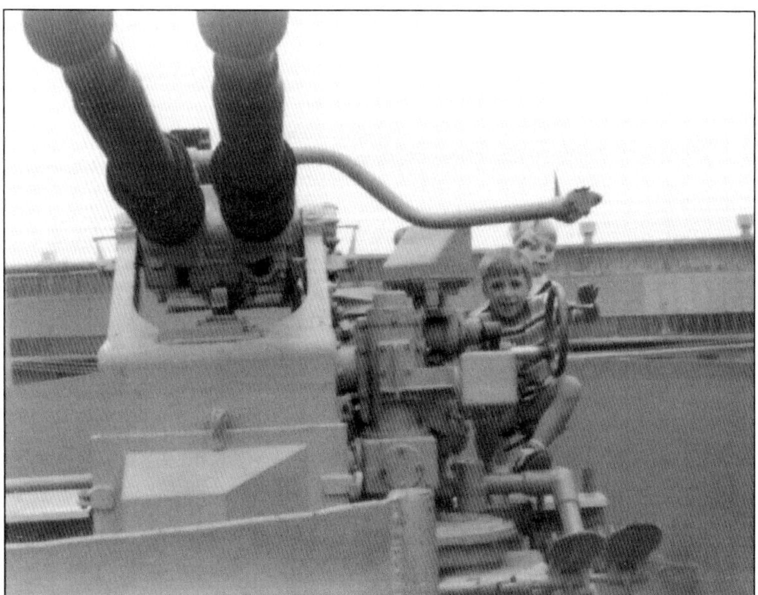

The author stands behind his older brother David on one of the stern 40-millimeter gun mounts on the *Massachusetts* in 1979. The quadruple 40-millimeter gun mount was a medium-range antiaircraft weapon that was standard on capital ships during World War II. (Author's collection.)

In the fall of 1981, the museum dedicated a World War II craft known as a Landing Craft Mechanized (LCM). These boats were used to transport tanks and troops for amphibious assaults upon the enemy, such as in the Pacific and on the beaches of Normandy. With a length of 50 feet and a crew of four, the LCM could carry a 30-ton tank or 60 soldiers.

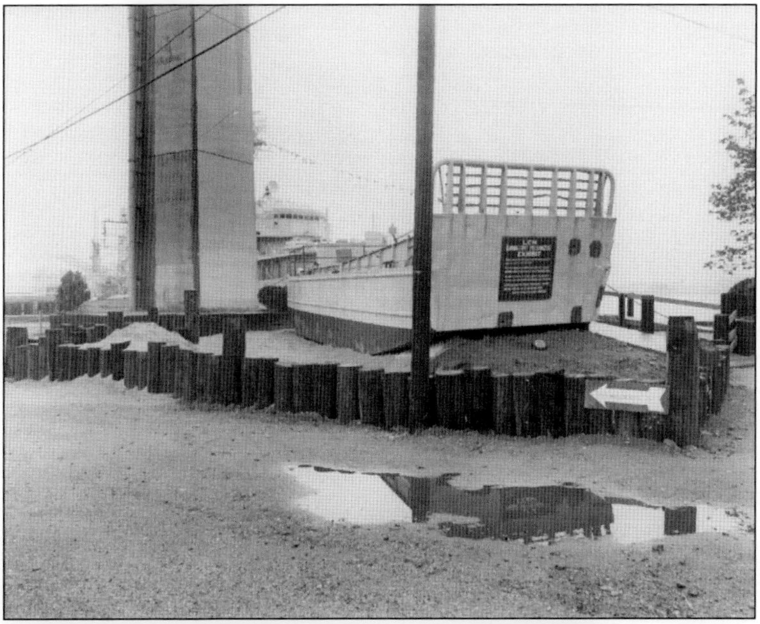

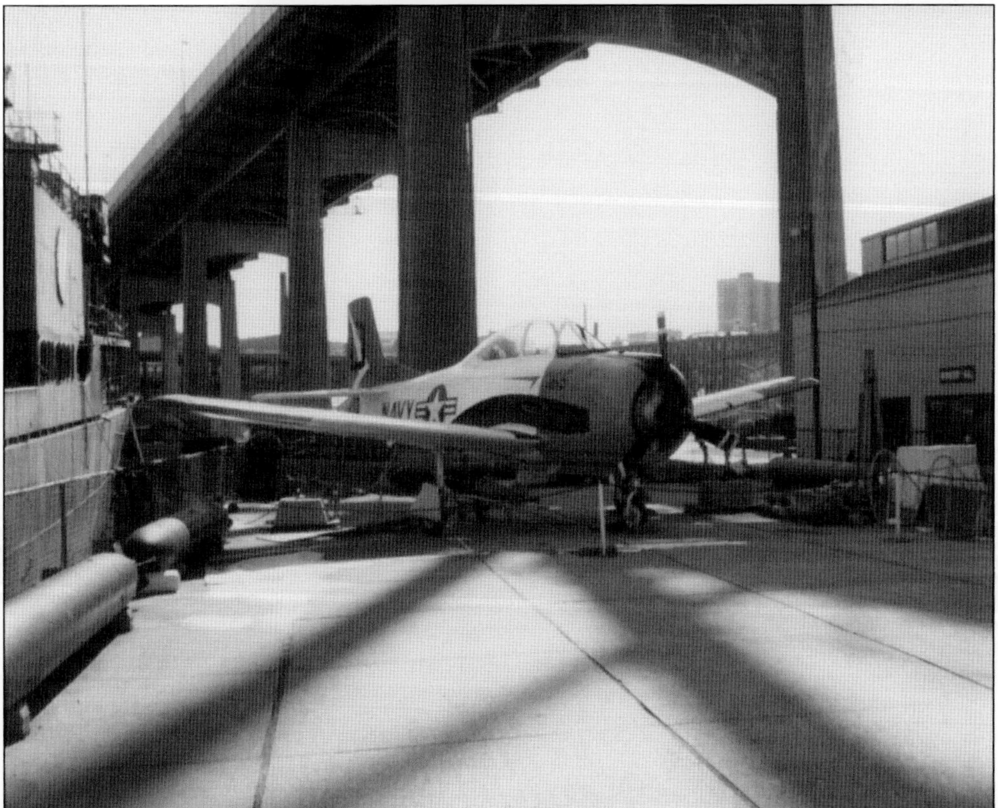

The year 1984 included the addition of a T-28 Trojan trainer airplane on the pier adjacent to the *Joseph P. Kennedy, Jr.* Successfully flown for the first time in 1949, later versions of the plane were ordered by the US Navy for carrier operations. The T-28 helped pilots transition to jet aircraft.

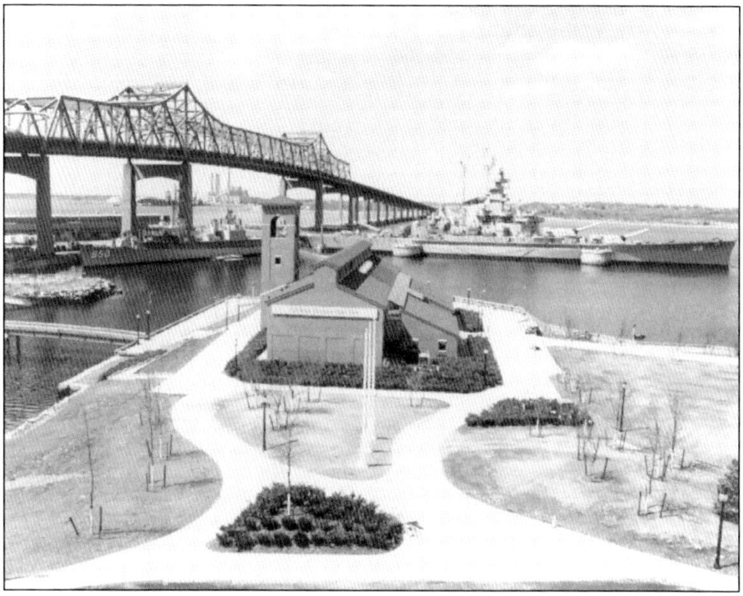

In August 1984, the Fall River Heritage State Park opened, with Gov. Michael S. Dukakis serving as the featured speaker. The 8.5-acre park has a boardwalk, benches, groves of trees, and a three-acre meadow perfect for summer concerts, craft festivals, and family picnics. Inside the visitors' center is an exhibit showcasing the history of Fall River, including several historic photographs.

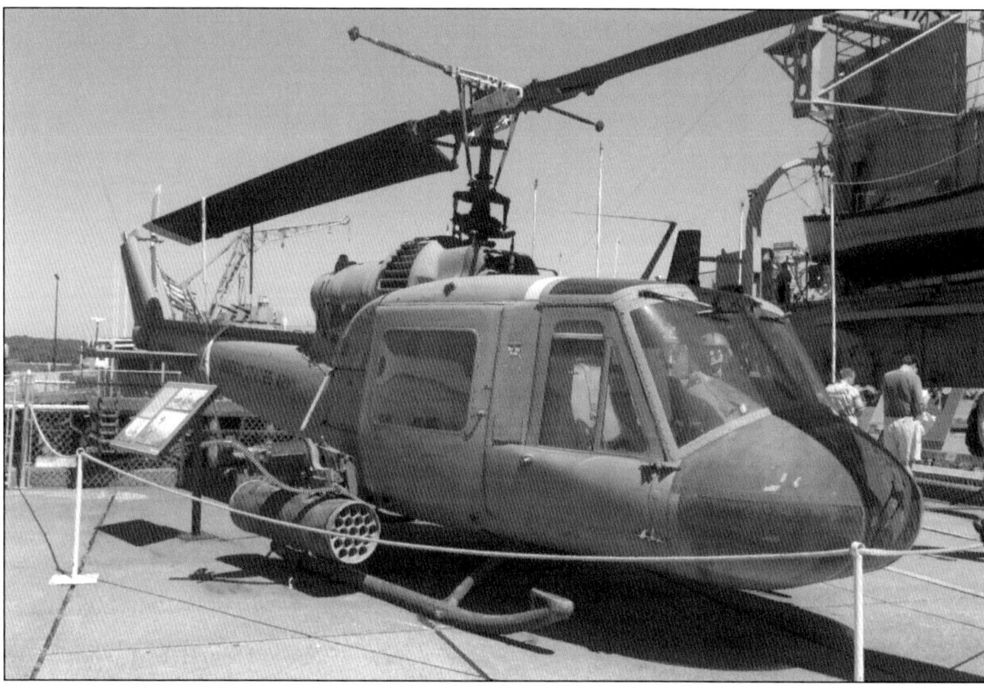

On Memorial Day 1993, the Vietnam Veterans of America, Westport Chapter 207, dedicated Huey Helicopter No. 66-60609. It was placed directly across from the T-28 airplane. The "609" served in Vietnam. The last combat unit she was assigned to was the 135th Assault Helicopter Company in Bear Cat, Republic of South Vietnam. The 135th's gun platoon was called the "Taipans." (Courtesy of Ted Hayes.)

Three

USS *Lionfish* (SS-298)

The Balao-class submarine *Lionfish* was commissioned on November 1, 1944, and her first commanding officer was Lt. Cmdr. Edward D. Spruance, son of the commander of the Fifth Fleet in the Pacific, Adm. Raymond Spruance. With a crew of over 60 sailors, she left for the Pacific on January 8, 1945, and began her first war patrol on March 19. After being fired upon by a Japanese submarine, she escaped and later surfaced to destroy a Japanese schooner on May 1. On July 10, she fired on an enemy submarine. When her captain looked through the periscope, he noticed a cloud of smoke on the horizon. In addition, her sonar man reported hearing noises consistent with a submarine imploding.

Decommissioned after the war, the *Lionfish* was recommissioned in 1951 and served as a training ship until she left on October 18, 1952, for a Mediterranean cruise. In 1960, she was used for Naval Reserve Training and, two years later, was reclassified an Auxiliary Research Submarine. She was struck from the Naval Register on December 20, 1971, and became a permanent memorial to all submariners at Battleship Cove on August 30, 1972.

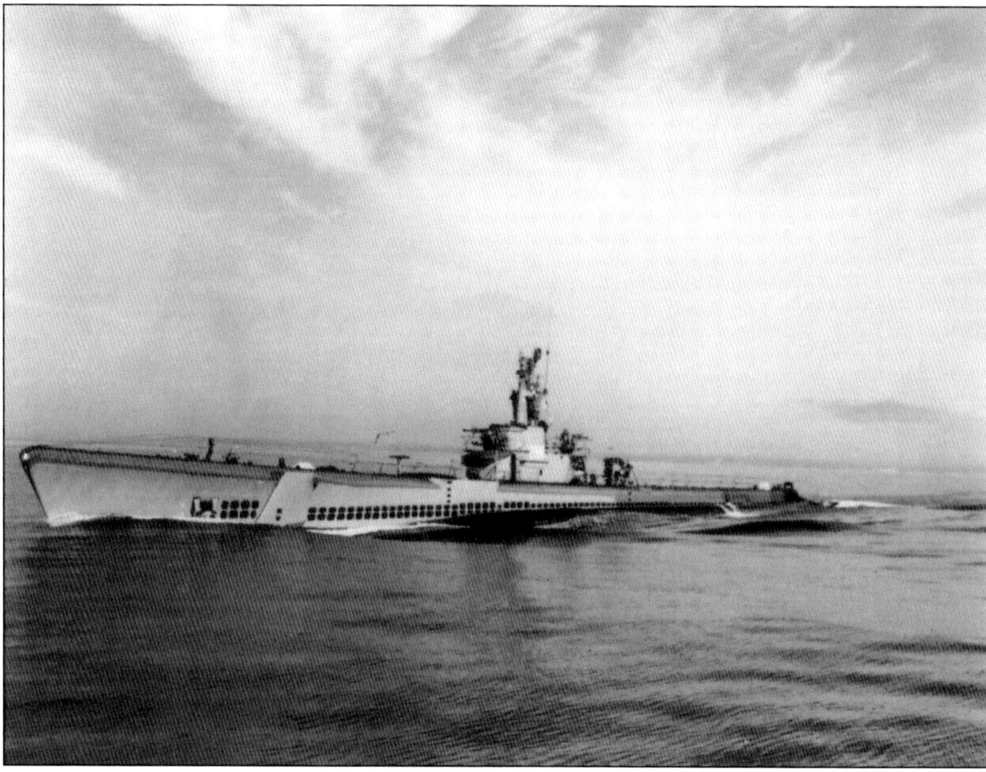

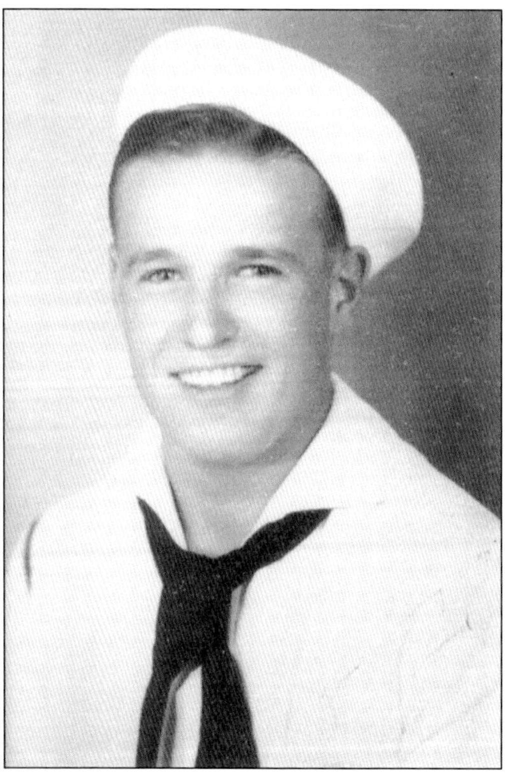

The USS *Lionfish* (SS-298), a 311-foot-long Balao-class submarine, was commissioned on November 1, 1944, in Portsmouth, New Hampshire. With a crew of 66, she could travel on the surface at 20 knots, and when submerged, at 8 knots. On March 19, 1945, she began her first war patrol, cruising in the Bungo Channel, a strait separating the Japanese islands of Kyushu and Shikoku. (Courtesy of the US Naval Institute.)

Howard L. Marx was born and raised in Buffalo, New York, and enlisted in the Navy at the age of 19. He arrived at Naval Station Newport for boot camp in March 1940. After graduating from submarine school in July, he reported aboard the USS *Bonita* (SS-165) in July. When war broke out, he made several patrols with the *Bonita*, and after passing the chief's exam, he was transferred to the *Lionfish* before her commissioning on September 27, 1944. (Courtesy of Catherine Marx.)

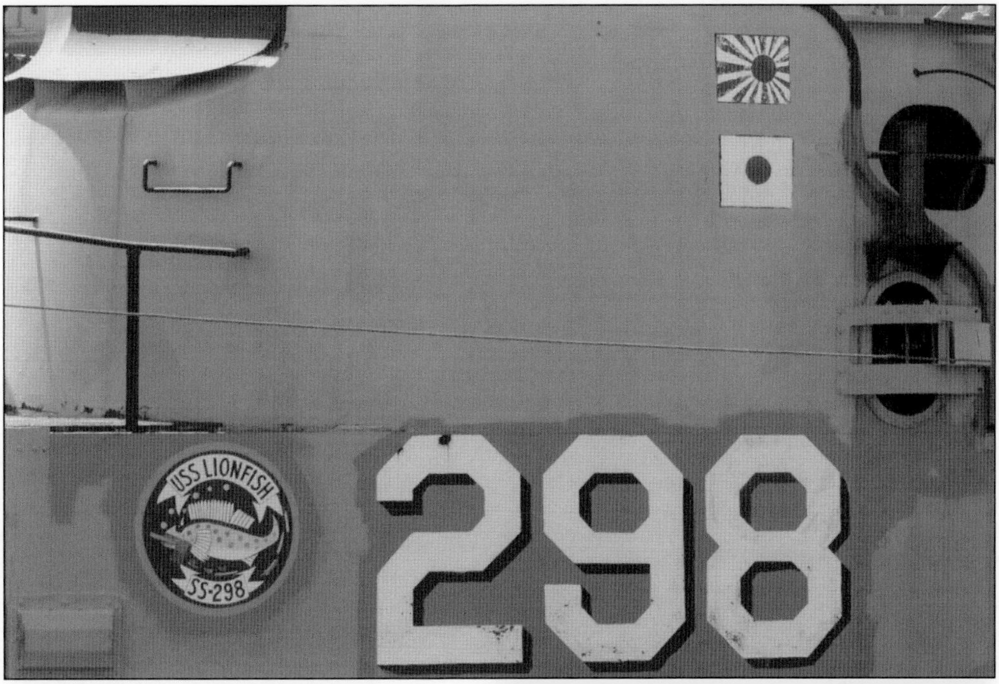

A close-up view of the *Lionfish*'s sail highlights the submarine's crest. On April 11, she was almost destroyed by an enemy sub. After destroying a Japanese schooner on May 1, she fired on a Japanese sub on July 10, and the crew felt they had destroyed it. (Courtesy of Ted Hayes.)

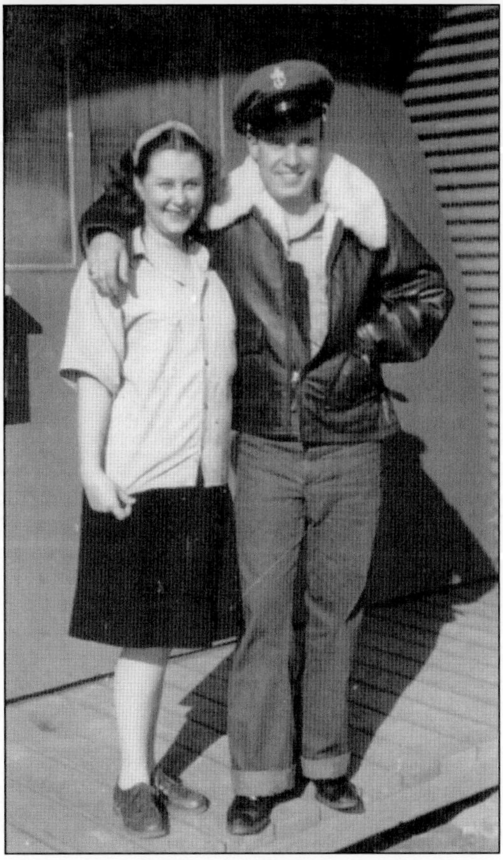

Chief Marx stands with his wife, Catherine "Kay" Marx. American submarines played a major role in the defeat of Japan. Although they comprised the smallest arm of the American military, they destroyed 55 percent of all Japanese shipping in the war. The "Silent Service" sank 1,113 merchant ships and over 200 warships, including 7 aircraft carriers. However, with a casualty rate of 22 percent, their contribution to the war effort came with a tremendous loss of life. There are 52 submarines, and over 3,500 sailors, considered to be on Eternal Patrol. (Courtesy of Catherine Marx.)

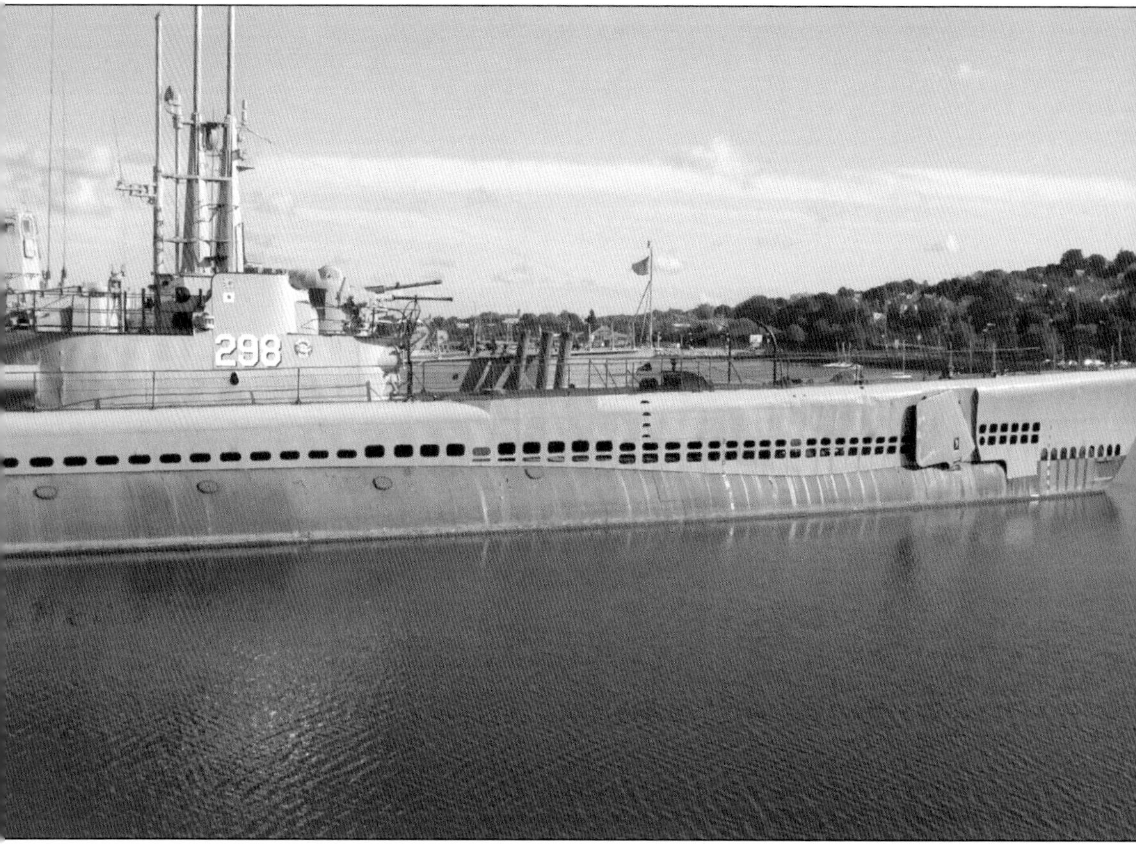

When the war ended, the *Lionfish* sailed for the West Coast and was decommissioned on January 16, 1945. She then entered the Pacific Reserve Fleet. She received one Battle Star for her service in World War II. On January 31, 1951, the *Lionfish* was recommissioned and served as a training ship for the Sonar School in Key West, Florida, for a couple of months. She was transferred to New London, Connecticut, where she continued to be used for training purposes until she was sent to the Boston Naval Yard to be overhauled. On October 18, 1952, she departed for a Mediterranean cruise in which she participated in NATO exercises and had liberty calls at Taranto and Naples, Italy. She was decommissioned again on December 15, 1953, and placed in the Atlantic Reserve Fleet. In 1960 she was used for Naval Reserve Training, and two years later was reclassified an Auxiliary Research Submarine. She was struck from the Naval Register on December 20, 1971, and became a permanent memorial to all submariners at Battleship Cove on August 30, 1972. (Courtesy of Ted Hayes.)

Four

USS *Joseph P. Kennedy, Jr.* (DD-850)

The destroyer *Joseph P. Kennedy, Jr.* (DD-850) was named after the eldest son of Joseph and Rose Kennedy. Built in Quincy, Massachusetts, the vessel was christened by Jean Kennedy on July 26, 1945. Commissioned at the Boston Navy Yard on December 15, 1945, she left for her shakedown cruise in February 1946. The "Jay Pee" cruised off the East Coast, in the Caribbean, and with the Sixth Fleet in the Mediterranean. During the Korean War, she screened aircraft carriers and provided plane guard duties. She rounded out her war career by protecting Formosa from an assault by Chinese forces and helped bombard the city of Wonsan.

After visiting Washington, DC, for the inauguration of Pres. John F. Kennedy, she entered the Brooklyn Navy Yard for an extensive overhaul. In September 1962, she hosted President Kennedy and his family for the America's Cup races.

During the Cuban Missile Crisis, the *Joseph P. Kennedy, Jr.* and another destroyer stopped and boarded the Russian chartered freighter *Marucla*. For the rest of the decade, she continued operating with the Sixth Fleet in the Mediterranean and was part of the afloat recovery teams for NASA's space program. Decommissioned in 1973, she was donated by the Navy to Battleship Cove and officially opened to the public in 1974.

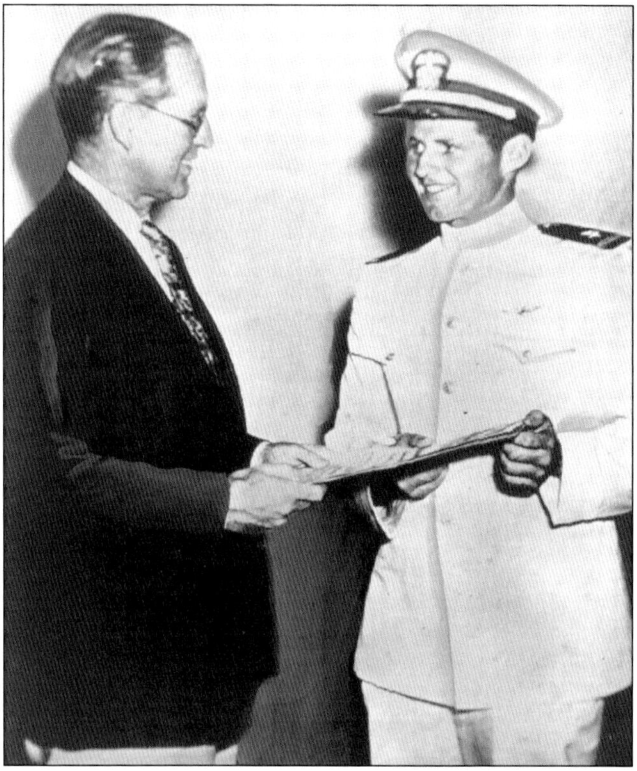

Joseph P. Kennedy Jr. was born on July 25, 1915, in Hull, Massachusetts. He graduated from The Choate School in 1933 and earned his degree at Harvard in 1938. While enrolled at Harvard Law School, he left one year shy of graduation and enlisted in the US Naval Reserve in June 1941. He volunteered for flight training, and as shown here, received his commission and wings from his father in the spring of 1942. (Author's collection.)

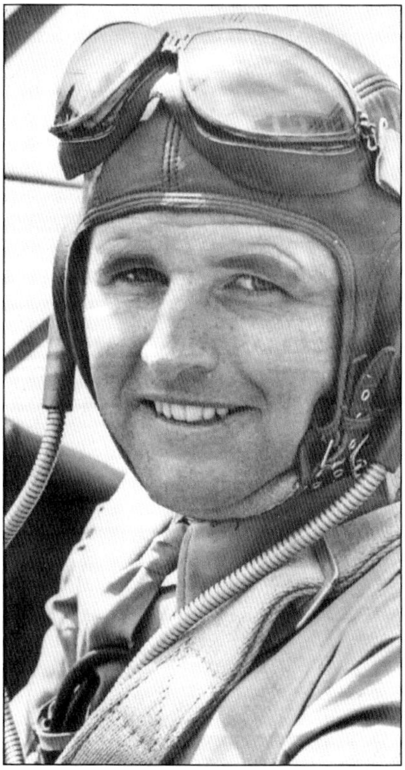

In September 1943, Kennedy was sent to England. For the next several months, he flew Liberators over the North Sea and the English Channel. In July 1944, he volunteered for a secret mission and earned the rank of lieutenant. In this top-secret mission, he and his copilot would fly a Liberator packed with explosives, then bail out while another plane used radio control to guide the drone into a V-2 rocket installation in France. On August 12, 1944, while over England, Kennedy was attempting to parachute from his Liberator bomber when it exploded prematurely. He was posthumously awarded the Navy Cross. (Author's collection.)

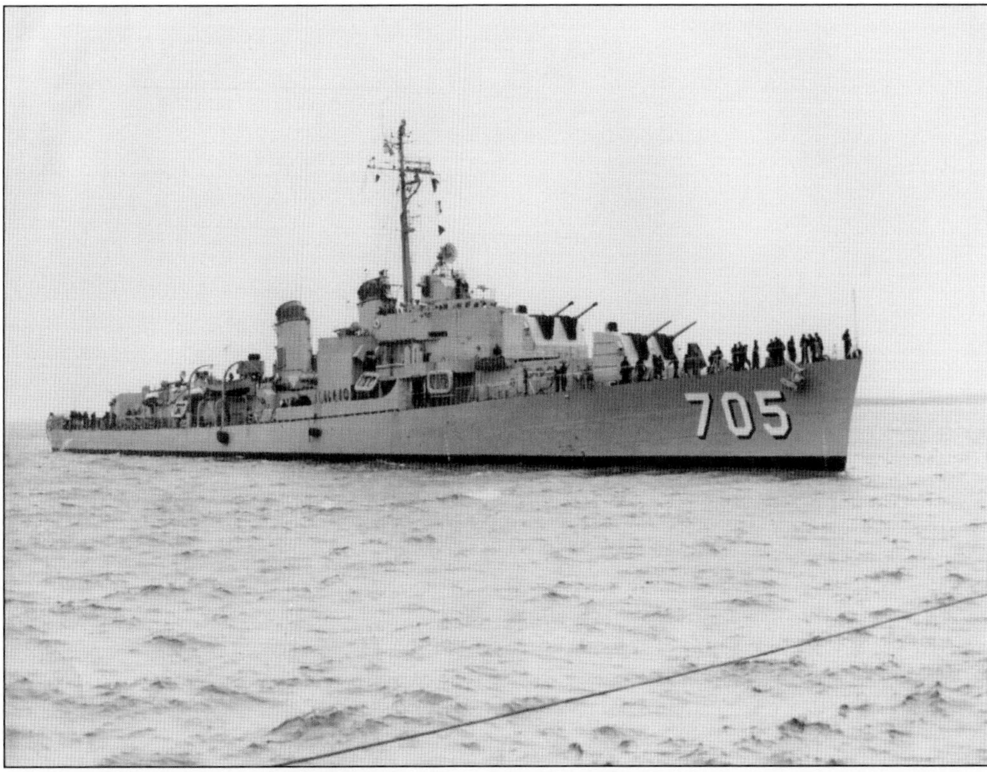

The Navy's destroyers of World War II were mainly of the Fletcher class or the later Sumner class, like the USS *Compton* (DD-705), shown here. The destroyers of the Sumner class were nearly identical to those of the Fletcher class, but their topside arrangement was much different. The next class of destroyer, the Gearing, would basically be the Sumner design with a 14-foot section added amidships to store more fuel. (Author's collection.)

The Navy awarded four Gearing-class contracts to Bethlehem Steel's Fore River Shipyard in Quincy, Massachusetts. Along with the *Kennedy*, it built the USS *Leonard F. Mason*, the USS *Rupertus*, and the USS *Charles H. Roan*. After the laying of her keel on April 2, 1945, the *JPK* begins to come to life along the Fore River on May 3, 1945.

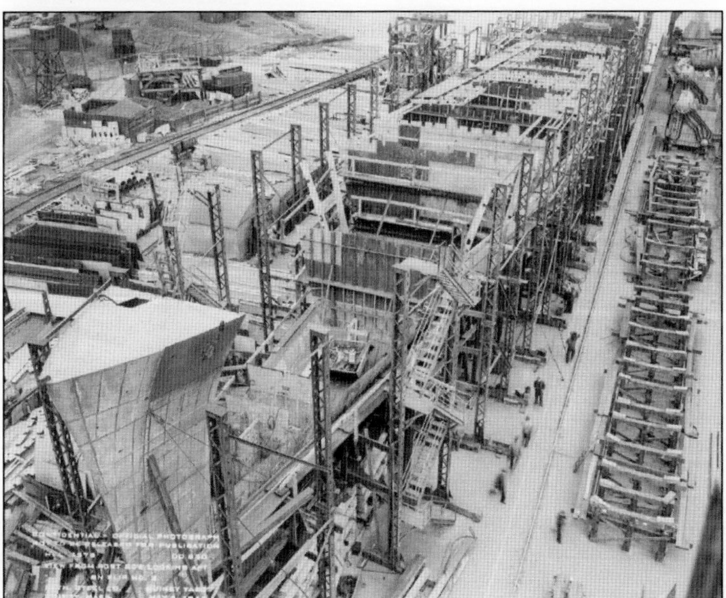

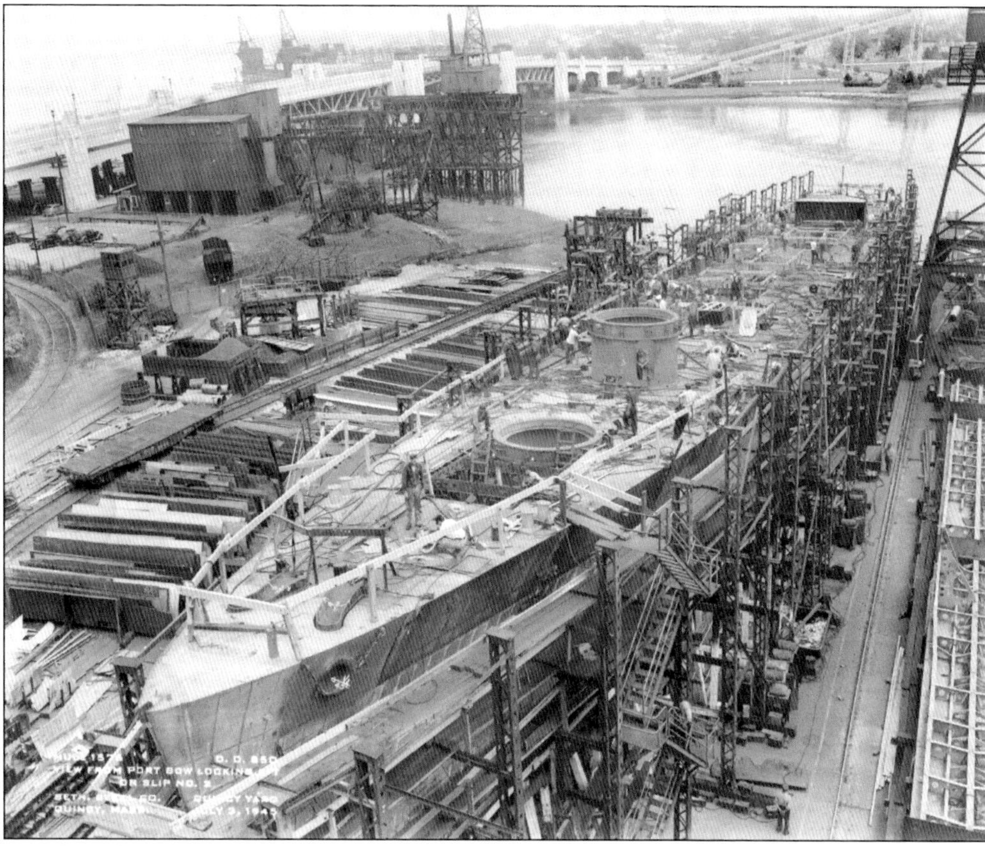

By July 3, all of her machinery, such as boilers and engines, had been installed and her hull was almost finished. The gun mount foundations of her two forward guns, Mount 51 and Mount 52, can be seen at center. At upper left is the Fore River drawbridge, which leads out to Boston Harbor's south channel, Nantasket Roads.

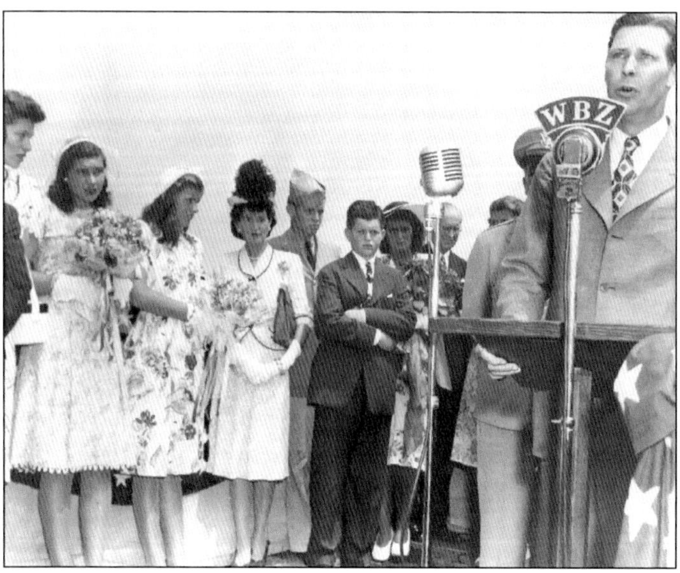

One day after what would have been Lieutenant Kennedy's 30th birthday, the destroyer named after him was ready to be launched on July 26, 1945. Although not yet a commissioned Navy ship, she was a step closer. Named after a native son, the commissioning was a major news story. Future senator Ted Kennedy (center) watches the ceremony. Over his right shoulder is his older brother Robert, and over his left shoulder is his sister Jean, the official sponsor of the ship.

Jean Kennedy, 17, her father, Joseph Sr., and mother, Rose, are all smiles prior to the launching. In honor of their son's memory, they created the Joseph P. Kennedy, Jr. Foundation in 1946. The foundation advocates for those with intellectual disabilities through public awareness campaigns and fundraising.

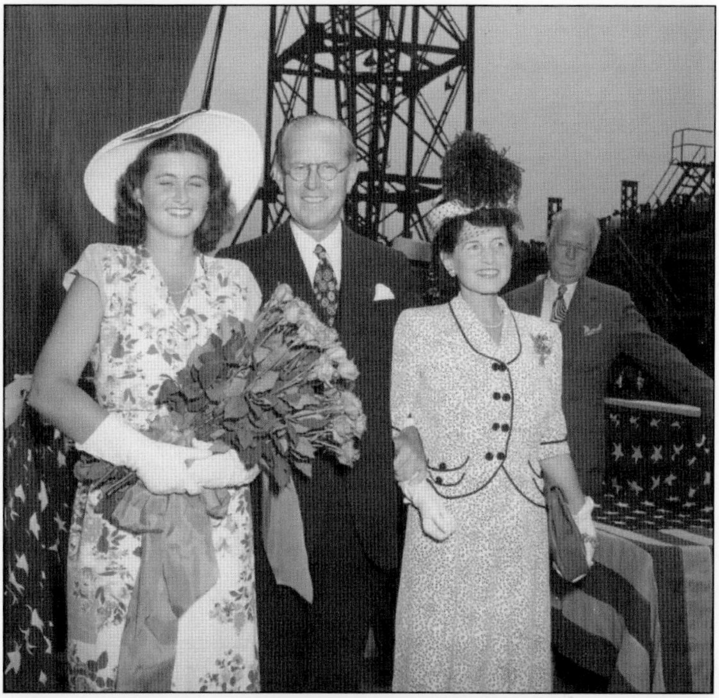

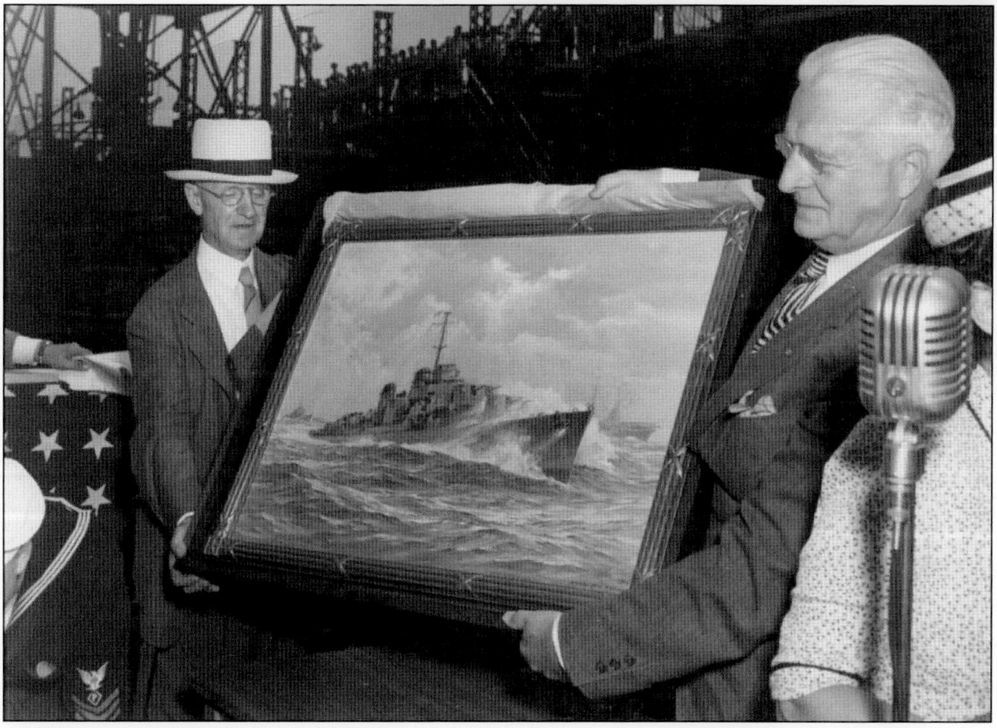

A painting of the USS *Joseph P. Kennedy, Jr.* escorting a carrier task force was presented to the family prior to the launching. Joseph Sr. was no stranger to either the Fore River Yard or the US Navy. In 1917, at the age of 29, he became the assistant general manager for the Quincy yard, which was booming as a result of America's entry into World War I.

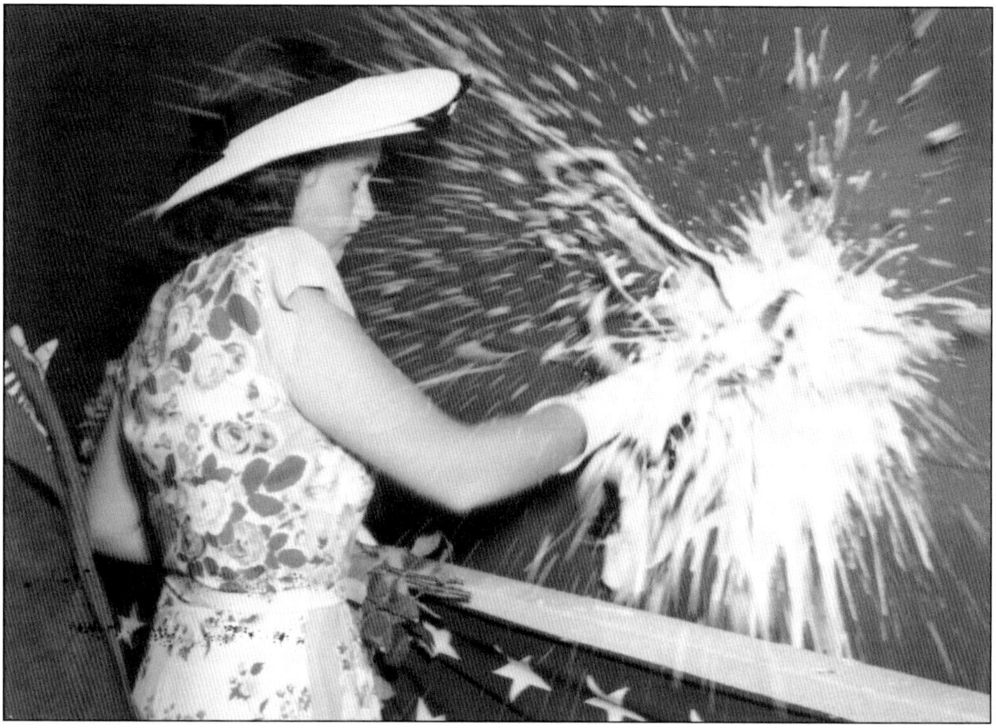

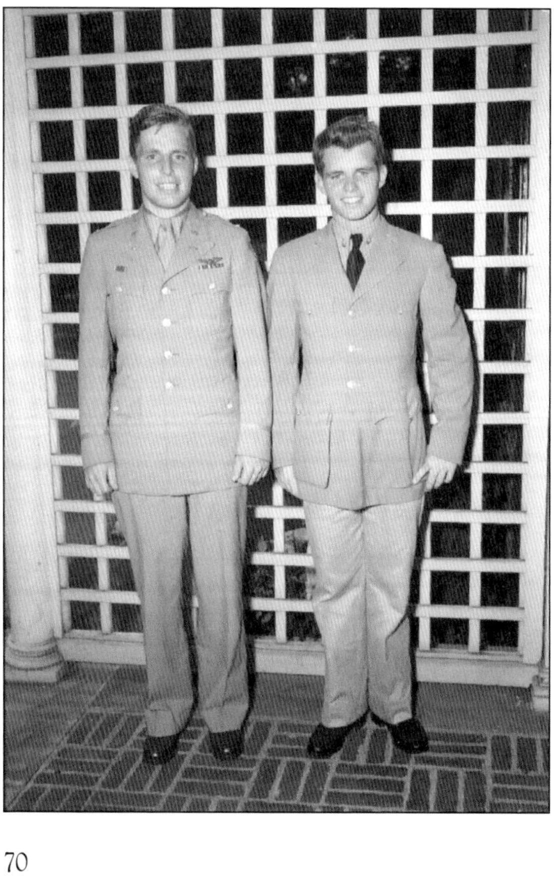

Jean Kennedy, the eighth child and youngest daughter of Rose and Joseph Sr., smashes a champagne bottle on the bow of a destroyer named for her eldest brother. At the time, the 2,400-ton *JPK* was the largest destroyer the Fore River Yard had ever built. With a thin hull and no armor, destroyers are affectionately called "tin cans" by their sailors.

An unknown sailor and Robert Kennedy (right) pose during a party held after the christening. Born 10 years after Joseph Jr., Robert enlisted in the Naval Reserve on October 5, 1943, just shy of his 18th birthday. Just two months before he joined the Navy, his brother Jack was almost killed when the PT-boat he was commanding was split in two by a Japanese destroyer. In 1946, Robert would serve aboard the *Kennedy*.

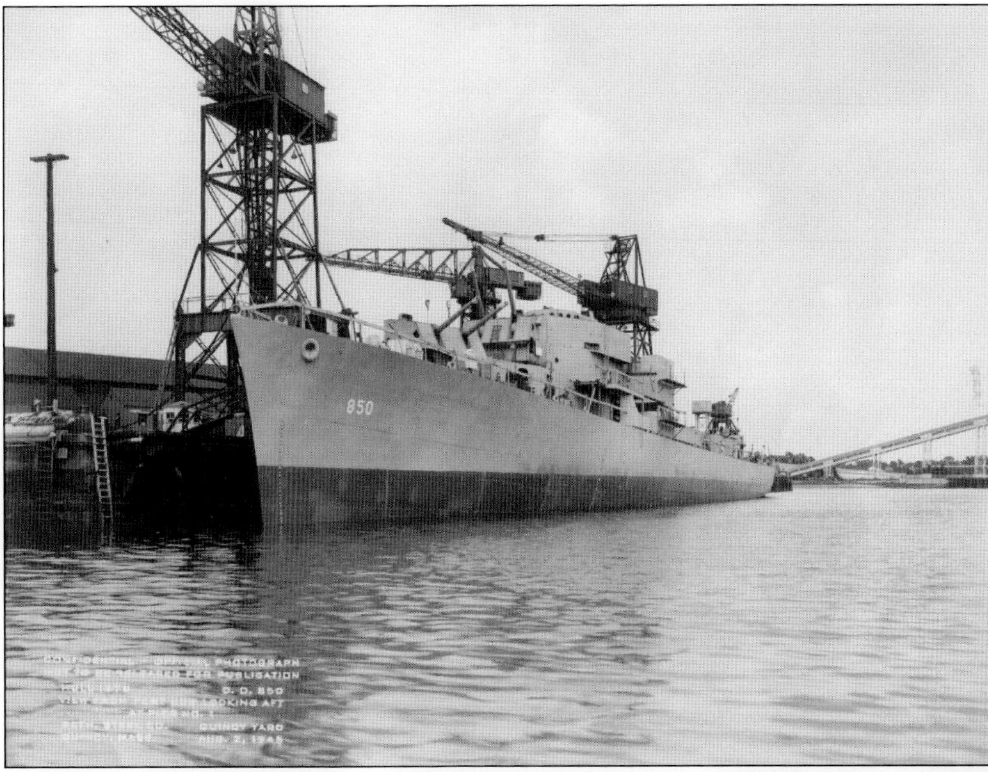

On August 2, 1945, the *Kennedy* continues to be fitted out at Pier No. 1. All three of its 5-inch, 38-caliber guns have been installed, and the portholes of her pilothouse can be seen. With little fuel, stores, and ammunition belowdecks, she rides very high out of the water.

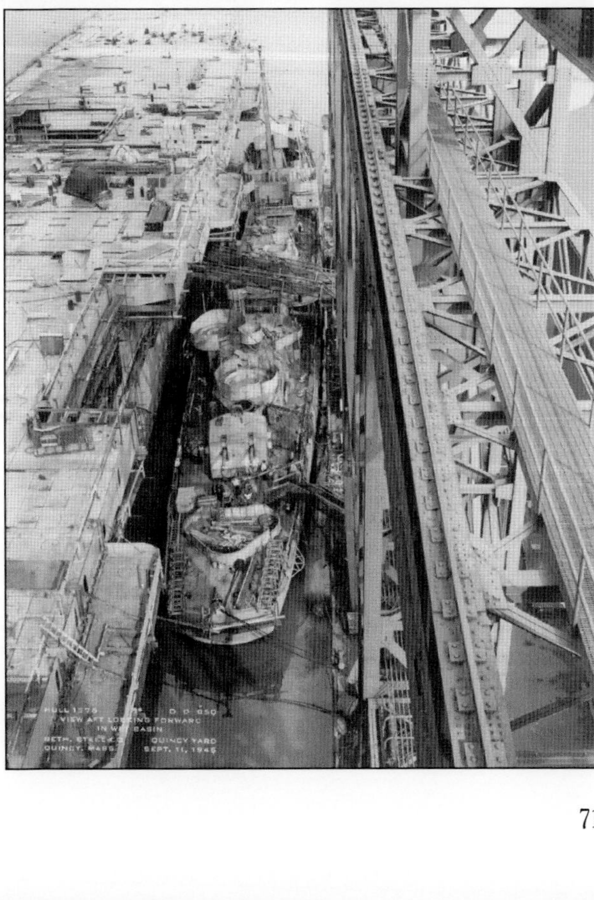

Seen here on September 11, 1945, the *JPK* is almost a complete warship. On the left is the Essex-class carrier the USS *Philippine Sea* (CV-47), which had been launched six days earlier. By this time, a good number of officers and enlisted personnel had reported aboard to familiarize themselves with their new home.

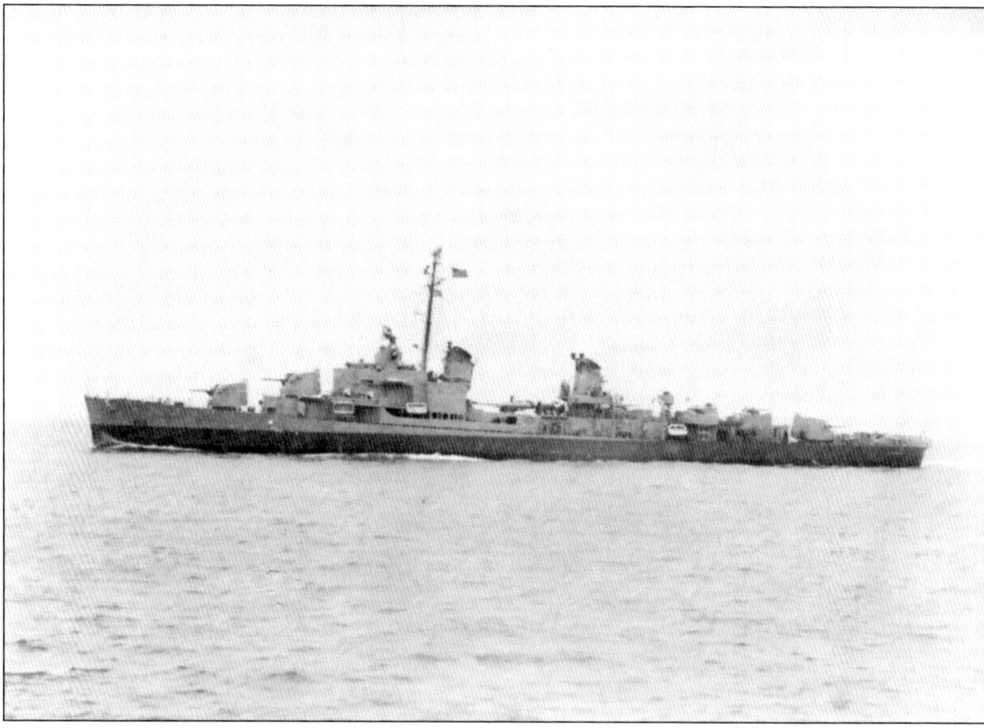

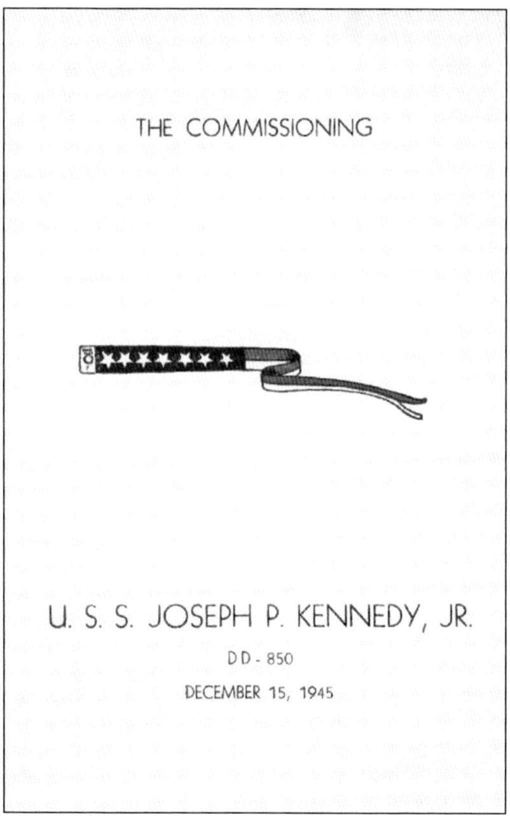

THE COMMISSIONING

U. S. S. JOSEPH P. KENNEDY, JR.

DD - 850

DECEMBER 15, 1945

The *Kennedy* steamed from the Fore River Shipyard to the Boston Navy Yard in a snowstorm on December 14, 1945, as she was going to be commissioned the next day. She was powered by four boilers driving two sets of steam turbines, which in turn drove her two propellers through reduction gears. The machinery was in alternating compartments, ensuring that one torpedo hit could not stop the destroyer dead in the water.

This is the front cover of the destroyer's commissioning program. After World War II, there was talk in the highest levels of the government to completely do away with the US Navy. Many leaders believed that America's next war would be against Russia and that victory would be won with the use of airplanes delivering atomic bombs.

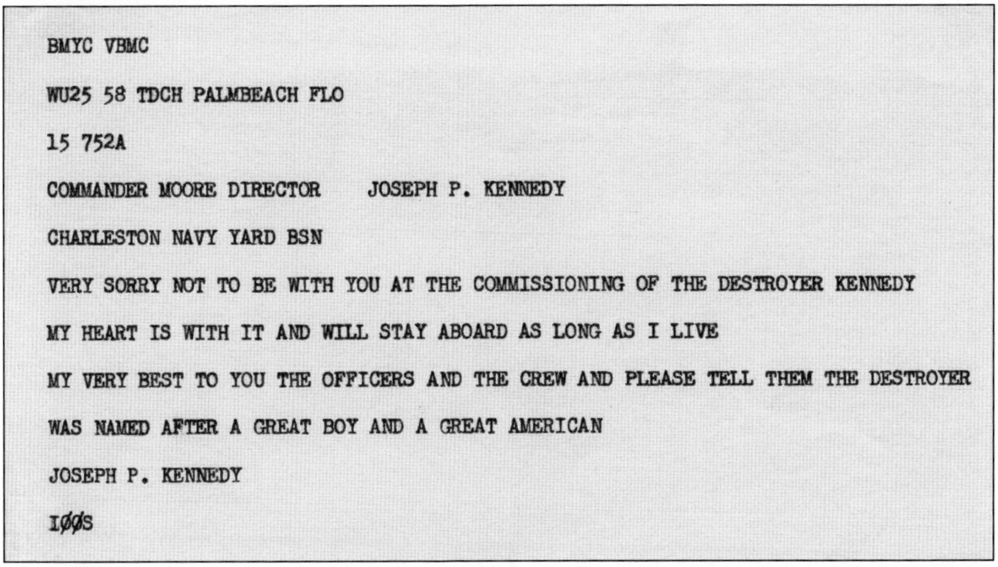

BMYC VBMC

WU25 58 TDCH PALMBEACH FLO

15 752A

COMMANDER MOORE DIRECTOR JOSEPH P. KENNEDY

CHARLESTON NAVY YARD BSN

VERY SORRY NOT TO BE WITH YOU AT THE COMMISSIONING OF THE DESTROYER KENNEDY

MY HEART IS WITH IT AND WILL STAY ABOARD AS LONG AS I LIVE

MY VERY BEST TO YOU THE OFFICERS AND THE CREW AND PLEASE TELL THEM THE DESTROYER

WAS NAMED AFTER A GREAT BOY AND A GREAT AMERICAN

JOSEPH P. KENNEDY

IØØS

Joseph Kennedy Sr., unable to attend the commissioning, sent this telegram from his home in Palm Beach, Florida, to the *Kennedy's* commanding officer, Cmdr. Harry G. Moore. Joseph, continuing his business interests, became focused on real estate. He began to invest most of his energies in the careers of his remaining sons, especially his second son, John.

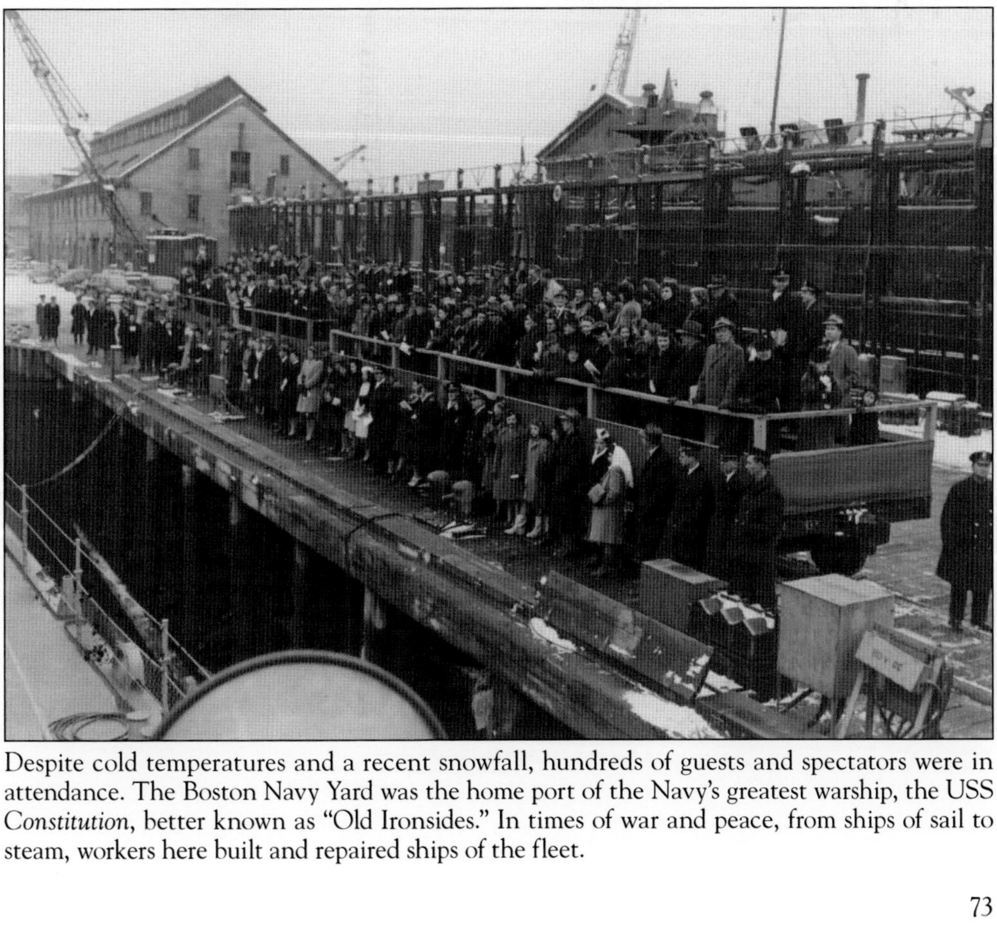

Despite cold temperatures and a recent snowfall, hundreds of guests and spectators were in attendance. The Boston Navy Yard was the home port of the Navy's greatest warship, the USS *Constitution*, better known as "Old Ironsides." In times of war and peace, from ships of sail to steam, workers here built and repaired ships of the fleet.

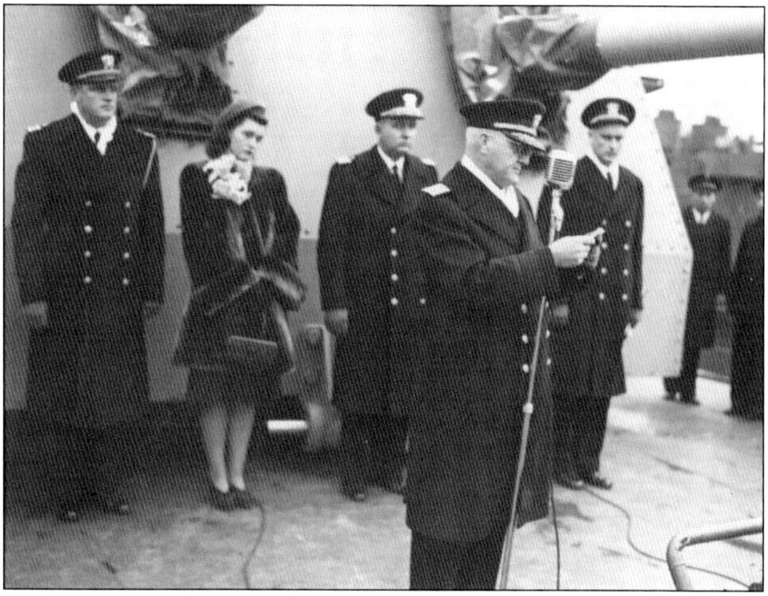

The featured speaker of the occasion, Rear Adm. Felix Gygax, commandant of the 1st Naval District, used the opportunity to deliver a strong plea for keeping intact the naval forces of the United States and firmly opposed the armed-forces unification plan proposed by the Army.

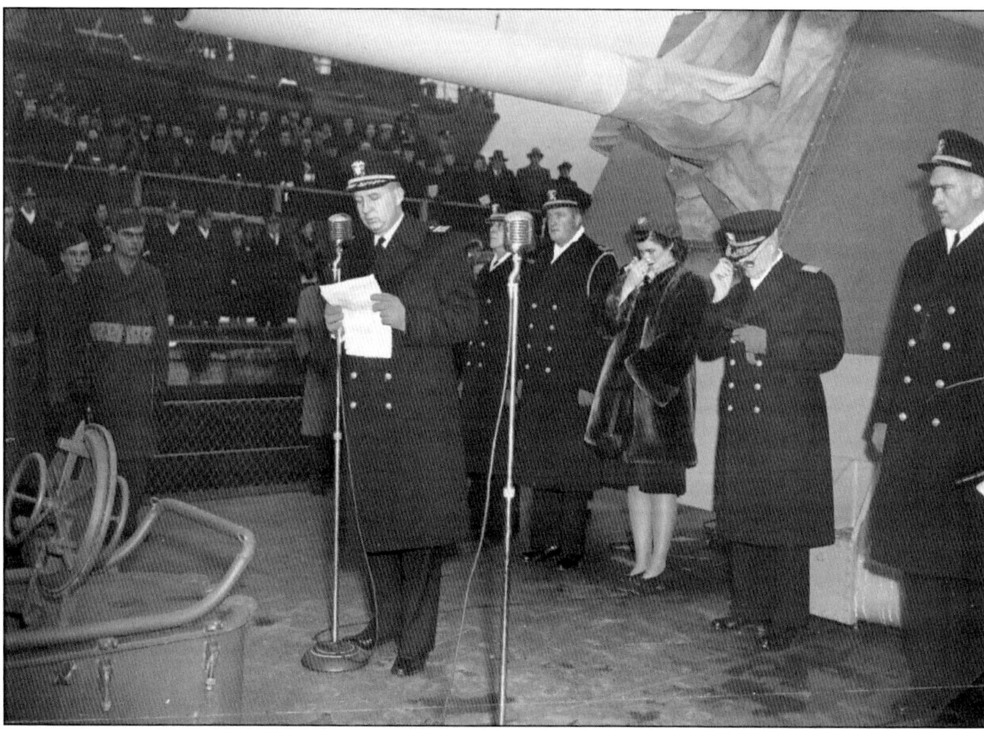

With the ship's sponsor, Jean Kennedy, behind him, Commander Moore reads his commissioning orders. A veteran of World War II, Moore knew destroyers, and he knew death. He became the commanding officer of the destroyer USS *Kidd* in August 1944. On April 11, 1945, a kamikaze plane with a bomb for payload slammed into the *Kidd* off Okinawa. The attack killed 38 men outright and wounded 55, several seriously, including Moore.

Although the *Joseph P. Kennedy, Jr.* carries no depth charges yet, this photograph provides an excellent view of the portside depth-charge track. When hunting a submarine, the charges rolled from the tracks by gravity when released mechanically or by a hydraulic system from the bridge. Sailors often referred to depth charges as "ash cans" because of their shape.

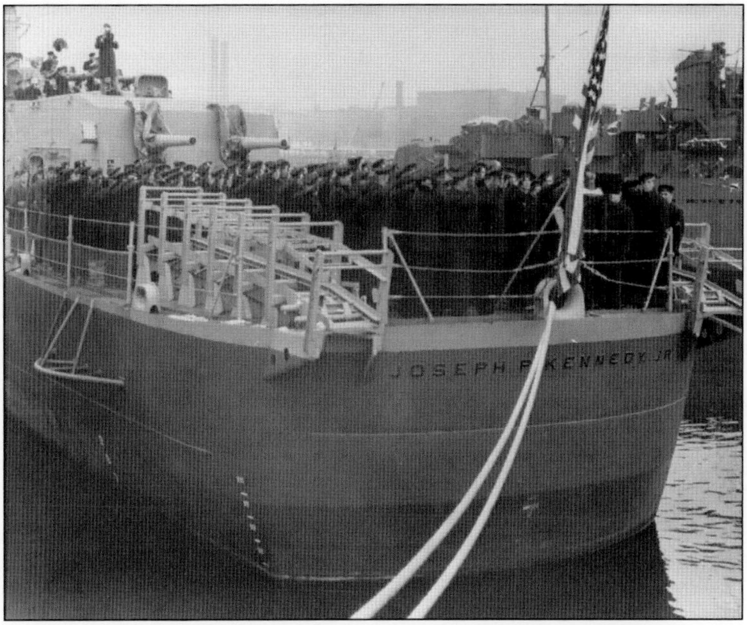

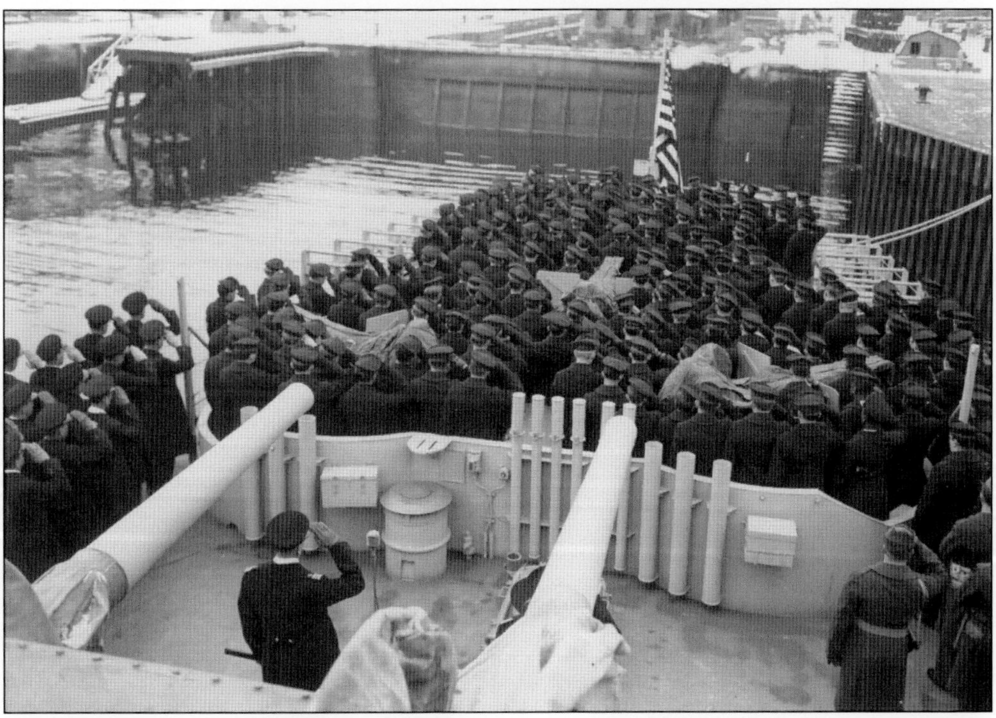

After the *JPK*'s first commanding officer, Cmdr. H.G. Moore, read his orders, the crew salutes the American flag. Besides Commander Moore, her crew was made up of 22 officers and 345 enlisted sailors. On February 4, 1946, the *JPK* steamed to the Caribbean for her shakedown cruise to ensure that everything worked on the ship and to provide the crew the opportunity to familiarize themselves with the newest class of destroyer.

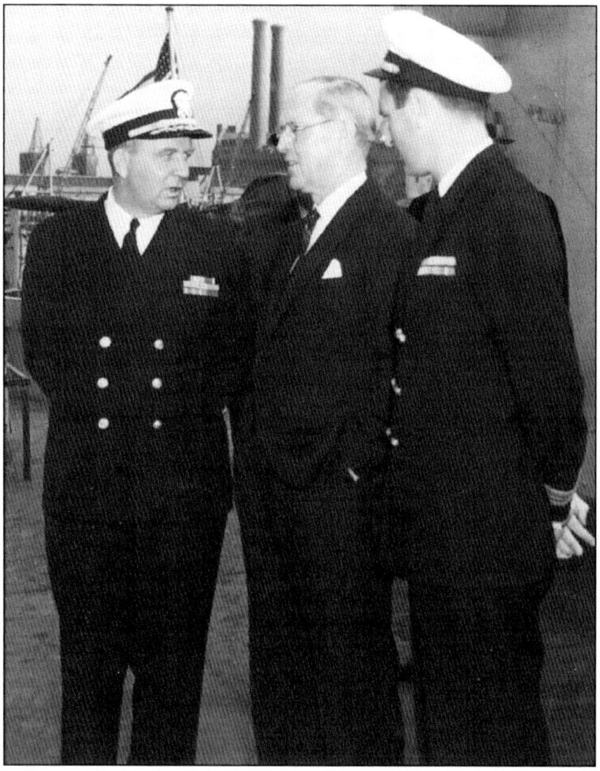

On April 11, 1946, Joseph Kennedy Sr., visiting the ship named after his oldest son for the first time at the Boston Navy Yard, was given a personal tour. While reviewing the sailors, he met his son, Robert, who had volunteered to serve aboard the *Kennedy*. At the time, Robert was working to earn the rate of radar man. The *JPK* soon left for her home port of Newport, Rhode Island, and participated in Naval Reserve training for the next several months.

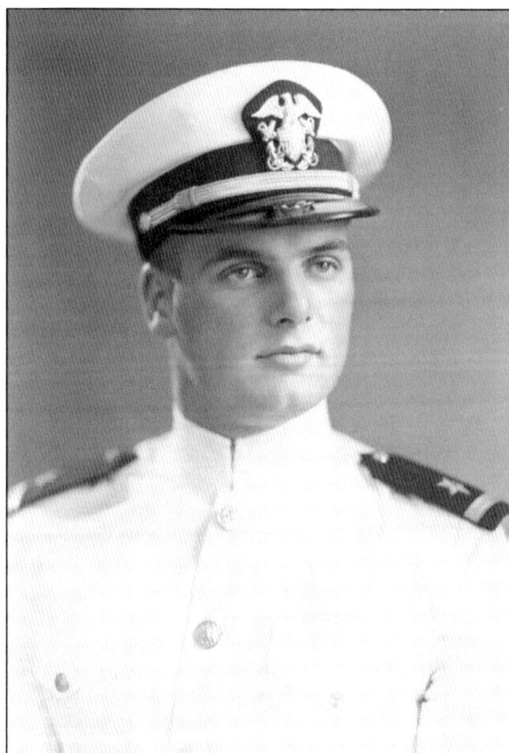

Ens. George West Jr. grew up in the same city that built the *Kennedy* and is believed to have been the youngest officer at the time of her commissioning. Ensign West was the assistant engineering officer aboard the *Kennedy* when she made a goodwill tour to South America for the inauguration of the president of Chile in November 1946. This would be the ship's only deployment to the Southern Atlantic during her entire career.

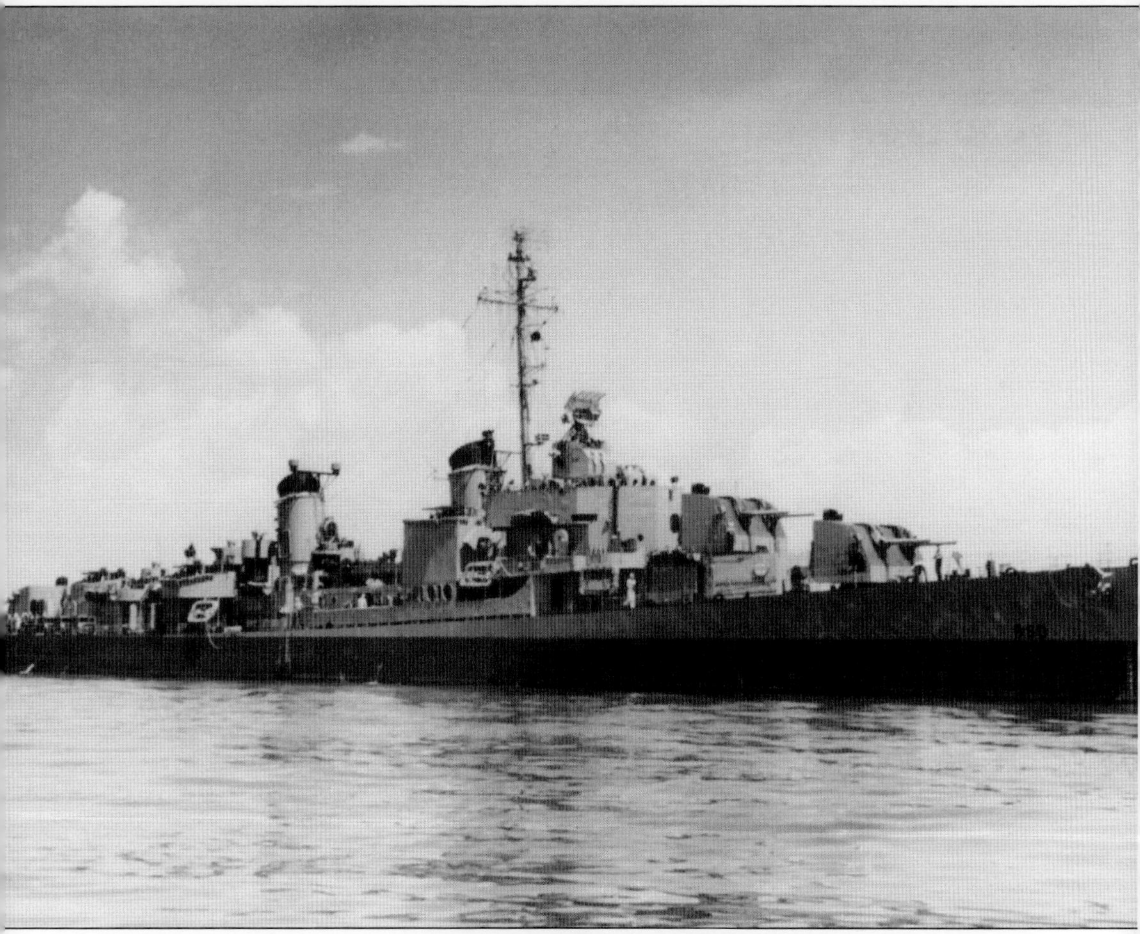

In the first half of 1947, the *Kennedy* conducted antisubmarine exercises off Rhode Island and then sailed with the aircraft carrier USS *Philippine Sea* to the Caribbean Sea. Retuning to Newport on May 5, she became the flagship of Destroyer Division 102, Destroyer Squadron 10 on May 15. A week later, she participated in antisubmarine exercises with the submarine *Finback* (SS-230).

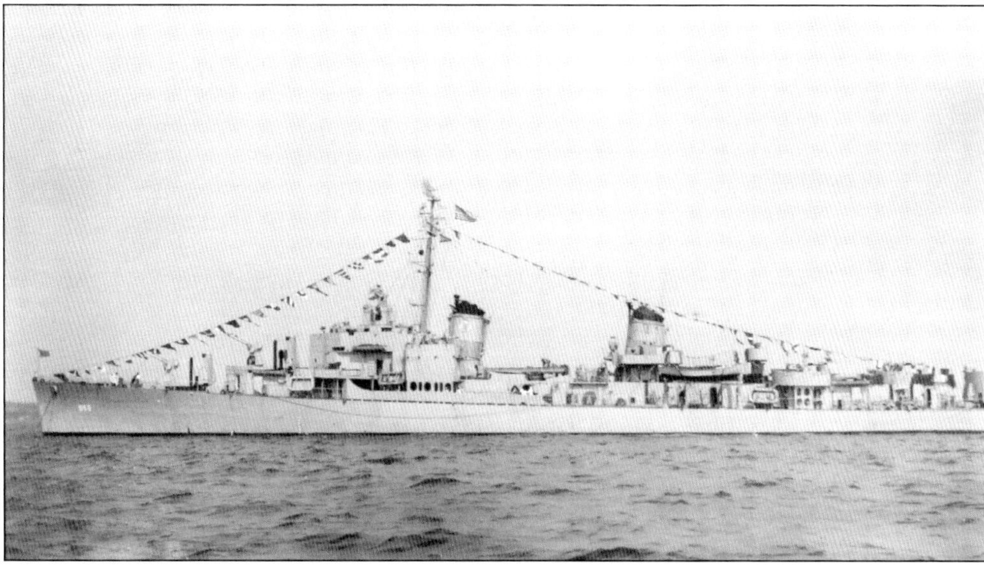

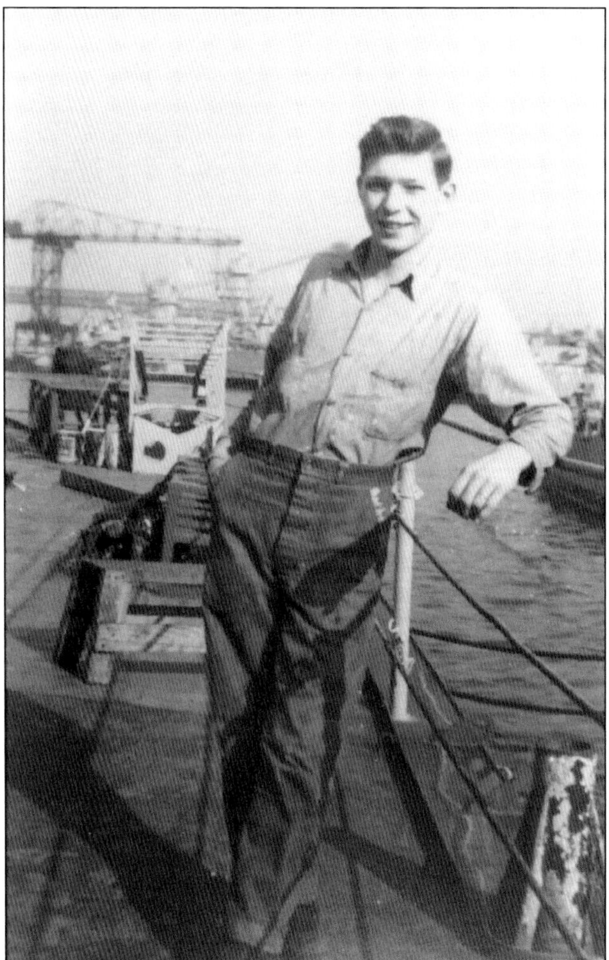

On June 20, the *Kennedy* arrived at New York City and moored off Poughkeepsie for the annual sailing regatta in the Hudson River. Here, she lies anchored on July 4, 1947, with flags flying from stem to stern, a custom called "dressing the ship." Ships of the Navy are dressed or full dressed on special occasions such as national holidays, or as a compliment to a foreign nation or distinguished person.

During the summer, the *Joseph P. Kennedy, Jr.* participated in a naval reserve officer training cruise from Newport to Argentia, Newfoundland. The *Kennedy* arrived in the Brooklyn Navy Yard in August for an overhaul. While the work was being done, Machinist's Mate Third Class Howard L. Bishop stood on the forecastle for this photograph. The battleship *New Jersey* (BB-62), serving at New York as flagship for Rear Adm. Heber H. McClean, commander, Battleship Division One, is in the background. Bishop served aboard the *JPK* from June 1946 until April 1949.

CPO Harold Davis, standing on the wing of the bridge, is using a navigational instrument called a pelorus. On March 1, 1948, the *Kennedy* arrived off Gibraltar for her first deployment with the newly created Sixth Task Fleet, later called Sixth Fleet, in the Mediterranean. These "gray diplomats" maintained the policies and prestige of America and ensured that the people of the Mediterranean lived in peace under governments of their own choosing.

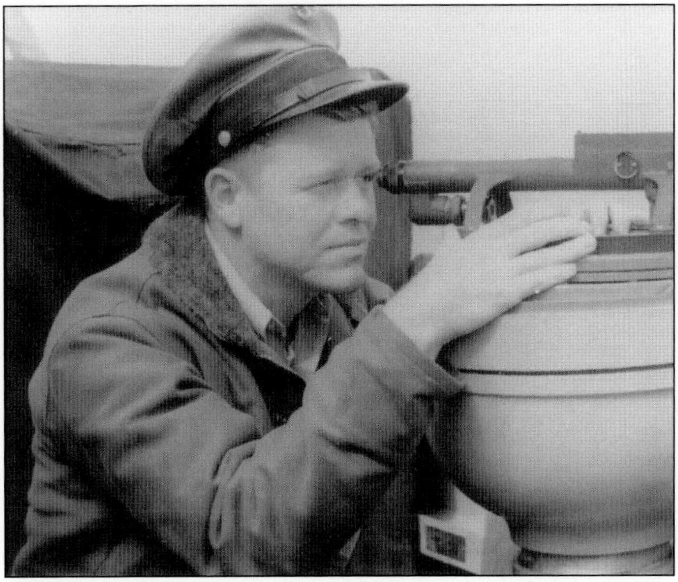

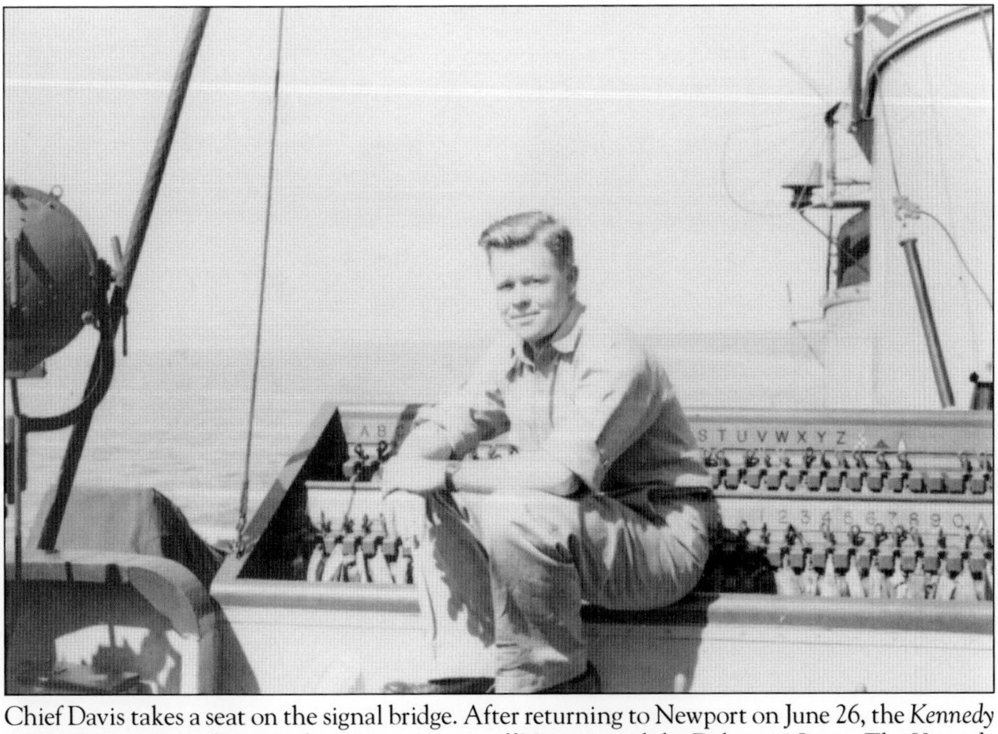

Chief Davis takes a seat on the signal bridge. After returning to Newport on June 26, the *Kennedy* was underway again for antisubmarine exercises off Virginia and the Delaware Capes. The *Kennedy* conducted another naval reserve training cruise off Cuba. In November, she was involved in Operation Barn Dance, a simulated search-and-destroy training mission against submarines.

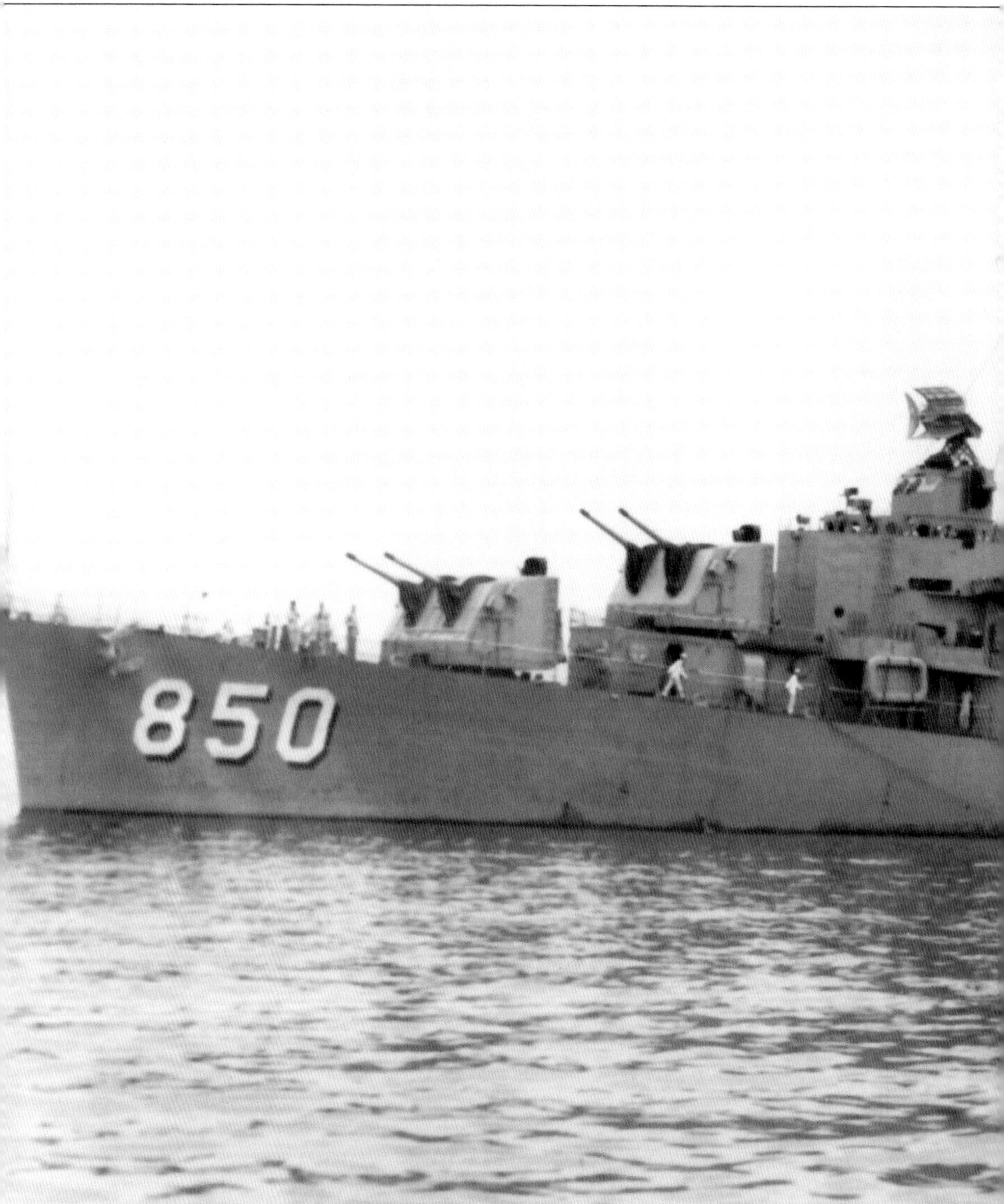

With the outbreak of the Korean War in 1950, the *Kennedy*, along with the three other destroyers of Destroyer Division 81, the *Rush*, *Fiske*, and *Hawkins*, practiced bombardment exercises as they prepared to be deployed in the combat zone. On January 3, 1951, under overall command of Capt. E.S. Von Kleeck, the destroyers left for Sasebo, Japan, via the Panama Canal. In February, the *Kennedy*, along with her fellow destroyers, joined Task Force 77 off Korea and screened the

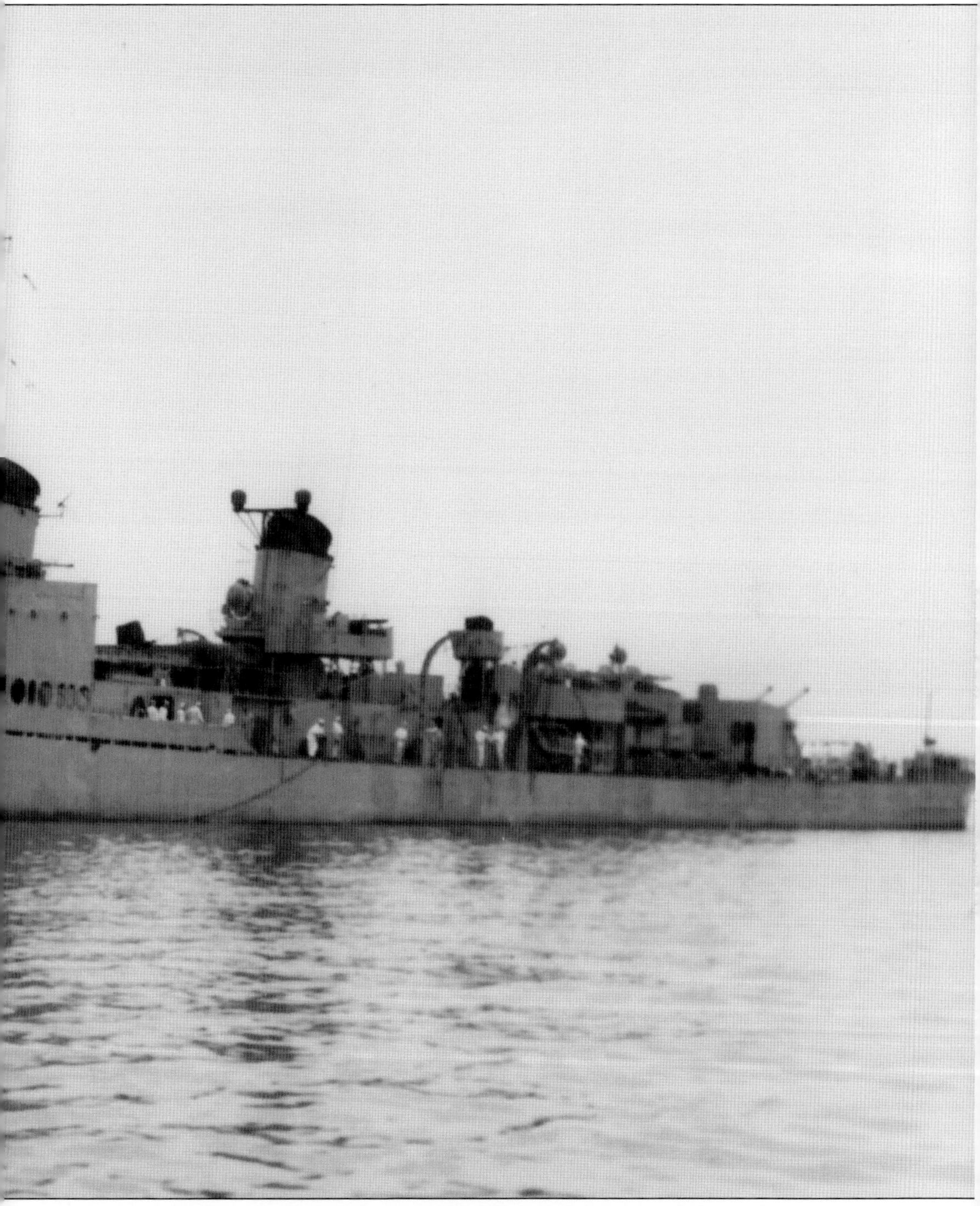

aircraft carriers *Princeton* (CV-37), *Valley Forge* (CV-45), and *Philippine Sea* (CV-47) as their aircraft pounded enemy positions. On April 8, she steamed between mainland China and Formosa as part of the Formosa Patrol. This show of force was intended to deter the Communist forces from an amphibious assault across the Formosa Strait. (Courtesy of the US Naval Institute.)

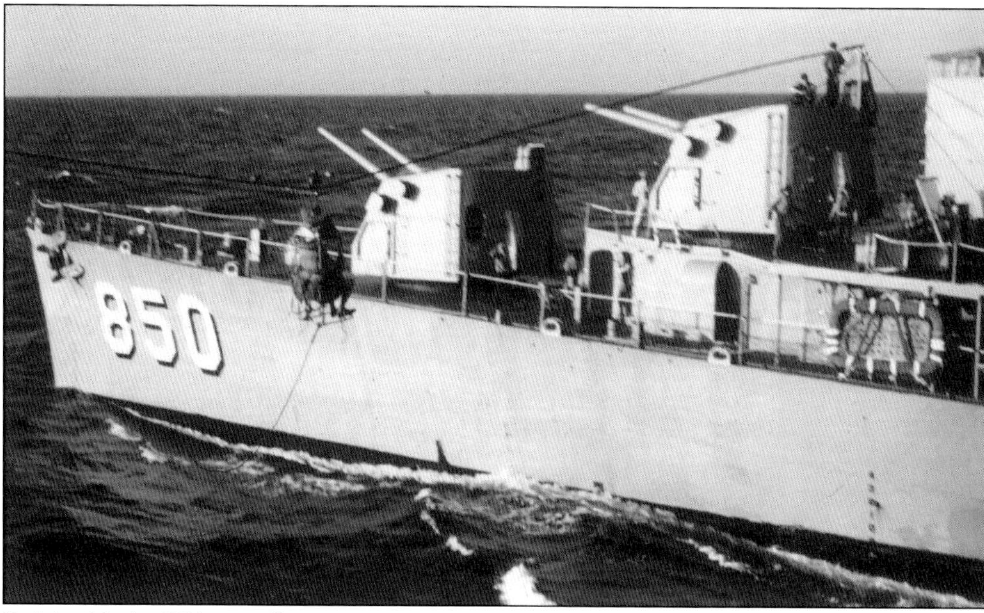

By May 20, the *JPK* was off Wonsan in North Korea and constantly firing her 5-inch, 38-caliber guns in shore bombardment and direct fire support for the troops ashore. On June 13, the *Kennedy's* role in the Korean War came to an end. For her service, the destroyer earned two Battle Stars. She headed to Sasebo, Japan, but soon left for Singapore, her first port of call on her around-the-world cruise. Here, a sailor from another destroyer is high-lined to the *JPK* by use of the bosun chair.

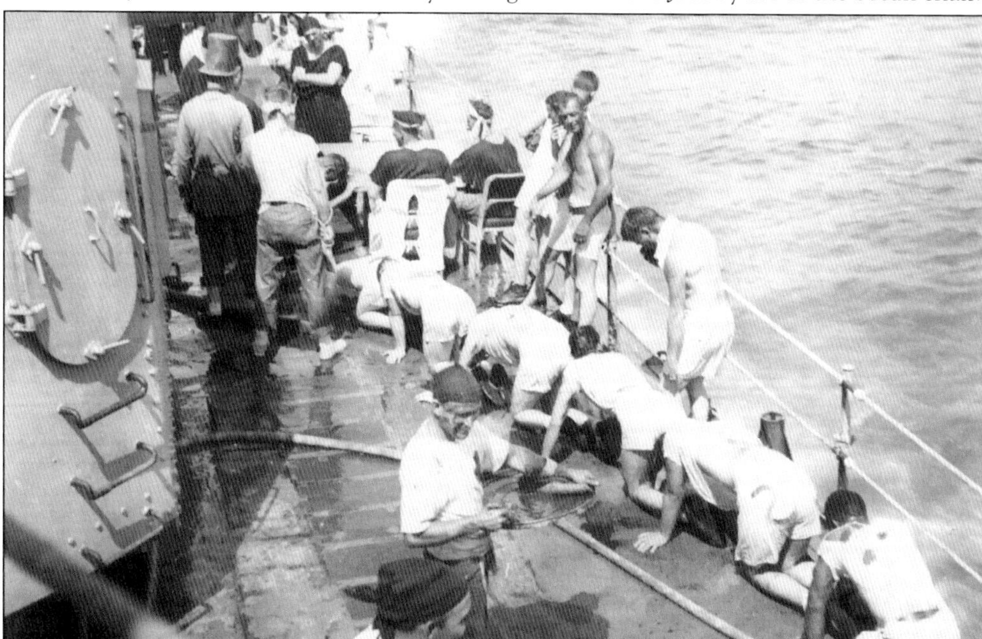

On June 27, on the Indian Ocean, the *JPK* crossed the equator. Anyone who had never crossed the equator before ("pollywogs") had to be initiated by those who had ("shellbacks"). At noon, all pollywogs had to report to the bow of the ship, get on their hands and knees, and crawl single file to the fantail, where the ceremony commenced. (Courtesy of Brad Strait.)

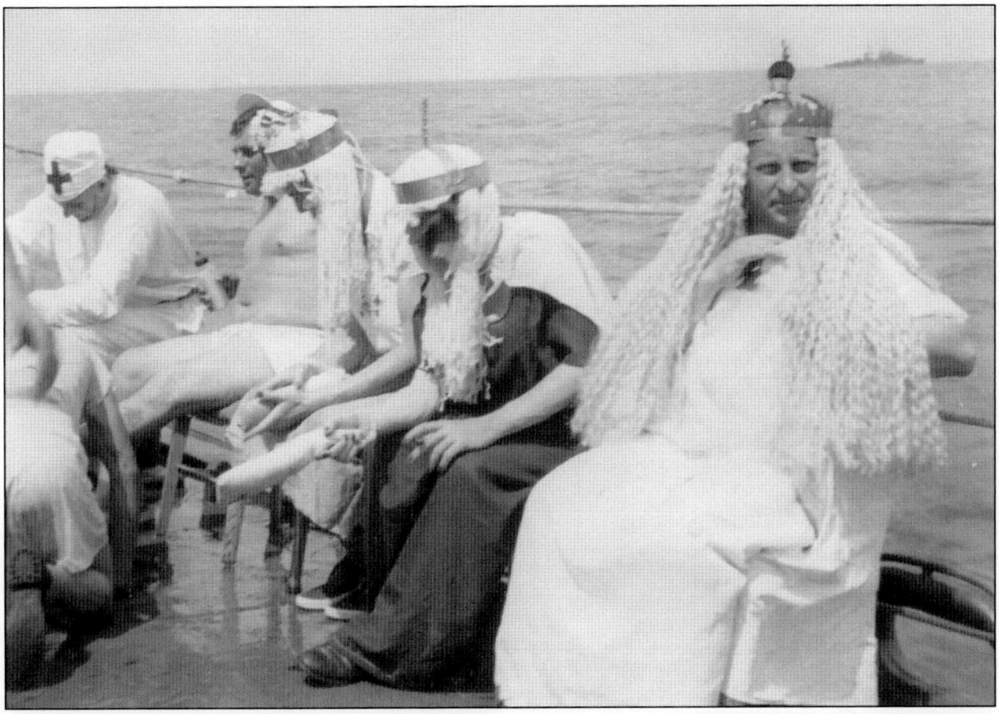

As they crawled, the pollywogs received their subpoena from Chief Radioman Robert Hahn and were hit by shellbacks with blackjacks, two pieces of canvas sewn together and filled with wet rags, for any reason they could come up with. After being doused with water from a fire hose, the pollywogs appeared before the Royal Court and were found guilty of all charges. They then had to kiss the Royal Baby's Belly and perhaps sing a verse of a popular song. (Courtesy of Brad Strait.)

After having their bodies covered in thick grease, the pollywogs reported to the Royal Barber, who would apply the Royal Shampoo, a double handful of burnt fuel oil mixed with graphite. After the shampoo, the Royal Barber removed random chunks of hair from their heads with dull scissors. (Courtesy of Brad Strait.)

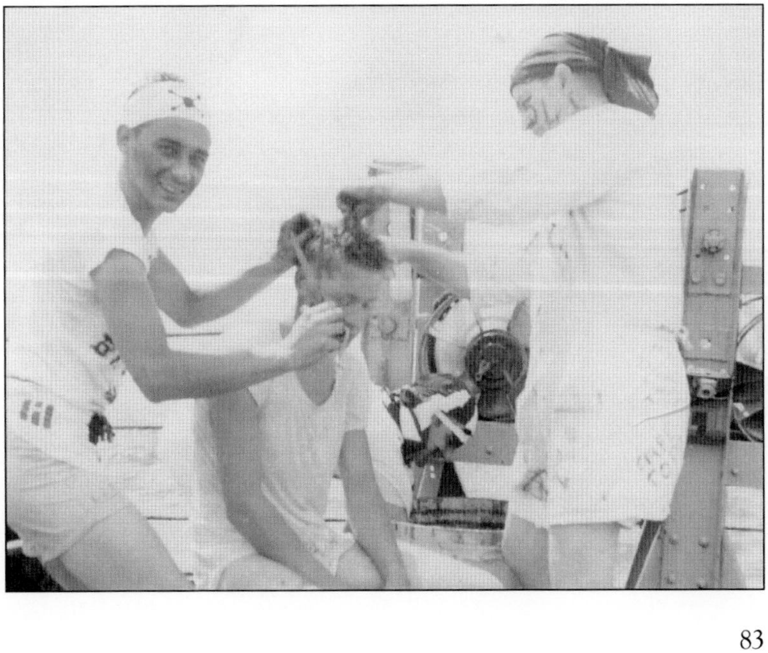

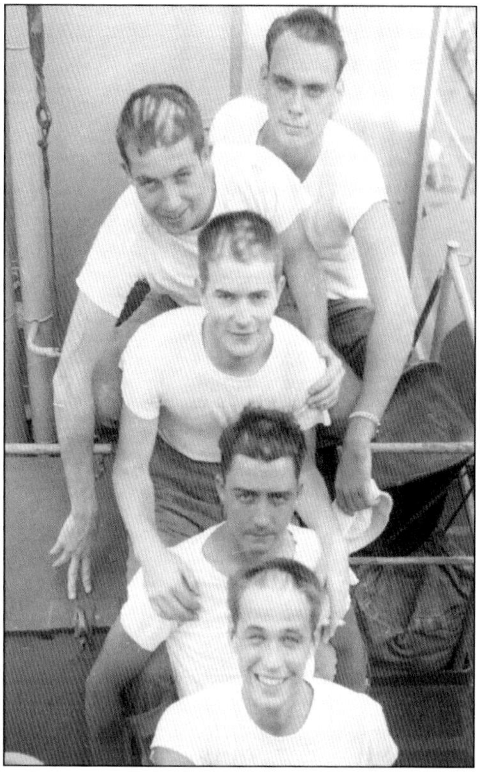

The day before the ceremony, Buddie T. Pender had been disrespectful to the shellback who was going to be the Royal Barber. He also made the mistake of telling the Royal Barber that when he returned home to Newport, he was going to get married. Pender soon learned that he should have kept his mouth shut. The ship's radio gang poses here after their haircuts. They are, from top to bottom, Robert Grimm, Gene Walker, David Simmons, Pender, and Donald Schultz. (Courtesy of Brad Strait.)

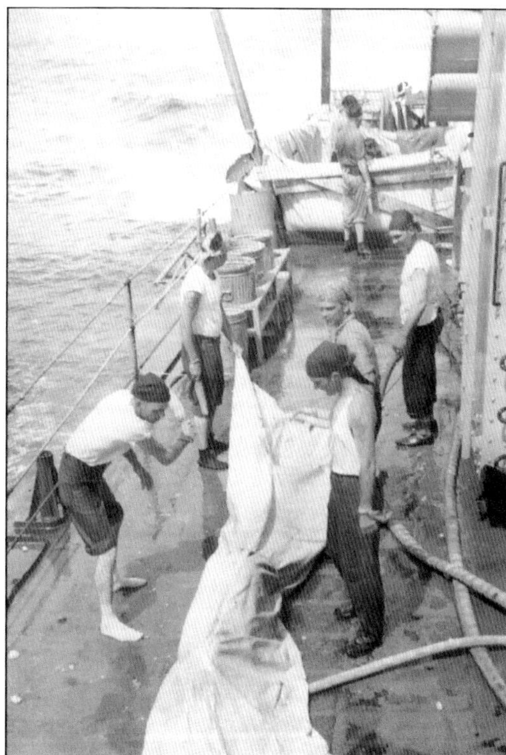

The pollywogs then had to crawl through a canvas slop-chute while being beaten by blackjack-wielding shellbacks. The chute, about 12 to 15 feet long, was filled with weeks-old garbage. The shellbacks added flour and water as well. The pollywogs had to squirm on their stomachs through this mess while being hit by the shellbacks. After being sprayed by a fire hose, the pollywogs officially became shellbacks. (Courtesy of Brad Strait.)

On June 29, the ship arrived in Colombo, Ceylon, and its softball team competed in the first annual Ceylon World Series. After beating the teams of fellow destroyers *Fiske* and *Rush*, the team advanced to the championship and won 7-5. After the *Kennedy* team's victory, the American ambassador presented the coach with a beautiful cup. Continuing on to Saudi Arabia, the *Kennedy* traveled through the Suez Canal and stopped at Port Said, Egypt. The crew stopped at Naples, Italy, on July 23 and at last arrived at Newport in August.

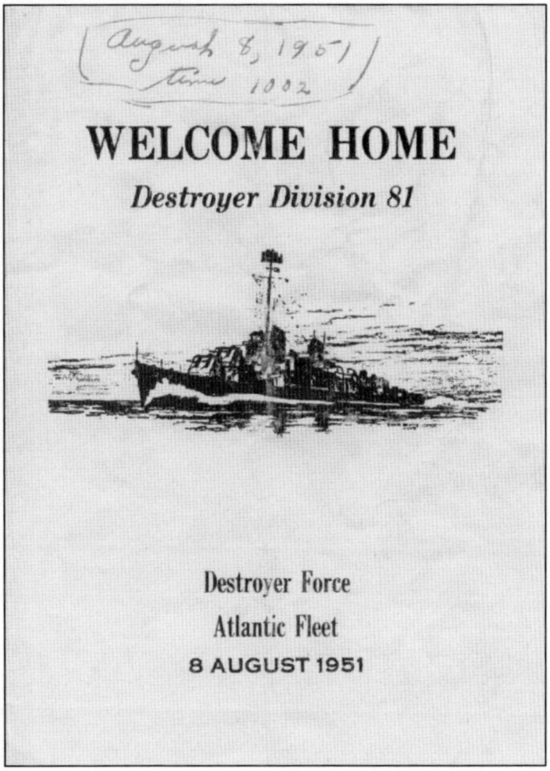

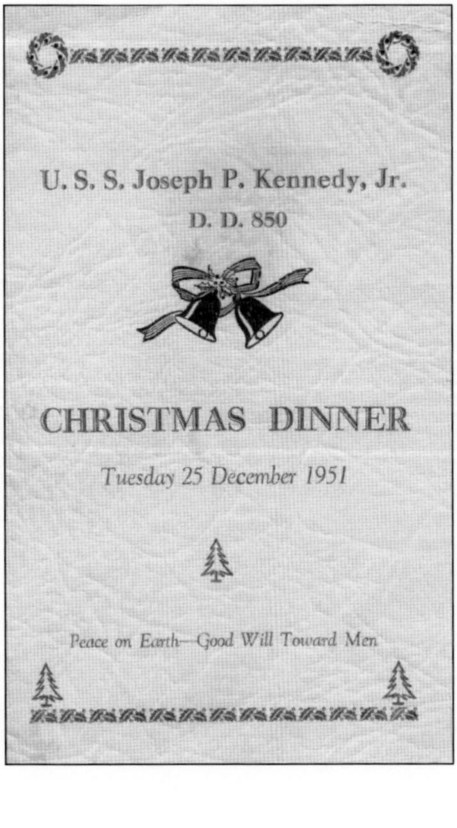

For the rest of the year, the destroyer conducted exercises off the Eastern Seaboard. Cmdr. Robert B. Lander took over as commanding officer in December 1951, and the crew celebrated Christmas in Newport, Rhode Island. During 1952, she participated in antisubmarine warfare exercises and became a "school ship" for the Fleet Training School at Newport.

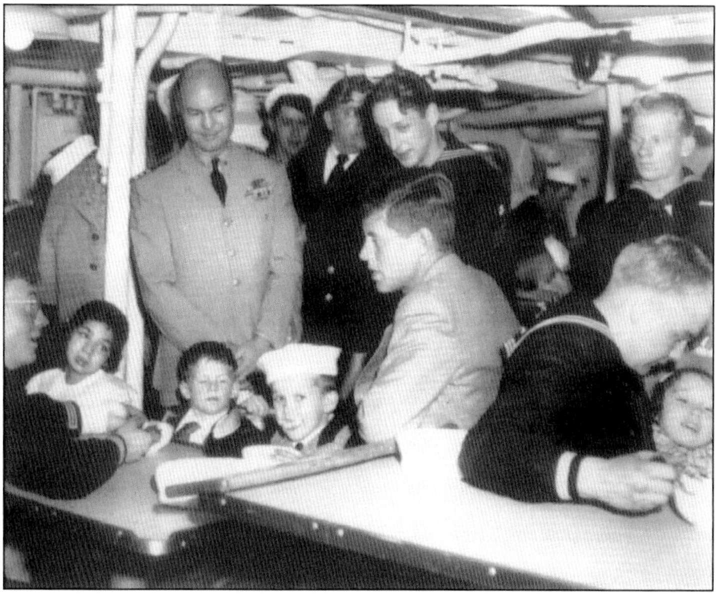

From January to May 1952, the *Kennedy* was overhauled in the Boston Navy Yard. In April, a party was held for disabled children on the mess deck. John F. Kennedy (seated, center), who had won his first election to the US Senate the previous November, participated in the activities. Standing at left is Commander Lander. On May 28, the ship steamed south for training off Guantanamo Bay. (Courtesy of Brad Strait.)

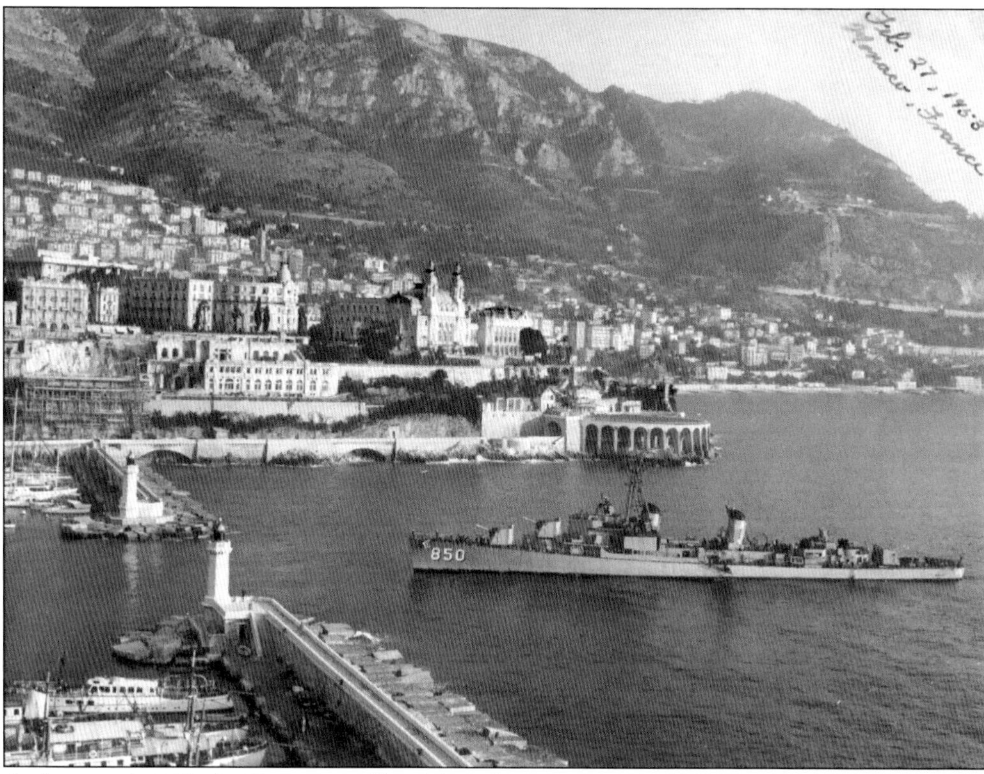

On January 7, 1953, the *Kennedy* and her fellow destroyers screened the Essex-class carrier *Tarawa* (CV-40) across the Atlantic for another Sixth Fleet deployment in the Mediterranean. Arriving in Trieste, Italy, on January 24, she spent the next several weeks training and making ports of call. The *Kennedy* is seen here on February 27 arriving at the city of Monaco, an independent principality and enclave within France. (Courtesy of Brad Strait.)

Through the help of a local harbor pilot, the *Kennedy* eases through the Monaco breakwater as she prepares to drop anchor in its main harbor. From ancient times until the 19th century, the port of Monaco was among the most important on the French Mediterranean coast. But by the 1900s, it had lost all commercial significance. (Courtesy of Brad Strait.)

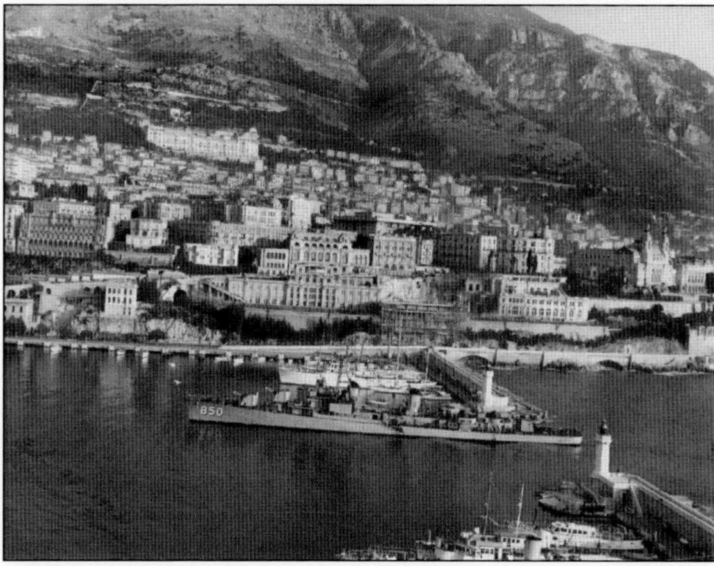

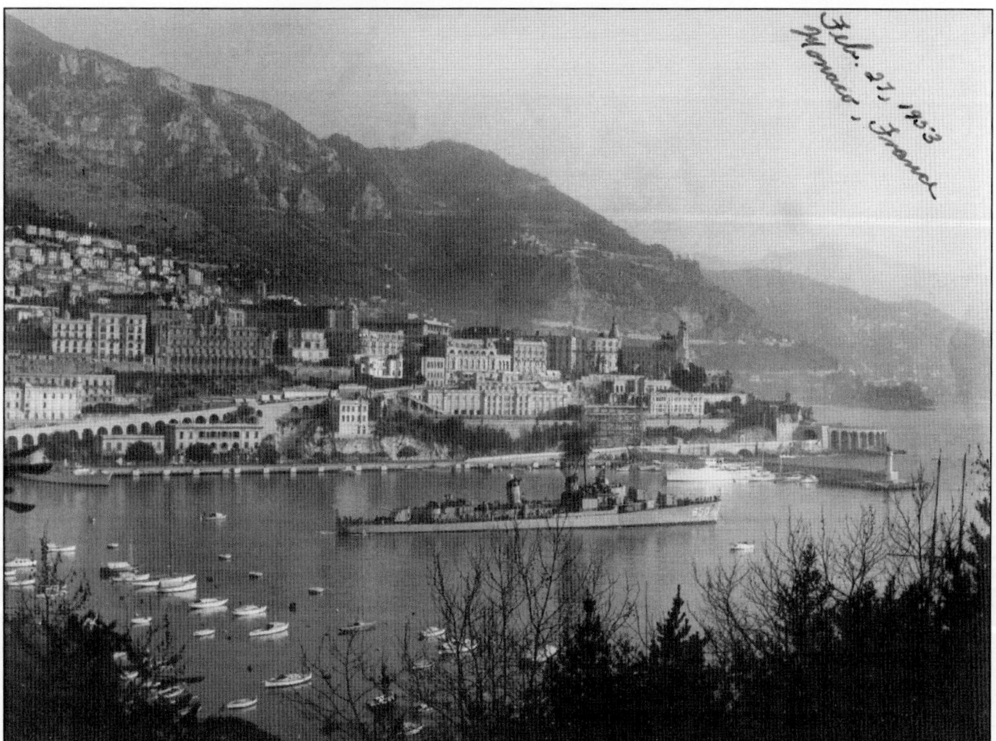

With the *Joseph P. Kennedy, Jr.* securely anchored, liberty parties wait to be ferried ashore, where they can relieve the stress and tension of shipboard life. To the left, beyond the small pleasure boats, is the business district, which includes open-air markets and the train station. On March 3, the *Kennedy* left Monaco and spent the next week conducting fleet exercises before arriving in Italy on March 10. After visiting Greece, Turkey, Spain, and France, the destroyer left for Newport on May 8. (Courtesy of Brad Strait.)

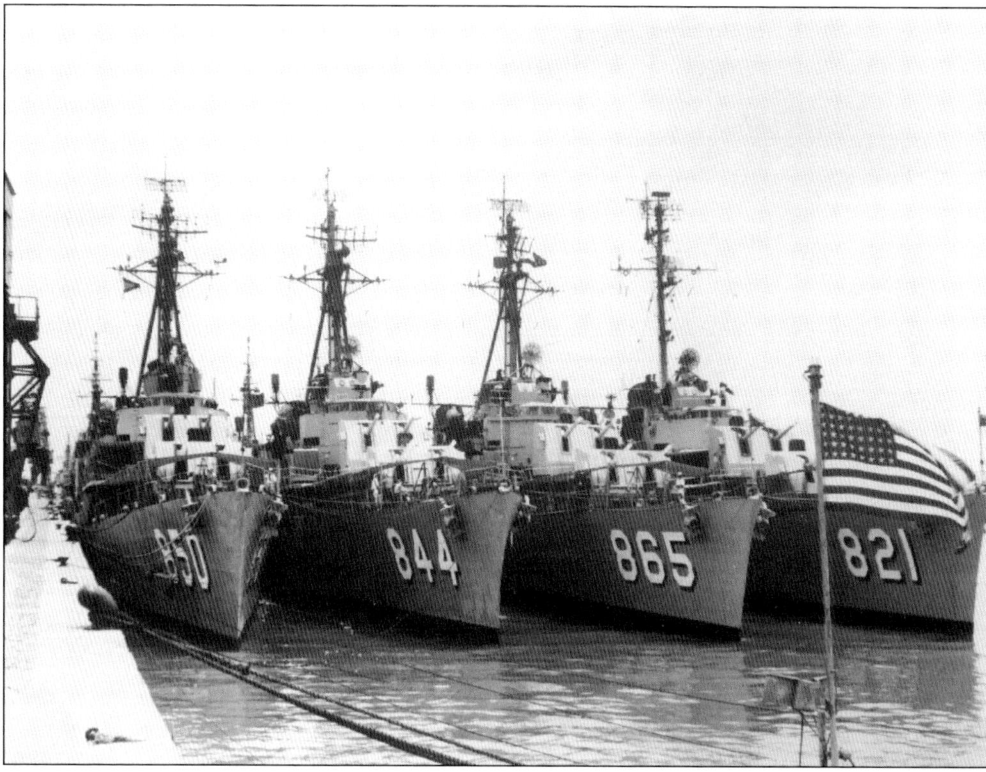

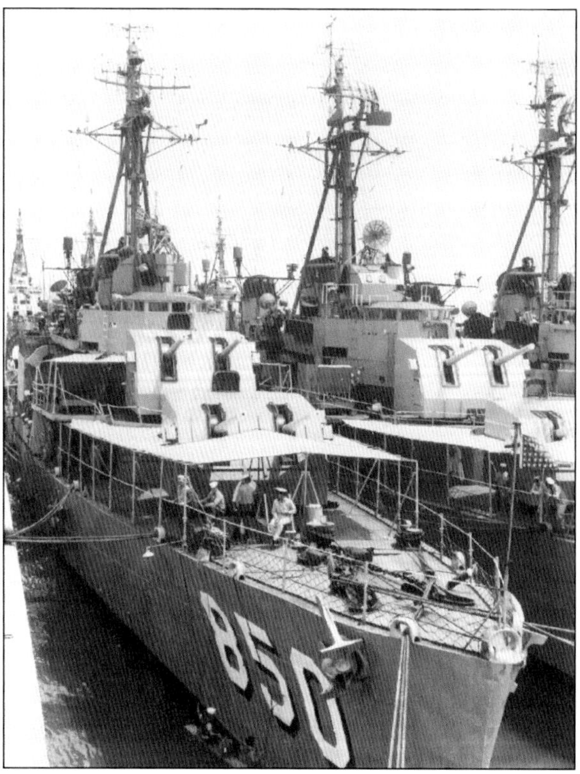

Destroyer Squadron 8 is seen here at Newport on May 18, 1953, after returning from its Mediterranean cruise. From left to right are the *JPK*, *Perry*, *Charles R. Ware*, and *Johnston*. The flag of Destroyer Squadron 8 flies from the mast of DD-850, as she is tied to the pier. The other destroyers are "nested" outboard of her. The *Kennedy* had a quick turnaround, departing Newport on May 25 to take part in antisubmarine exercises off Halifax, Nova Scotia.

The destroyer is a jack-of-all-trades ship, built to hunt down and destroy submarines. It also must pick up pilots in the water, provide antiaircraft support, and conduct shore bombardments. She faces attacks not only from ships, planes, and submarines, but also from the elements. Here, the crew chips and paints the hull while in port.

In September 1953, Cmdr. W.R. McKinney became the commanding officer of the destroyer. This is the cover of the Thanksgiving menu for that year. Nothing was left off the menu. Appetizers included shrimp cocktail, cream of pea soup, and a salad. The main course was roast turkey, mashed potatoes, sweet potatoes, string beans, and cranberry sauce. For dessert, the sailors enjoyed fruitcake and ice cream. The last items on the menu were cigars and cigarettes.

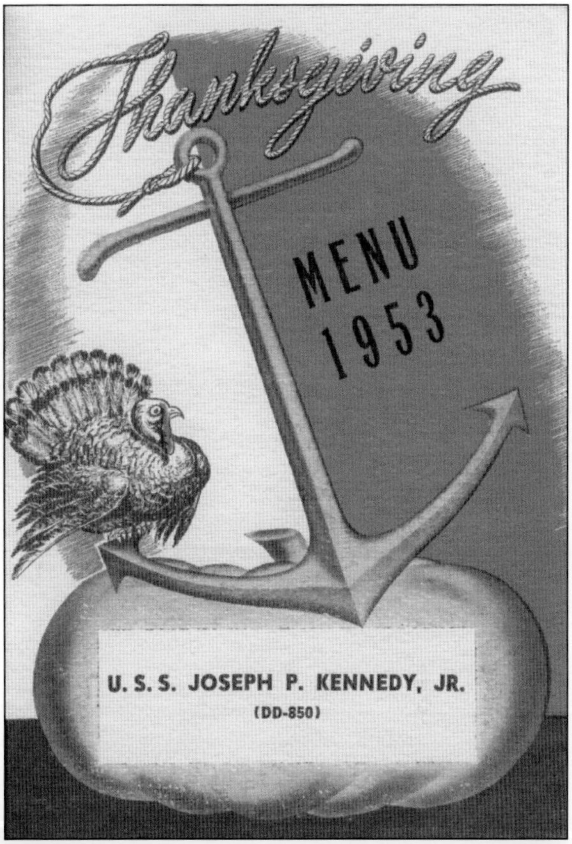

On January 5, 1954, the *Kennedy* left Newport for another deployment to the Mediterranean, arriving off the port city of Tangier in Morocco after two weeks at sea. Sailors are anxious and excited as they prepare to leave on liberty. The sailor at center has been assigned shore patrol duty. It will be his responsibility to keep his shipmates out of trouble and to break up any fights that occur.

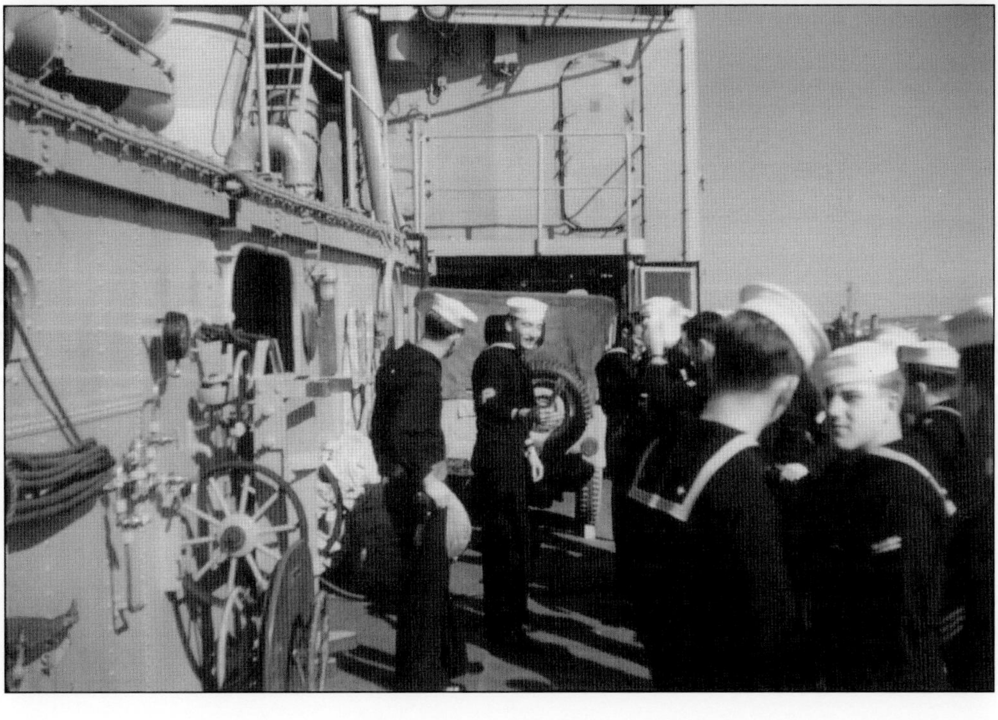

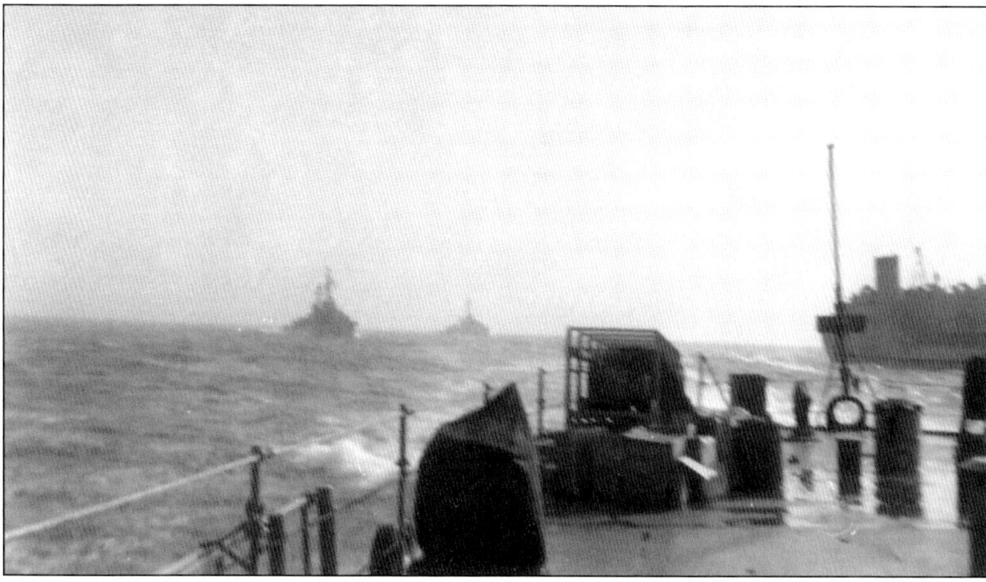

This photograph, taken from the *Kennedy*, shows a fellow destroyer in the distance. Centered on one or two aircraft carriers, the Sixth Fleet consisted of destroyers, cruisers, and submarines, along with its self-sustaining vessels such as tankers, storeships, and refrigerated vessels. In addition, several amphibious ships carried a battalion of Marines for emergency contingencies. (Courtesy of Brad Strait.)

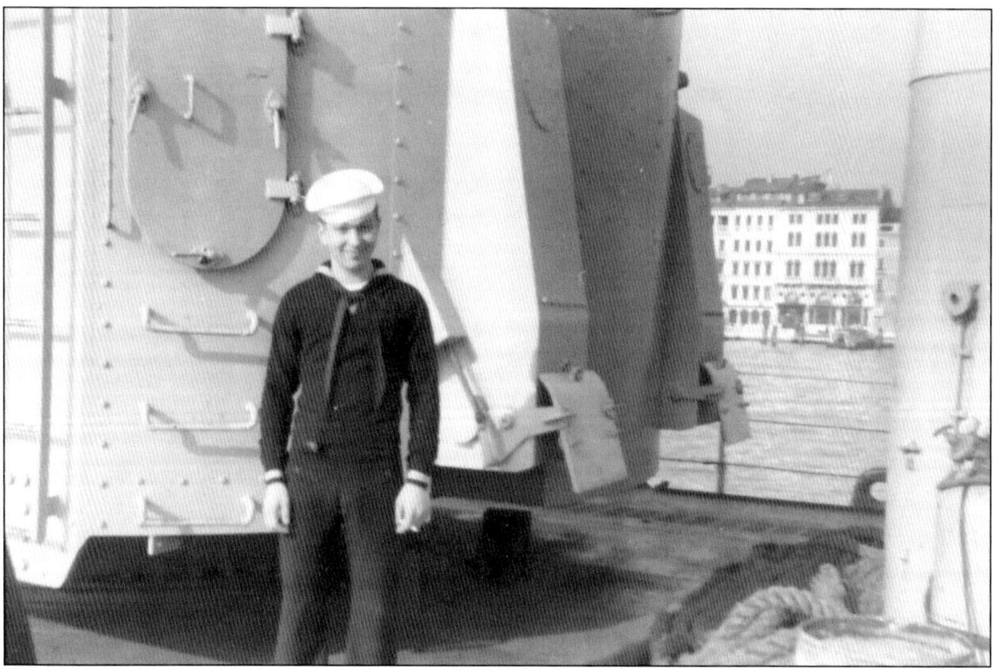

An unidentified sailor in dress blues prepares to leave the *Kennedy* for liberty at Venice, Italy. In the 1300s, after battling its rival republic, Genoa, Venice became the Christian world's leading maritime state. With a mighty shipbuilding arsenal, the city was known as "Queen of the Seas." Its maritime supremacy steadily declined in the 1500s, as most of its seagoing trade was captured by the Portuguese, Dutch, and English. (Courtesy of Brad Strait.)

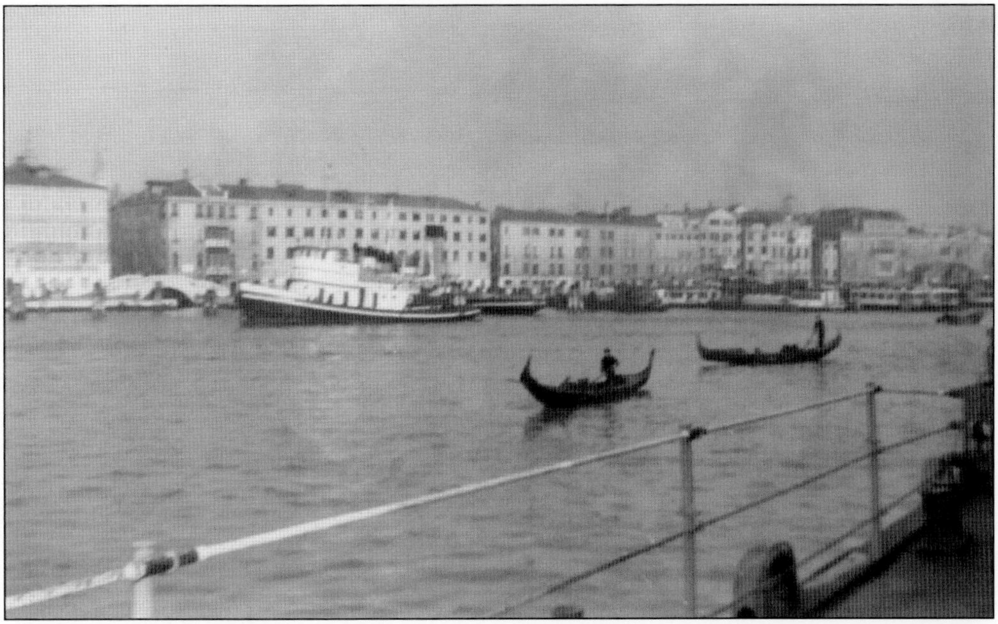

Here, two gondolas paddle by the destroyer. A harbor tugboat is visible in the background, and beyond it, the city. Venice was built on 118 alluvial islets, so gondolas are ideal for traveling through the many narrow and winding canals that traverse the city, including the Grand Canal that snakes through the heart of Venice. (Courtesy of Brad Strait.)

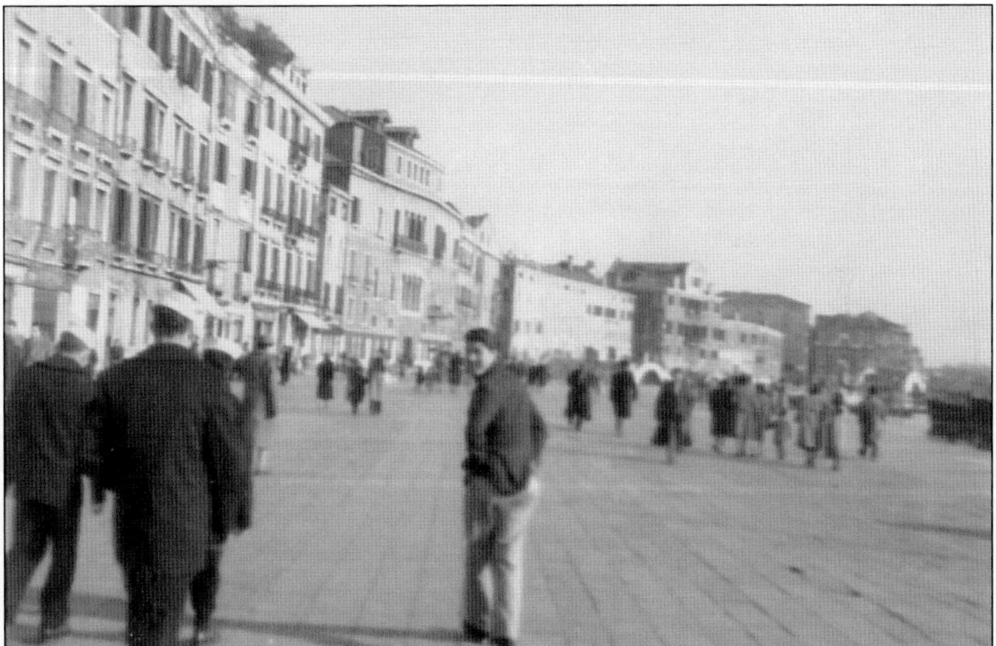

Kennedy sailors (left) begin their liberty. Shore patrol parties will be on the watch to make sure they stay out of trouble. Venice is a compact city that is free of automobiles, so many a sailor traveled by foot. Hundreds of footbridges cross the canals, and narrow lanes lead to hidden squares filled with shops and cafés. (Courtesy of Brad Strait.)

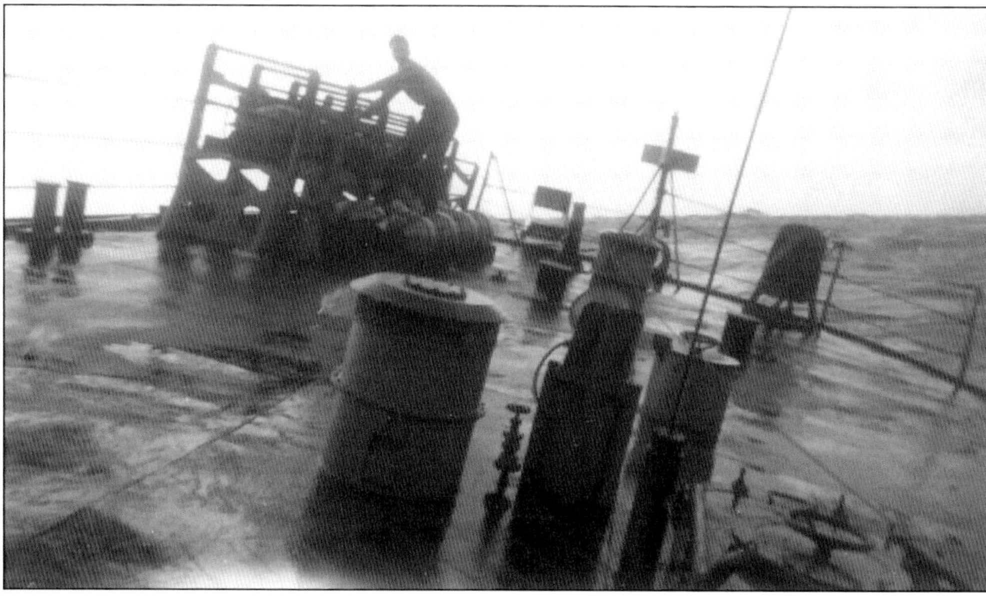

Boiler Tender Milton Walton stands on depth charges as the *Kennedy* rolls to port. He served aboard the ship from 1952 to 1955. Sailors of the Sixth Fleet were always busy, whether at sea, as shown here, or in port. Intensive maintenance was the standing order, as the ocean and air could destroy the ship just as quickly as the enemy. (Courtesy of Brad Strait.)

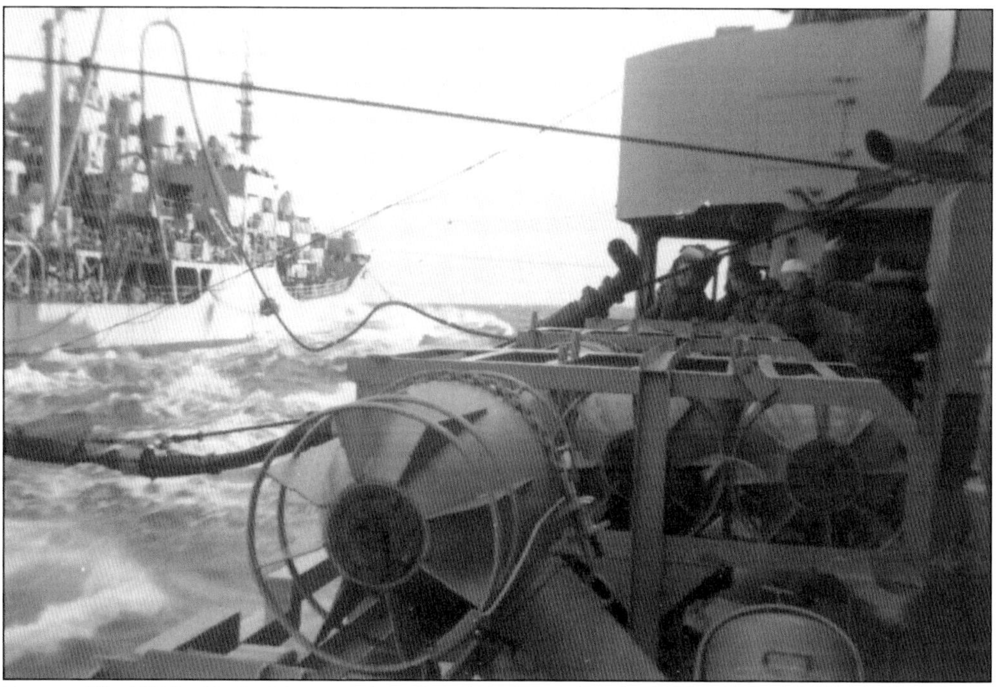

During World War II, the Navy perfected underway replenishment, the ability of auxiliary ships to transfer fuel, ammunition, and stores to vessels while steaming on a parallel course. This task was hazardous and strenuous for the sailors. Due to the high speeds needed to conduct flight operations with the carriers, destroyers must take on fuel every three to four days. This photograph was taken as the *Kennedy* refueled from the USS *Elokomin* (AO-55). (Courtesy of Brad Strait.)

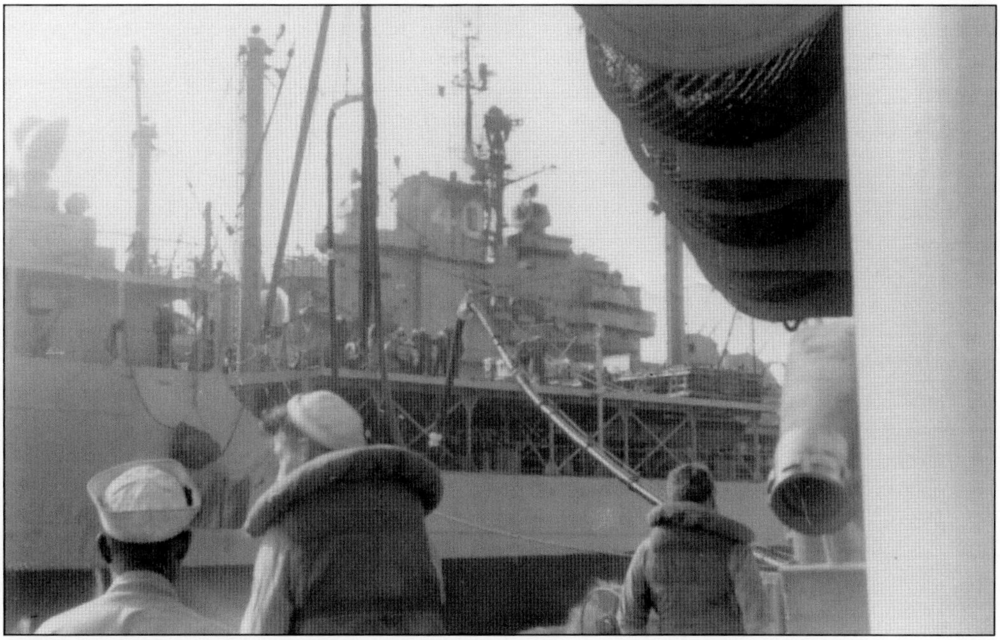

During an underway refueling, the oiler would steam at a constant course and speed while the *JPK* came alongside at the same course and speed, between 80 and 100 feet apart. The crews would string highlines between the two ships, and hoses would be manually drawn from the tanker to the destroyer's fuel inlets. At this time, the tin cans did not have power winches. Visible on the other side of the *Elokomin* is aircraft carrier *Tarawa* (CV-40). (Courtesy of Brad Strait.)

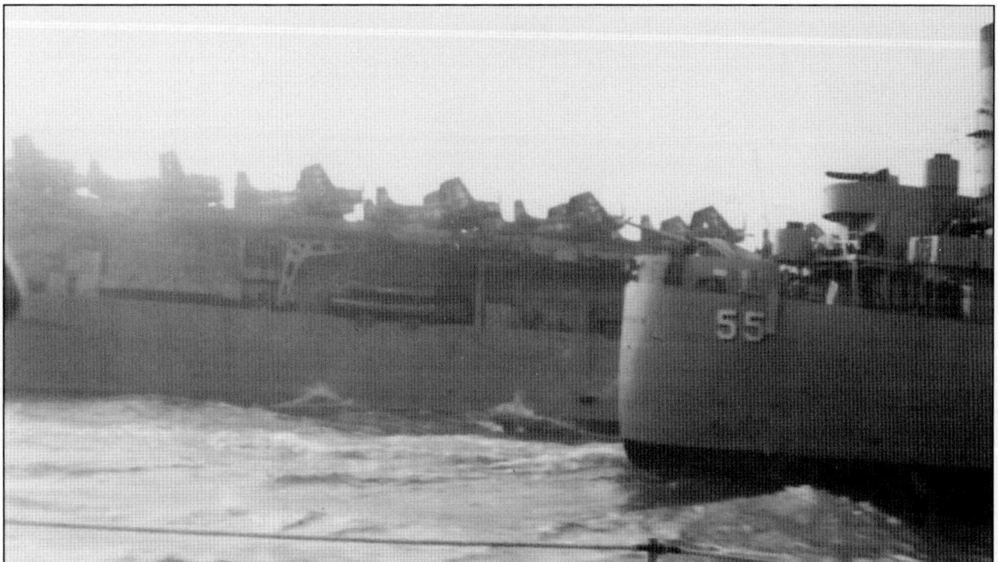

When receiving ammunition or stores, the same procedure would be used, except the goods would arrive at the *JPK*'s limited deck space and would have to be immediately stored below by the crew. Even those sailors offwatch would have to help out. Unless the seas were too rough, underway replenishments were conducted during day and night in all kinds of weather. (Courtesy of Brad Strait.)

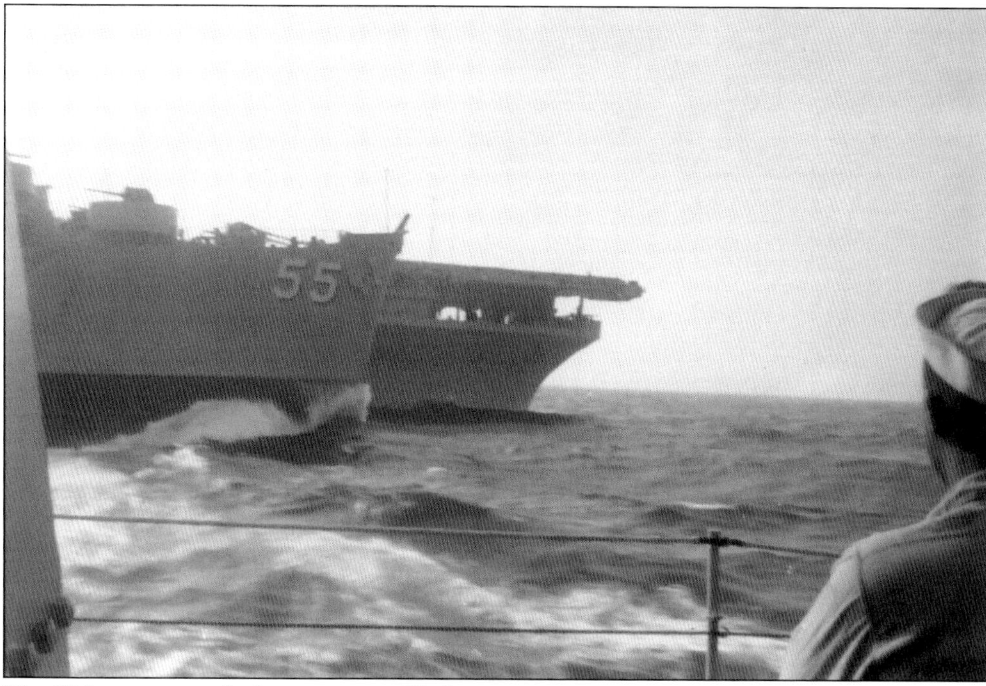

The *Elokomin*, named after a river in Washington State, refueled the *Kennedy* and the carrier *Tarawa* simultaneously. Based at Norfolk, she had serviced the ships of the fleet since 1943 and made numerous deployments with the Sixth Fleet. The *Tarawa* was commissioned just a week before the *JPK* in 1945. Assigned to mothball status in 1949, she was placed back in active duty with the outbreak of the Korean War in 1950. (Courtesy of Brad Strait.)

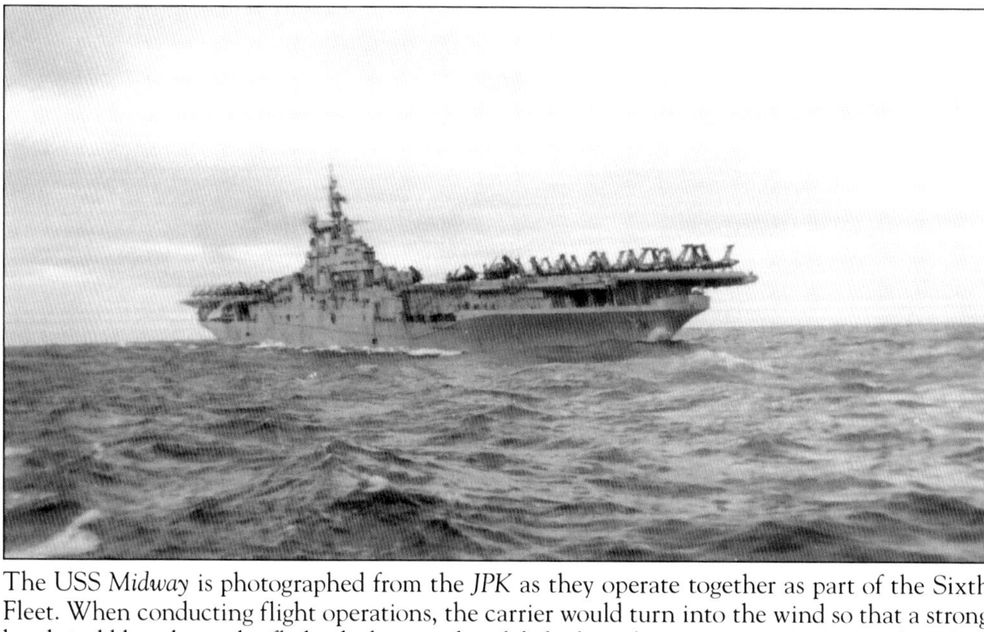

The USS *Midway* is photographed from the *JPK* as they operate together as part of the Sixth Fleet. When conducting flight operations, the carrier would turn into the wind so that a strong headwind blew down the flight deck, providing lift for launching or recovering aircraft. When plane guarding for the carriers, the *Kennedy* usually would steam about 1,000 yards behind and with the carrier to starboard. (Courtesy of Brad Strait.)

On March 22, 1954, the crew had liberty in the Italian city of Naples. In the background is the active volcano Mount Vesuvius. Each sailor was a roving ambassador for the United States, and as such, emphasis was placed on their good behavior. Over time the Sixth Fleet was nicknamed the "friendly fleet," as parties were often thrown for local children aboard the ship, and sailors donated clothing to the needy. In addition, the *Kennedy* often came to the aid of local fishermen and other mariners in distress. (Courtesy of Brad Strait.)

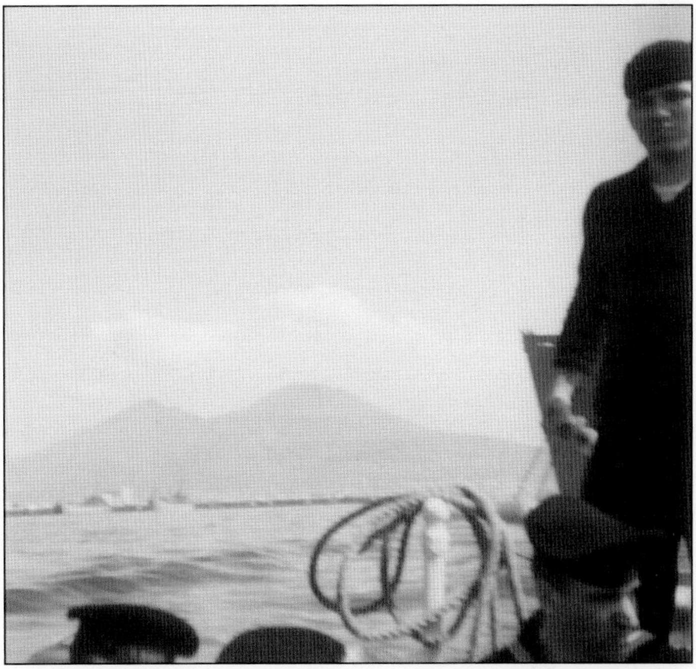

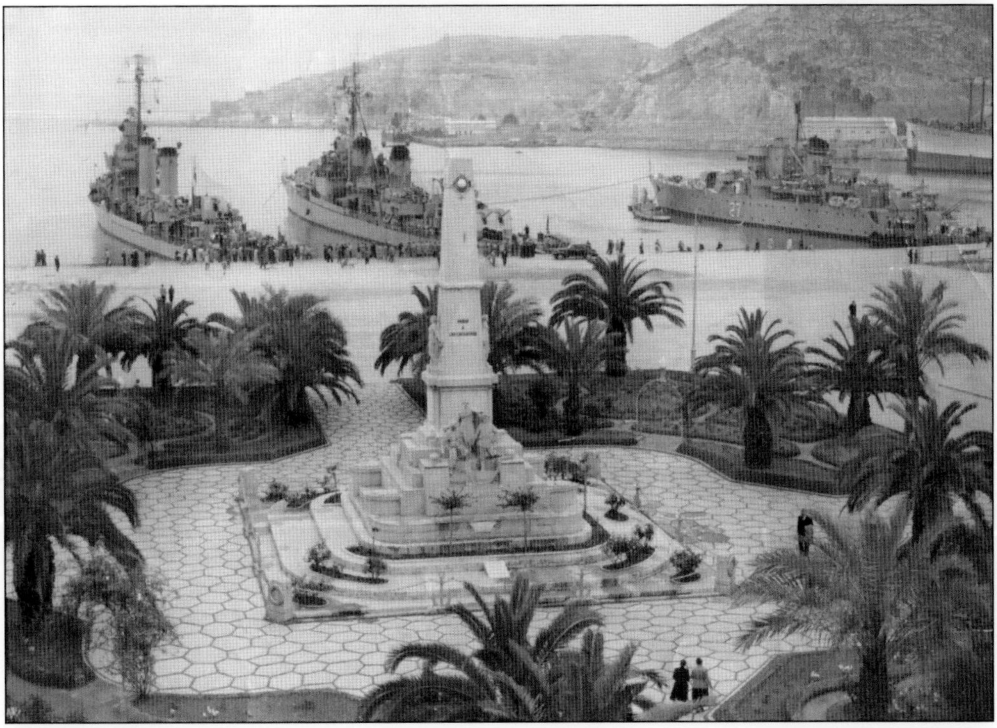

The *Kennedy* lies between two other warships in Cartagena, Spain. In the foreground is the Monument to the Heroes of Santiago de Cuba and Cavite, a war memorial erected in honor of the Spanish sailors who died in combat with the US Navy in waters off Cavite and Santiago on the Philippine and Cuban coasts. (Courtesy of Brad Strait.)

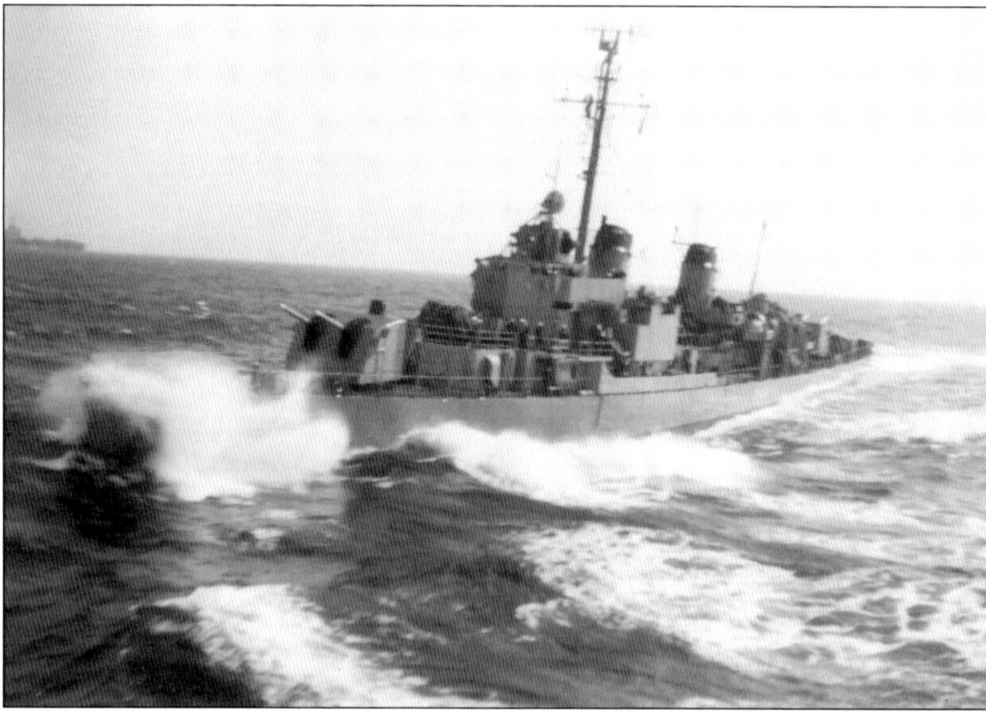

On April 14, 1954, another destroyer pulls alongside the *Kennedy* off Menton, France, to transfer bags of much-anticipated mail. Life aboard ship often consisted of standing watches, eating, and sleeping, with not much to break up the monotony. However, mail call was an event that the sailors loved, as it connected them with loved ones and events back in America. The *Kennedy* arrived home in Newport on May 26.

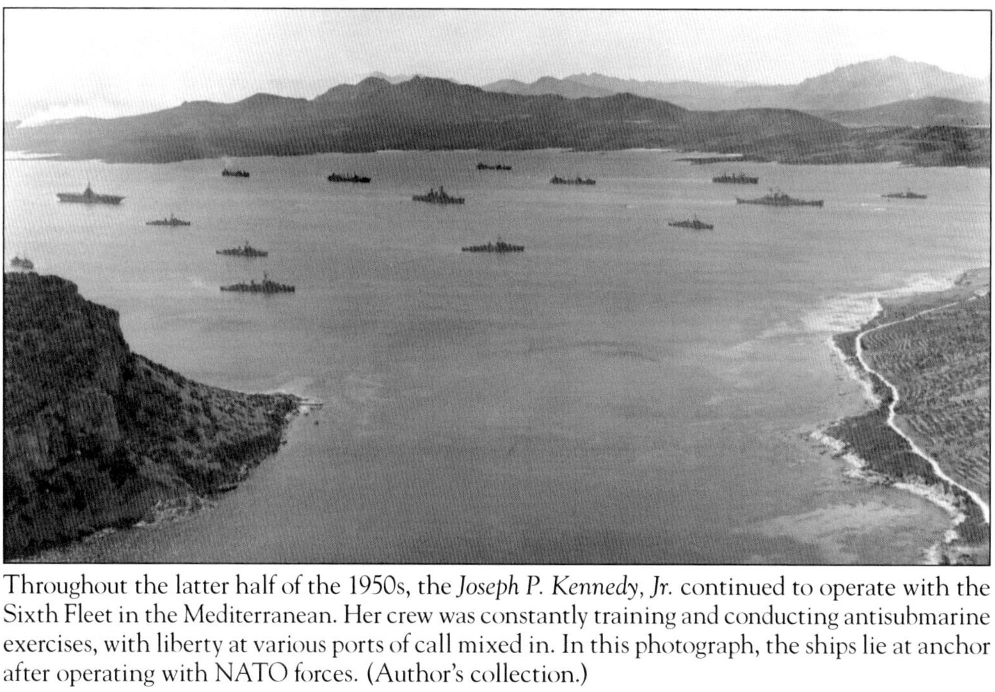

Throughout the latter half of the 1950s, the *Joseph P. Kennedy, Jr.* continued to operate with the Sixth Fleet in the Mediterranean. Her crew was constantly training and conducting antisubmarine exercises, with liberty at various ports of call mixed in. In this photograph, the ships lie at anchor after operating with NATO forces. (Author's collection.)

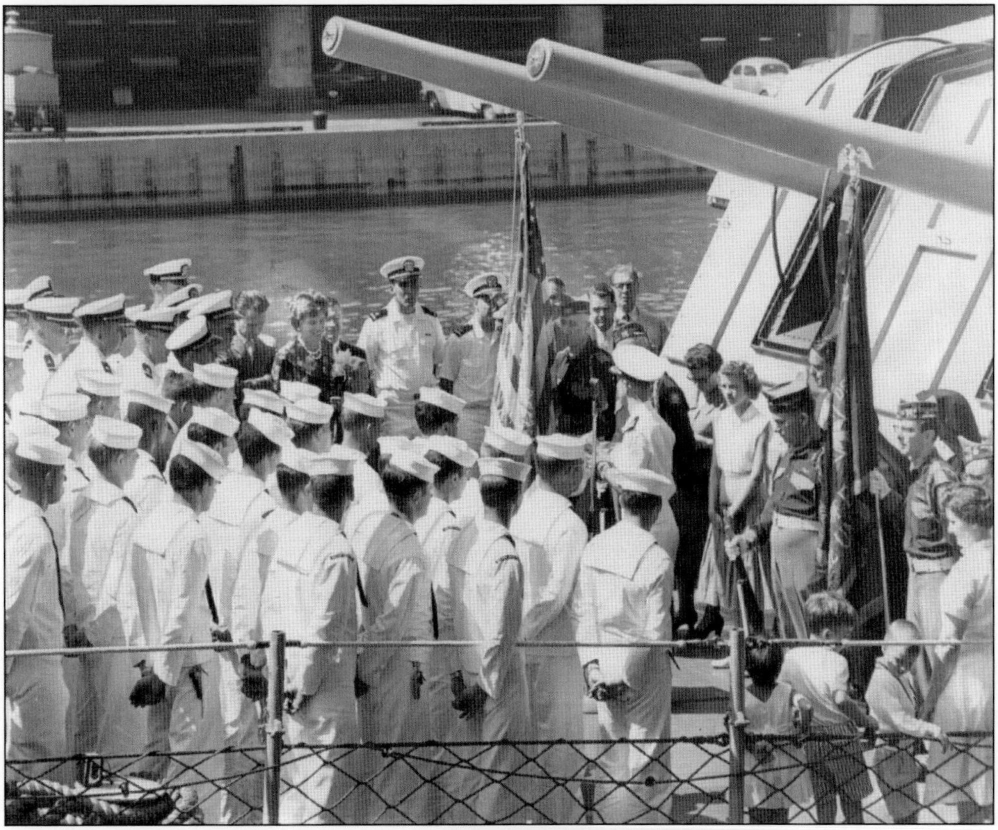

In the late 1950s, the *JPK*, along with other Navy ships, participated in midshipmen cruises for the Naval Academy. This gave the cadets the opportunity to receive a better understanding of life at sea and provided hands-on experience. On June 26, 1959, she entered the St. Lawrence Seaway and took part in ceremonies commemorating its opening. On July 2, she steamed to call on the city of Chicago, as shown here. (Author's collection.)

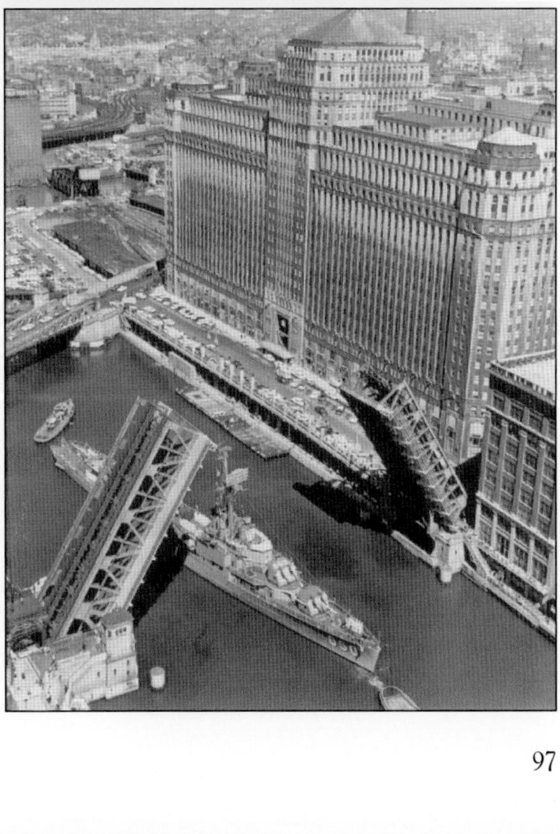

On July 10, the *Kennedy* left Chicago and headed to Lake Michigan to visit the cities of Milwaukee and Detroit. The building shown here in Chicago is the Merchandise Mart, owned by the father of the ship's namesake, Joseph P. Kennedy Sr. After visiting the cities, the destroyer steamed back to the Atlantic Ocean on August 6.

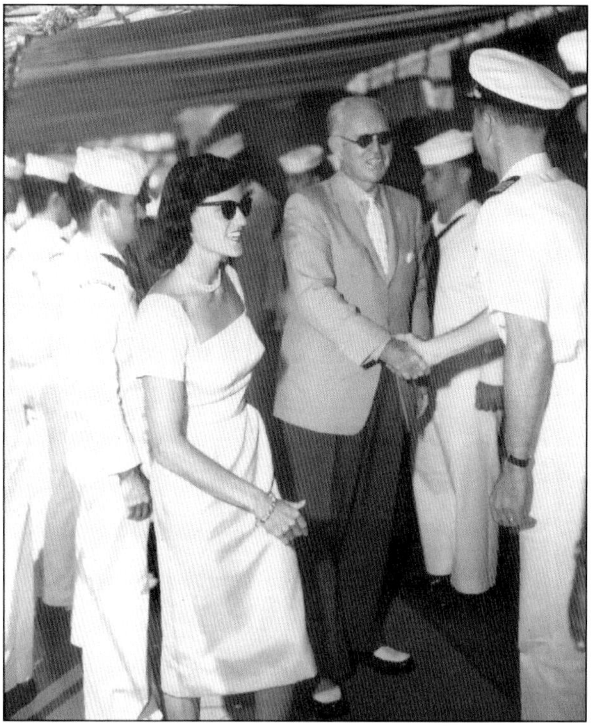

In the summer of 1960, the *Kennedy* left Newport for a deployment with the Sixth Fleet. She continued her traditional roles of escorting and providing plane guard duties for two aircraft carriers, USS *Forrestal* (CVA-59) and USS *Franklin D. Roosevelt* (CVB-42). On August 9, she was visited by Joseph P. Kennedy Sr. and his niece, Ann Gargan, off Cannes, France.

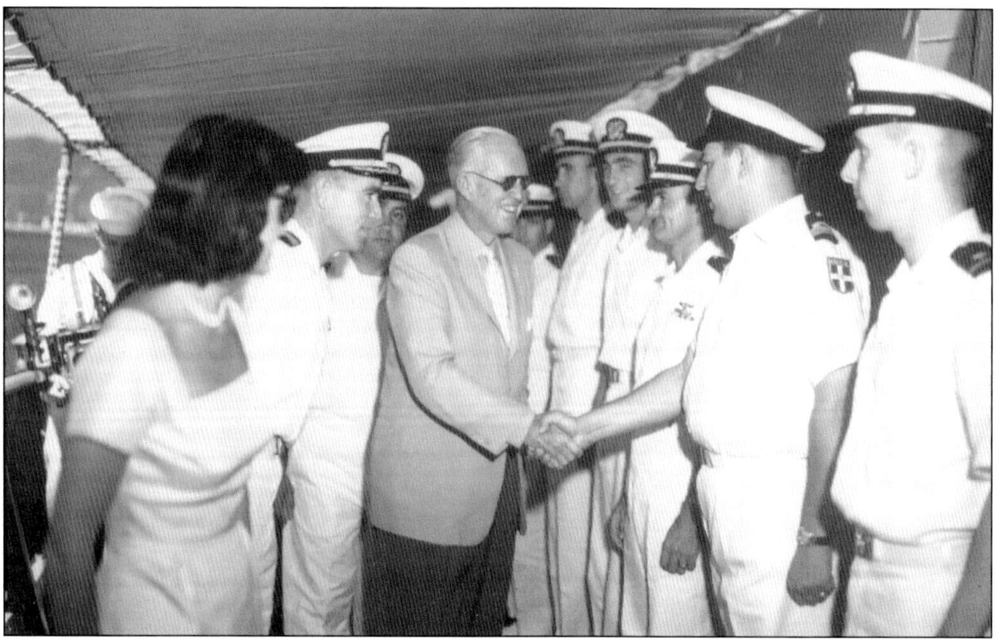

Joseph Kennedy Sr. and Ann Gargan were provided with a tour of the ship from top to bottom, and they enjoyed a meal with the ship's officers in the wardroom. Joseph Kennedy had spent the majority of the year gathering support for his son John, who was running for the Democratic ticket in the upcoming presidential election. Gargan, orphaned by the time she was 10, was the daughter of Rose Kennedy's sister. Forced to leave the convent two months before she took her vows, she became a quasi-member of the Kennedy family.

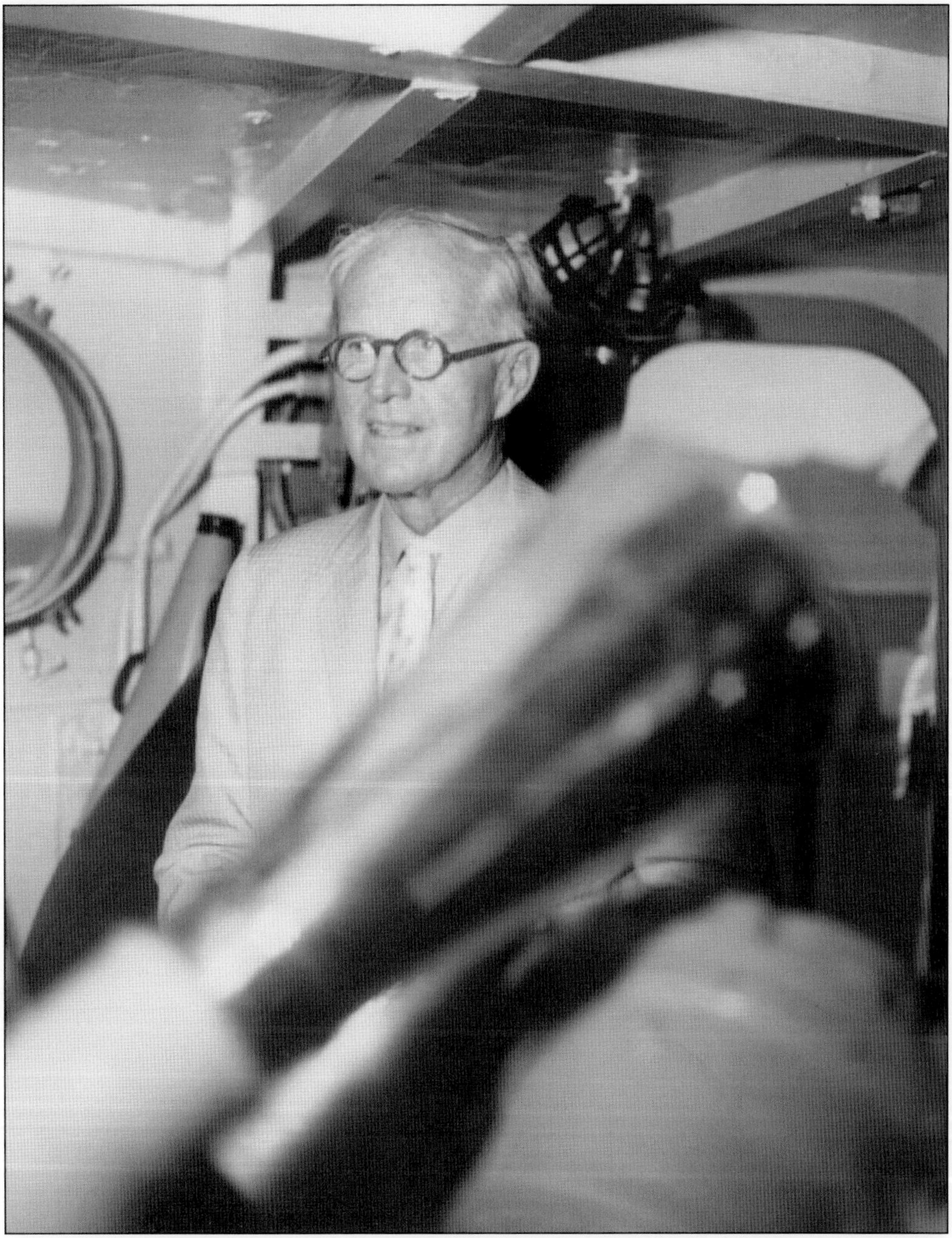

After Kennedy and Gargan left the destroyer, the *Kennedy* continued her deployment with the Sixth Fleet. On October 15, she returned home to Newport. A month later, her namesake's brother John, a Navy hero in his own right, became the 35th president of the United States. In honor of the president, the Navy sent the destroyer to Washington for the inauguration in January 1961. The ship's captain, Cmdr. Mark G. Tremaine, spent the week as an aide to former *JPK* sailor and soon-to-be attorney general, Robert F. Kennedy.

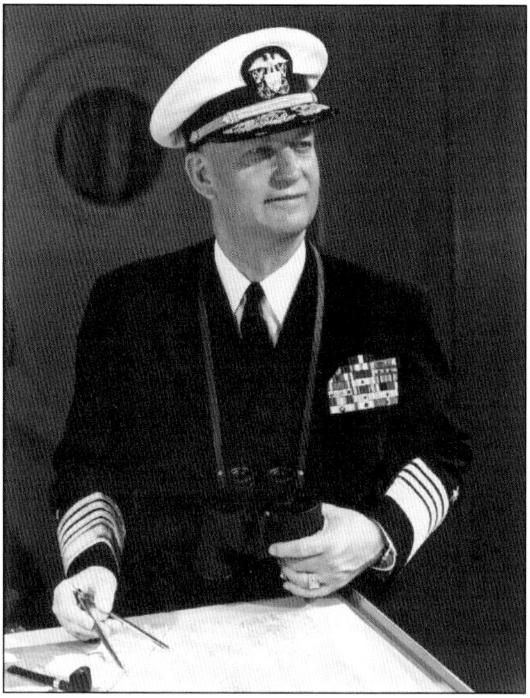

If there is one person who represents destroyers, it would be Adm. Arleigh "31 Knot" Burke. Best known for his exploits during World War II as commander of Destroyer Squadron 23, he was appointed chief of naval operations in 1955. Facing major cuts in defense spending by the Eisenhower administration and an increasing number of Soviet fast-attack submarines, Burke found a way to extend the life of his destroyers through the Fleet Rehabilitation and Modernization Program (FRAM).

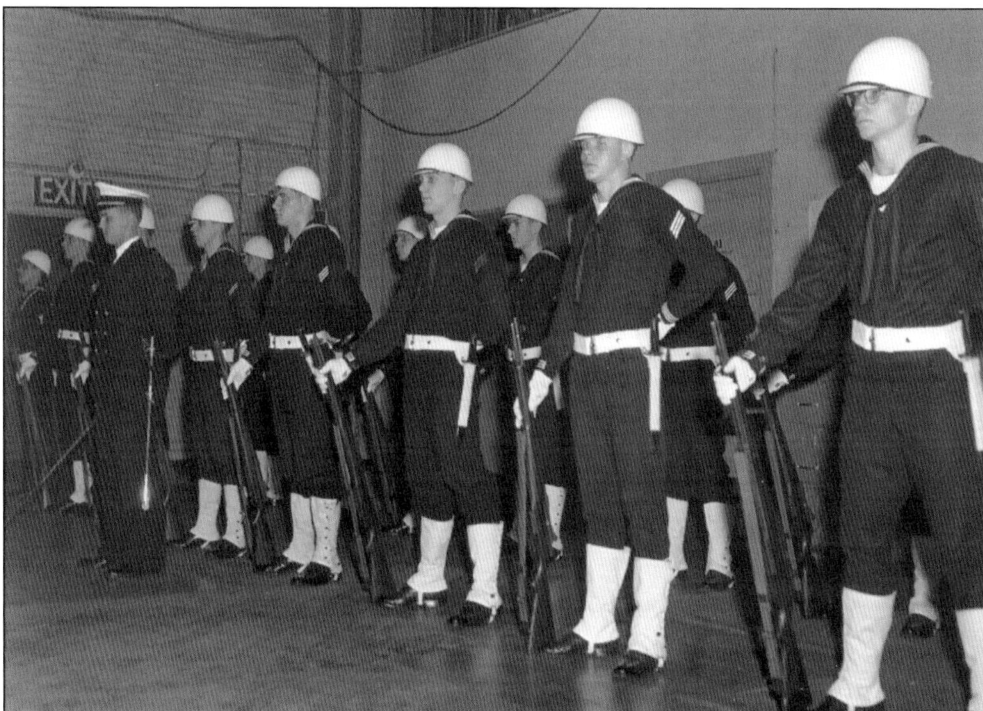

On July 1, 1961, the *Kennedy* docked at the Brooklyn Naval Yard for her FRAM overhaul. She received the new SQS-23 sonar, MK 32 triple torpedo tubes were installed in place of her second gun mount, and her entire superstructure was removed, modernized, and rebuilt with aluminum. On February 23, 1962, the ship's honor guards prepare for a Change of Command Ceremony.

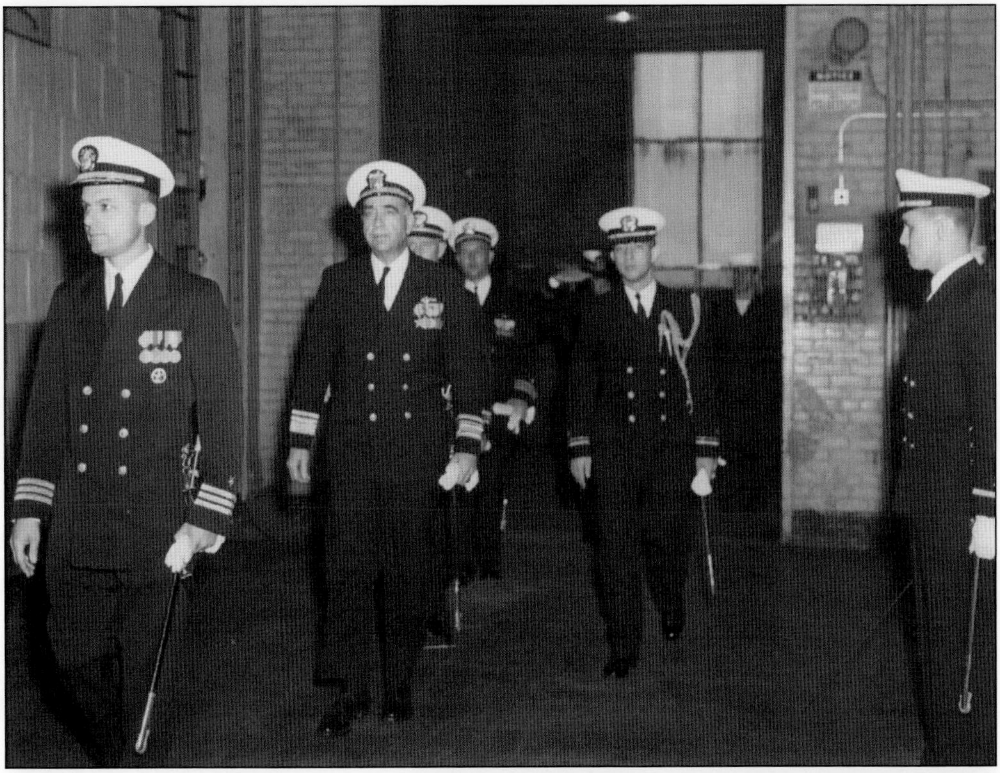

The Change of Command Ceremony is led by the relieving commander officer, Cmdr. Nicholas Mikhalevsky (left), followed by Rear Adm. G.H. Wales (second from left), commandant of the 3rd Naval District. Cmdr. Mikhalevsky was commissioned an ensign in 1945 and had most recently been the commanding officer of another Gearing-class destroyer, the USS *Robert H. McCard* (DD-822).

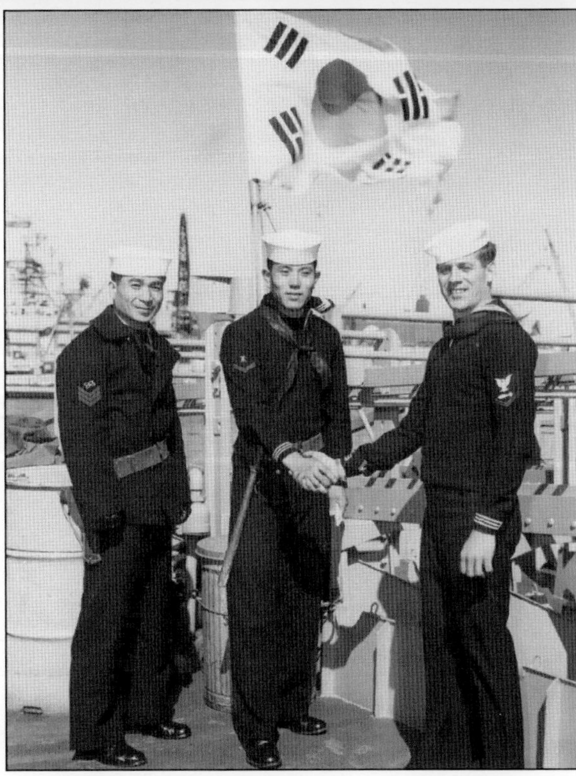

During March and April 1962, while undergoing her FRAM at the Brooklyn Naval Yard, the crew was paid a visit by the South Korean Navy as one their destroyer escorts arrived in New York City. Bonded by serving their countries on the high seas, both officers and crew paid host to one another on their ships. After touring the South Korean ship, one of the *Kennedy*'s sailors poses for a photograph.

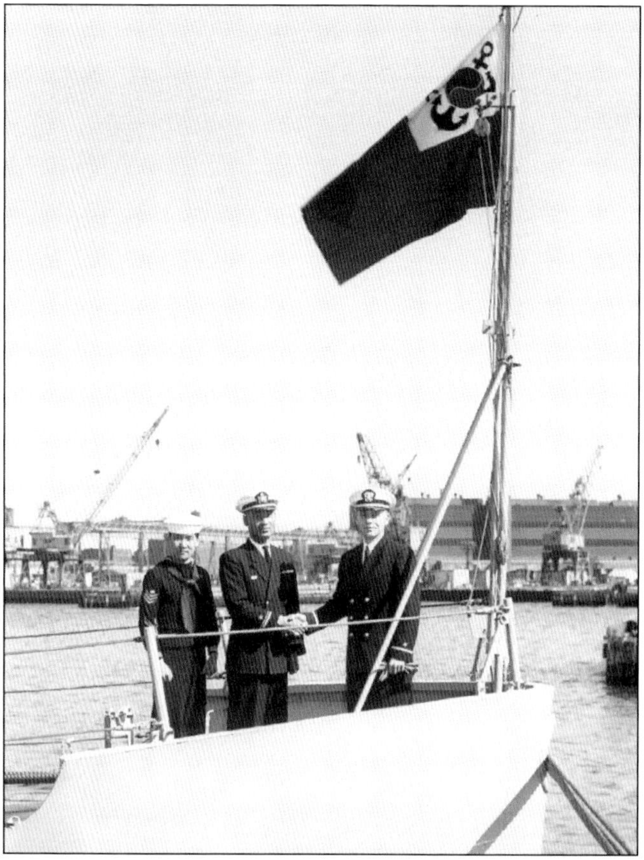

The Republic of Korea Navy (ROKN), established on September 5, 1948, is the oldest branch of the South Korean Armed Forces. With the outbreak of war in 1950, the navy exemplified itself by overpowering the enemy on both the east and west coasts. Ensign Yonkers was photographed with an officer and enlisted sailor of the ROKN on March 26, 1962. The naval jack of the ROKN flies to the right of Ens. Yonkers.

Another change resulting from the FRAM overhaul was that the ship received a modernized and enlarged bridge. On the far right is the captain's chair. At center is the helm with compass repeater. (Courtesy of Ted Hayes.)

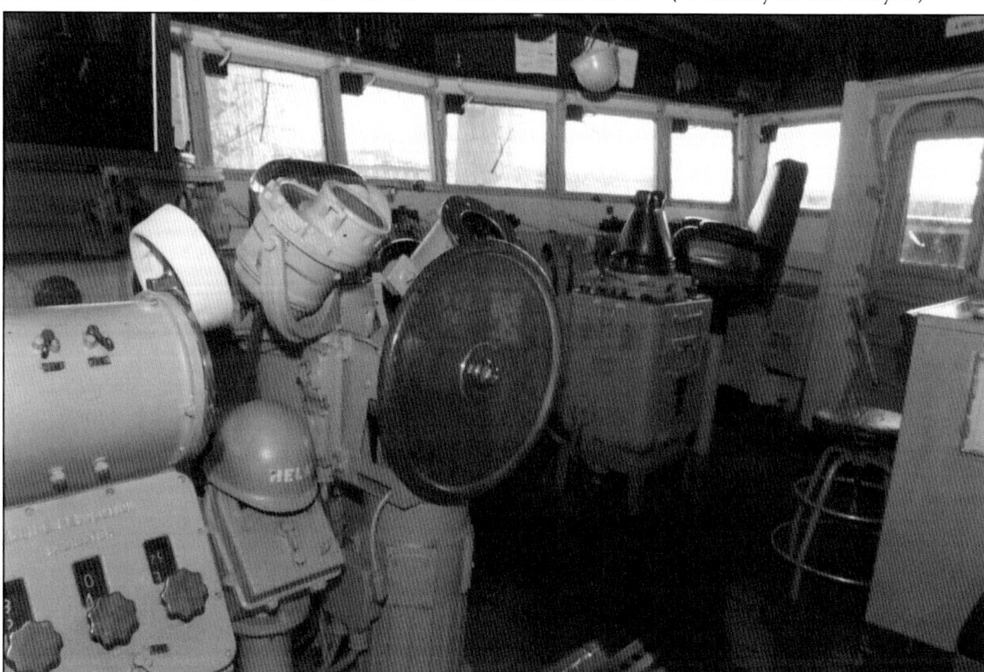

New "stand-off" weapons systems, which operated at a greater distance from the enemy, were installed. These were called Anti-Submarine Rocket (ASROC) and Drone Anti-Submarine Helicopter (DASH). Located behind the forward stack, the ASROC launcher (shown here) has four double-celled boxes housing eight ASROC missiles in an over-and-under arrangement. The mount could be rotated, and each double-celled box could be elevated independently to its firing angle of 45 degrees. (Courtesy of Ted Hayes.)

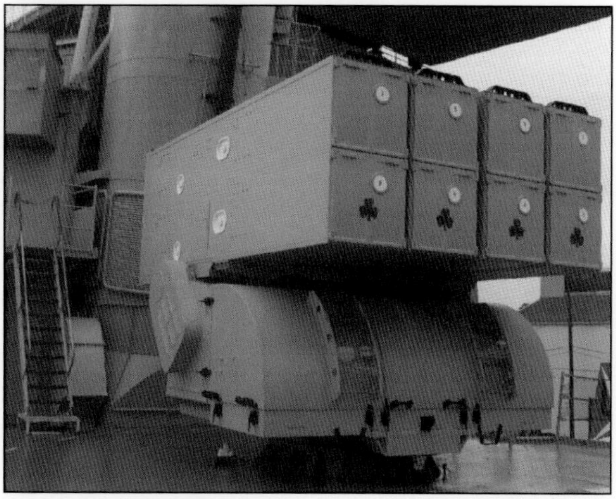

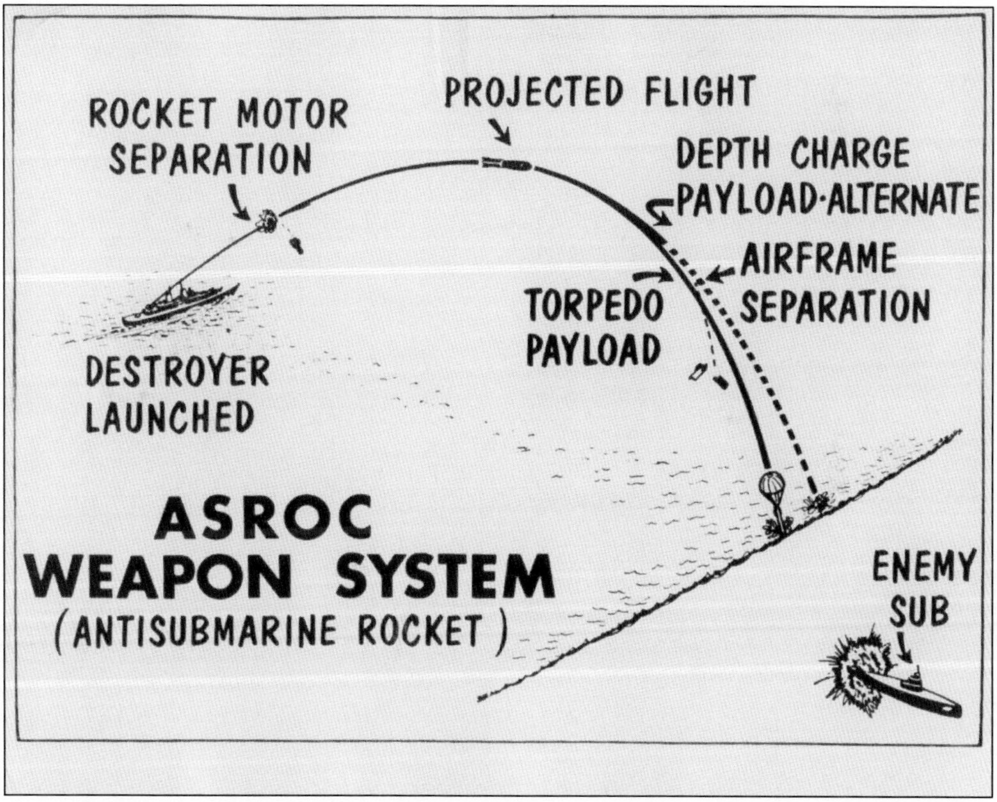

The ASROC was a solid-fuel, rocket-propelled, ballistic missile that could carry a payload of either a torpedo or a nuclear depth charge. When a submerged submarine was detected, the fire control system would compute its course and speed and spin the launcher in the direction of the sub. Once the missile was launched, both the rocket motor and airframe assembly would be separated from the payload at predetermined points in flight. Once in the water, the torpedo homed in for the kill while the depth charge exploded at a preset depth. (Author's collection.)

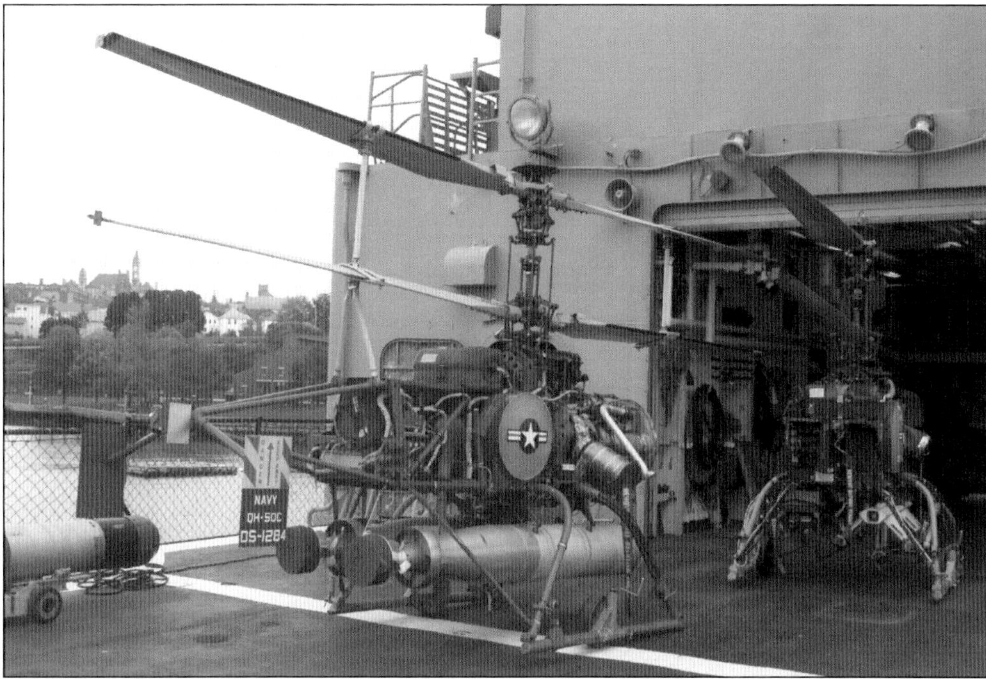

The other "stand-off" weapon system installed on the *Kennedy* during her FRAM was the DASH. To accommodate the DASH, a hangar and flight deck had to be built behind the aft stack. The droned coaxial, 900-pound helicopter carried a payload of two Mark 44 torpedoes. It was operated by a remote control station aboard ship and had a range of 22 miles. (Courtesy of Ted Hayes.)

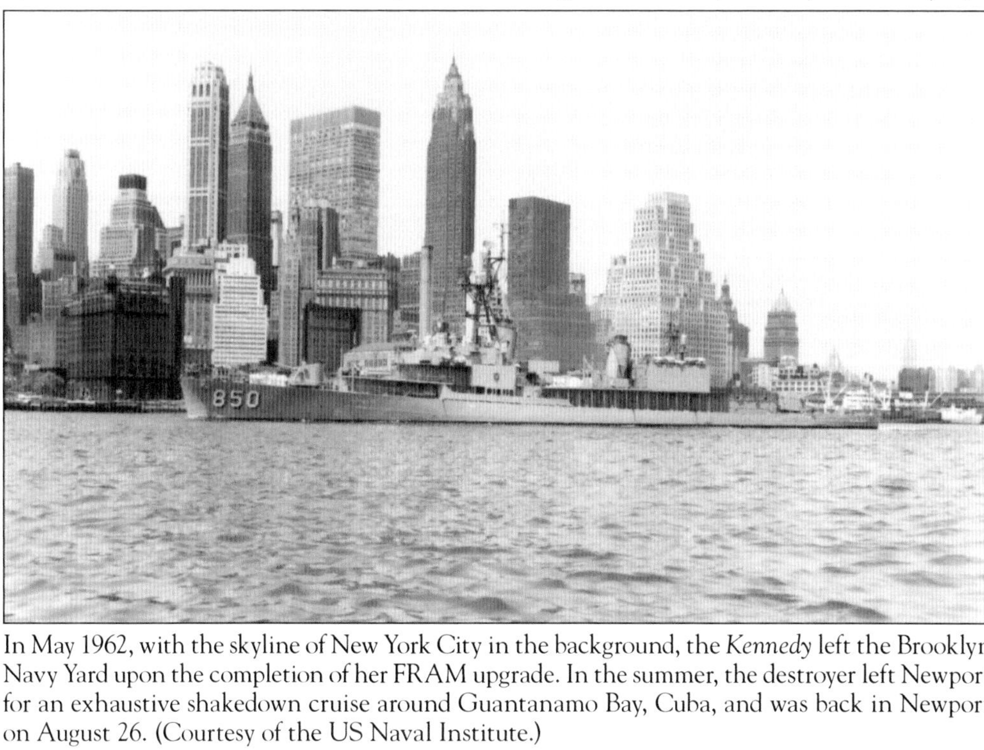

In May 1962, with the skyline of New York City in the background, the *Kennedy* left the Brooklyn Navy Yard upon the completion of her FRAM upgrade. In the summer, the destroyer left Newport for an exhaustive shakedown cruise around Guantanamo Bay, Cuba, and was back in Newport on August 26. (Courtesy of the US Naval Institute.)

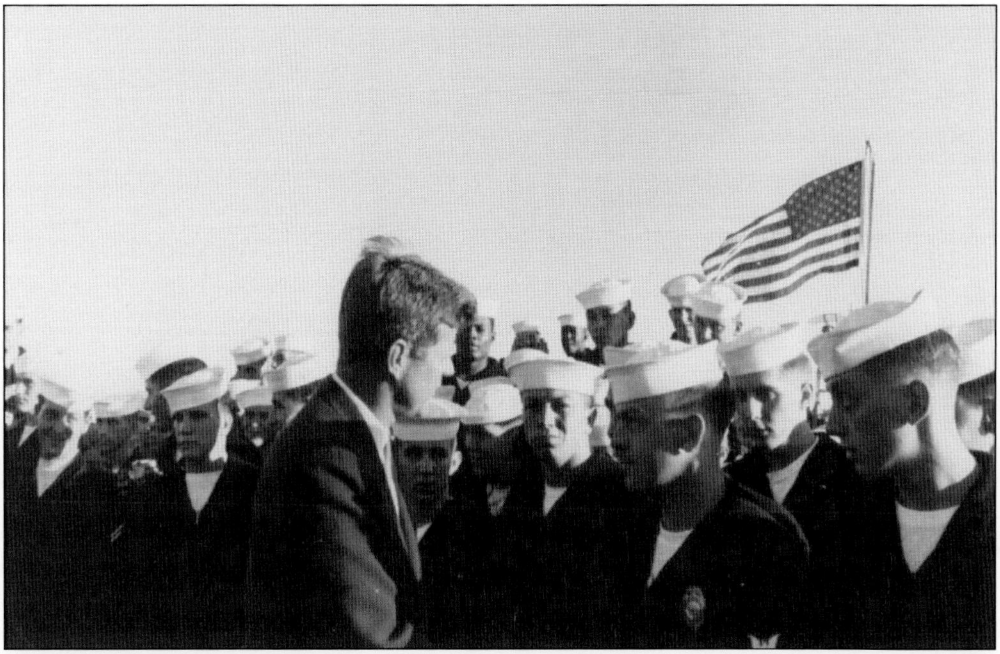

President Kennedy greets *JPK* sailors during the America's Cup races off Newport in September 1962. Commander Mikhalevsky, with the support of his chain of command, had personally extended an invitation to the president to visit the destroyer named for his older brother and receive a ship model that the crew had made. Mikhalevsky suggested that the America's Cup would provide a possible opportunity for the visit, which was accepted by the White House.

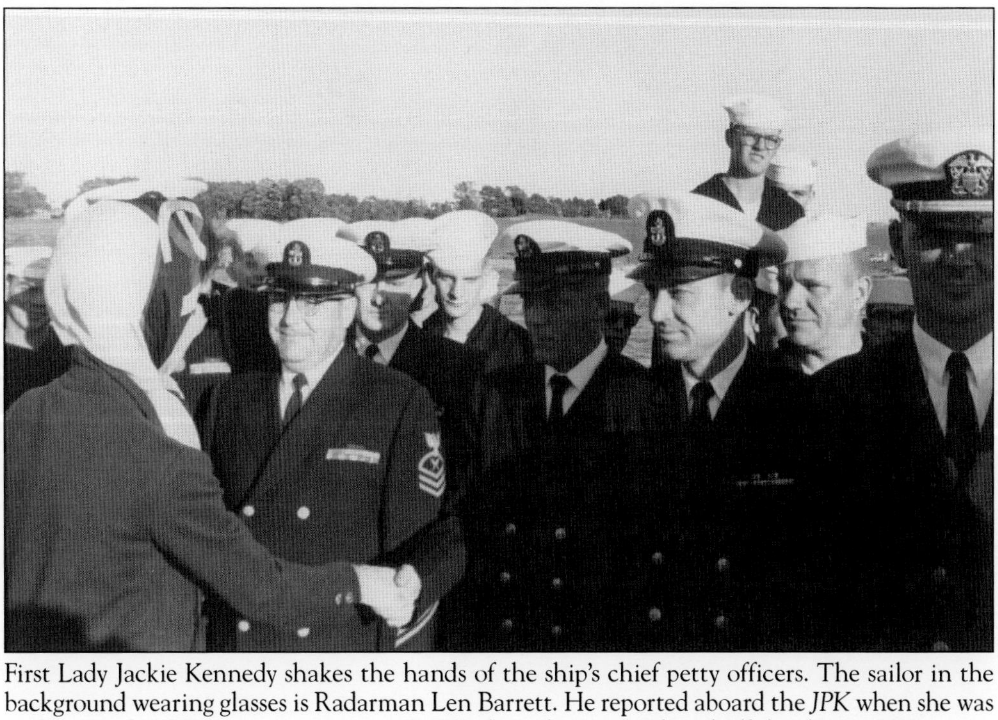

First Lady Jackie Kennedy shakes the hands of the ship's chief petty officers. The sailor in the background wearing glasses is Radarman Len Barrett. He reported aboard the *JPK* when she was undergoing her FRAM conversion in New York, and was transferred off the ship in 1964.

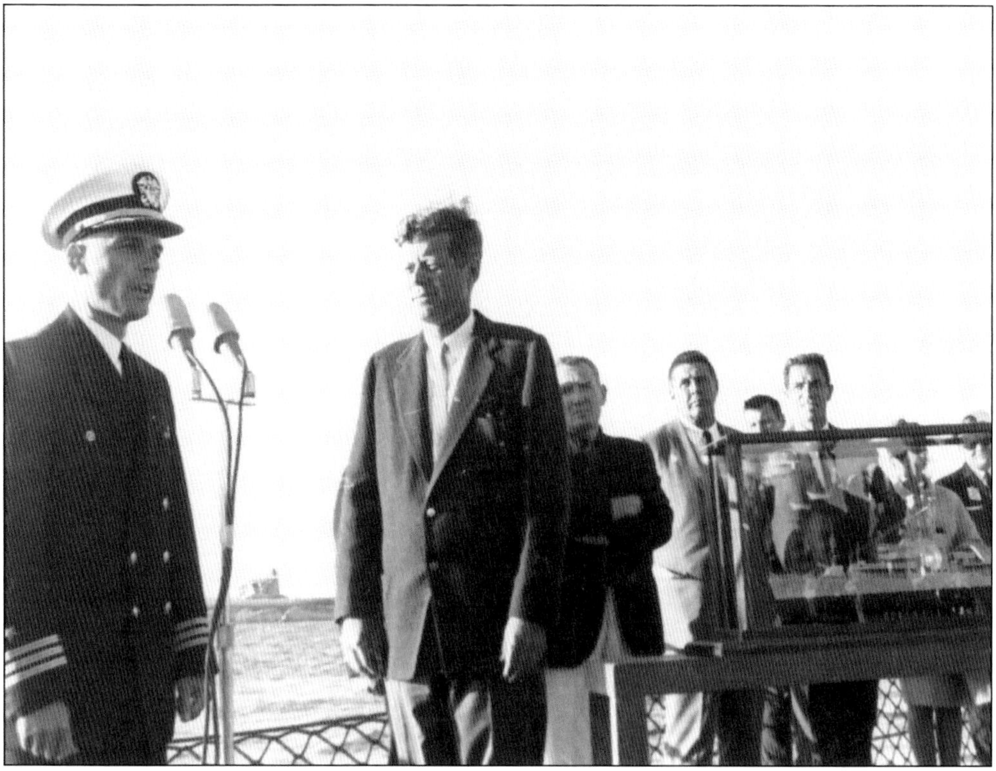

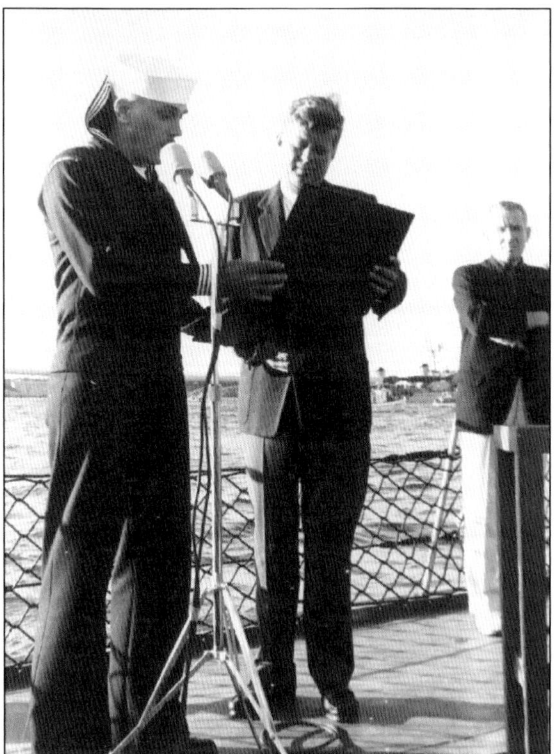

Standing on the fantail, Commander Mikhalevsky thanked President Kennedy for accepting the invitation to visit the *Joseph P. Kennedy, Jr.* and presented him with a model of the ship. The presentation took place on the day after the first America's Cup race was completed. John John and Caroline Kennedy were aboard the ship in the morning. John John was decked out in a sailor's outfit, and Caroline was shown a demonstration of signal flags.

Electrician's Mate Gilbert M. Olsen, senior man of the ship's Enlisted Welfare and Recreation Committee, spoke after his captain and told President Kennedy that the crew felt proud to serve on the ship. He then gave the president a schematic, signed by the crew, describing the principal characteristics of the model.

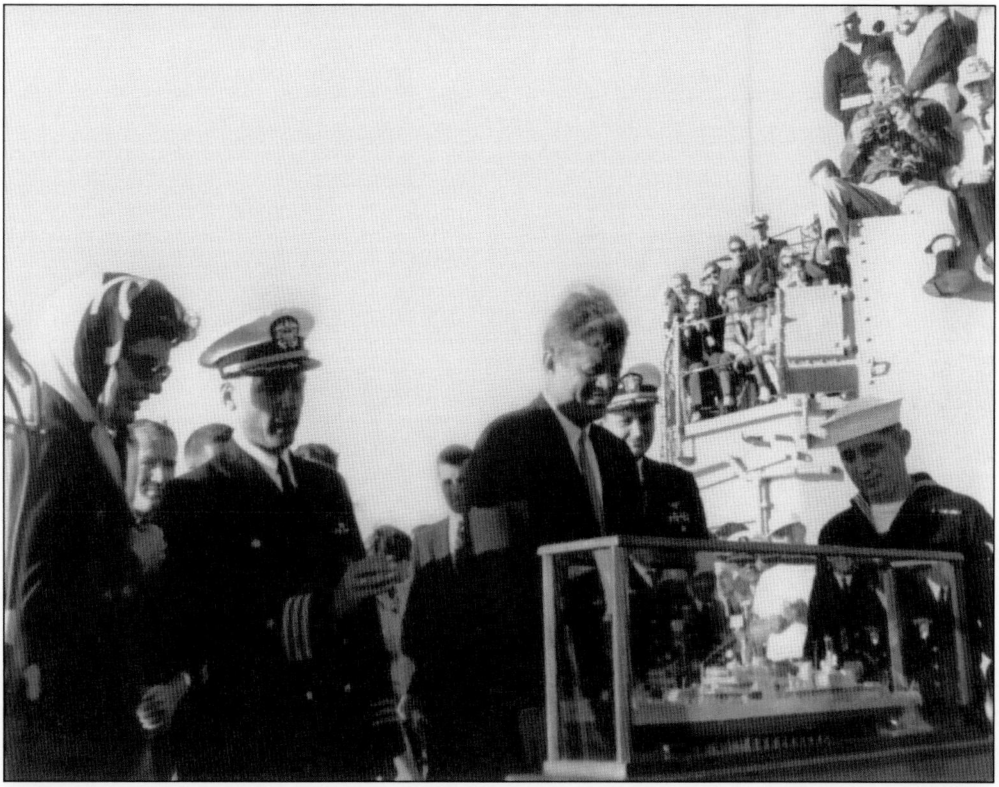

Shown here admiring the details of the ship's model are, from left to right, Jackie Kennedy, Commander Mikhalevsky, President Kennedy, and the sailor who made the model. In his remarks, Kennedy expressed how much the ship meant not only to himself but to his entire family. He went on to conclude that whatever was down the road for the country and the Navy, the *JPK* would play "an important and forward part." Those words would prove prophetic just over a month later off Cuba, during the Cuban Missile Crisis. (Courtesy of Dr. Peter Mikhalevsky.)

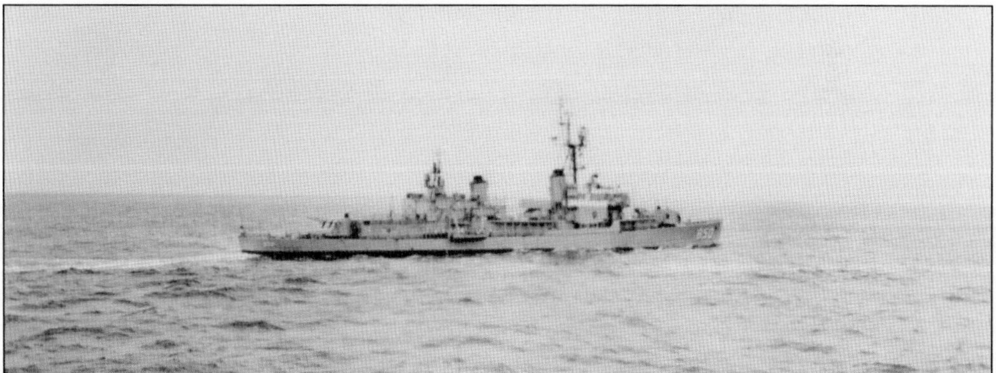

With the development of the Cuban Missile Crisis, the *Kennedy*, along with several other Navy ships, left Newport, Rhode Island, for Cuba on Monday, October 22. When the naval quarantine went into effect at 10:00 a.m. on October 24, the *Kennedy* was escorting auxiliary vessels. On October 26, both she and another destroyer, the USS *John R. Pierce* (DD-753), stopped the Russian-chartered cargo ship *Marucla*. In this photograph, the boarding party prepares to lower the whaleboat. (Courtesy of National Archives.)

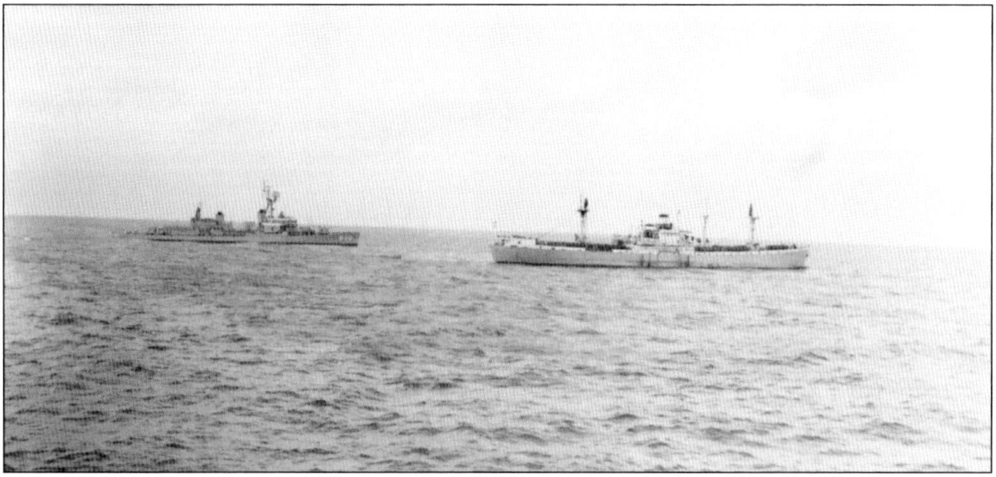

The whaleboat, made up of both *Kennedy* and *Pierce* sailors, heads for the *Marucla*. The freighter was registered to the country of Lebanon, and its sailors were from Greece. After a two-and-a-half-hour search, no prohibited cargo was found, and she was allowed to proceed to Havana. The *Kennedy* continued operating in the area until she arrived home on December 7. (Courtesy of National Archives.)

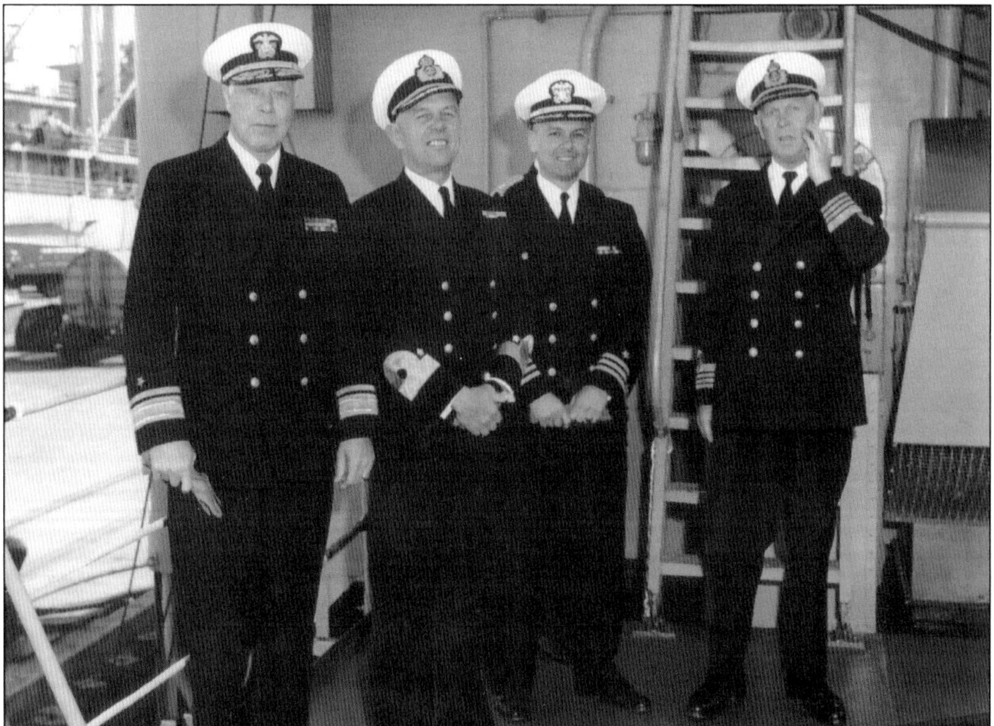

Shown here are, from left to right, Rear Adm. R.H. Speck, commander of the Atlantic Fleet Cruiser-Destroyer Force; Vice Adm. Ake Fredrick Lindemaim, commander in chief, Royal Swedish Navy; Commander Mikhalevsky; and Commodore Anders G. Nilson, Swedish Royal Navy, naval attaché in Washington, DC. They were photographed on the ASROC deck while touring the destroyer on April 12, 1963. (Courtesy of Dr. Peter Mikhalevsky.)

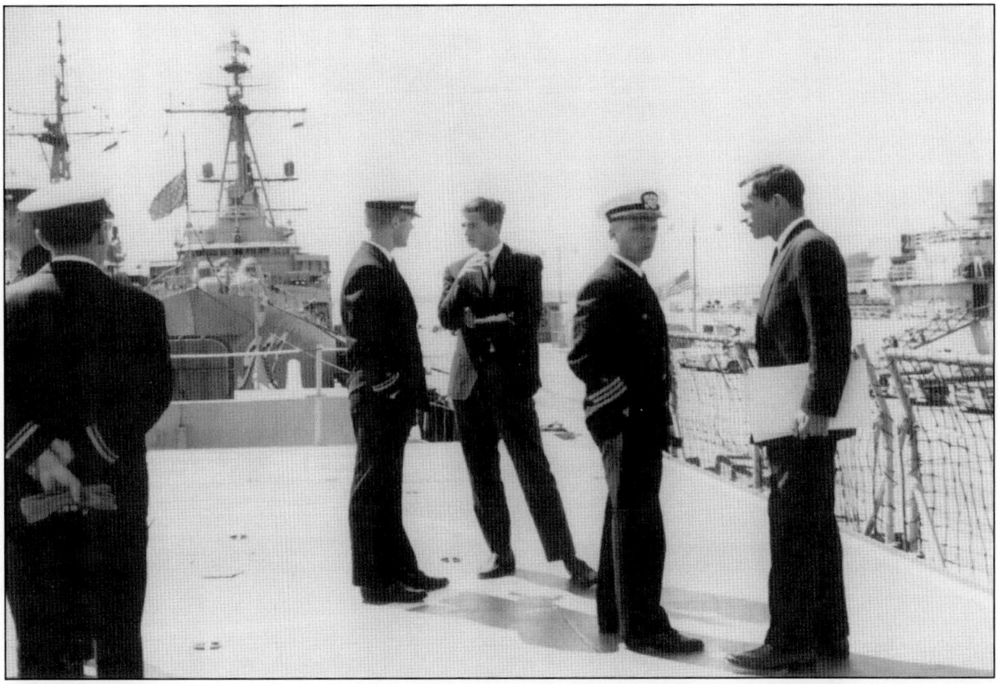

Rhode Island senator Claiborne Pell (far right) chats with Commander Mikhalevsky on the DASH helo deck on April 25, 1963. In the background, talking with another naval officer, is Prince Hans Adam of the Principality of Liechtenstein. A student at Harvard University at the time, he was staying with the senator and his wife over Easter weekend when they visited the *Kennedy* and other ships of Atlantic Fleet Cruiser-Destroyer Force in Newport. (Courtesy of Dr. Peter Mikhalevsky.)

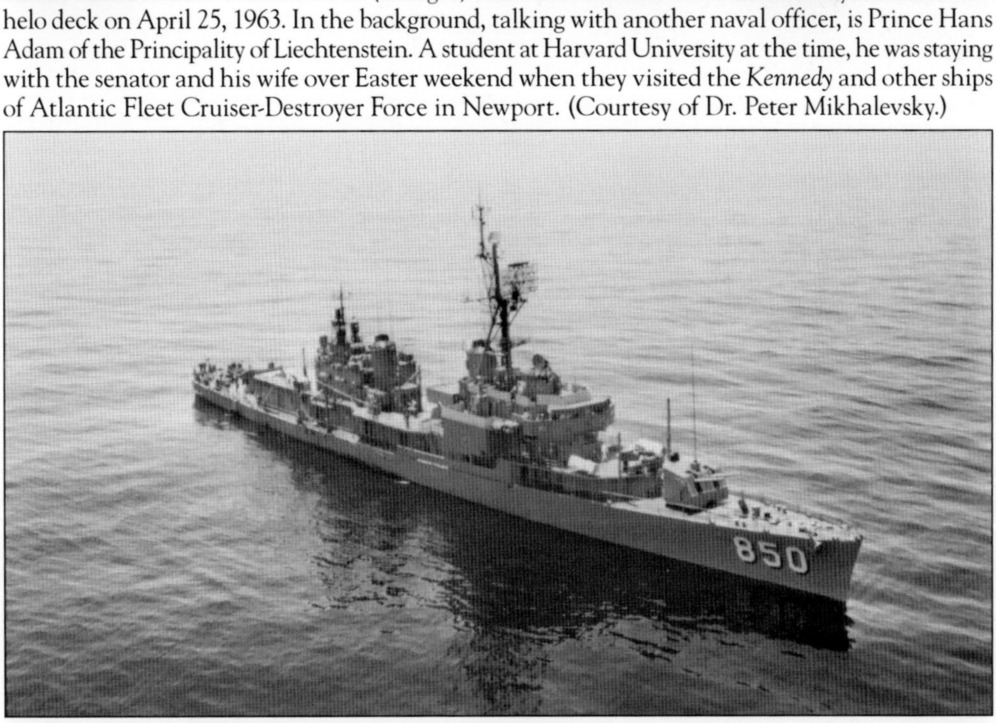

In the summer of 1963, Naval Academy midshipmen boarded the Kennedy for a seven-week training cruise, which ranged from Bermuda to Halifax, Nova Scotia. That same summer, the Jay Pee became the second ship in the Atlantic Fleet to qualify in the operation of the DASH. (Courtesy of National Archives.)

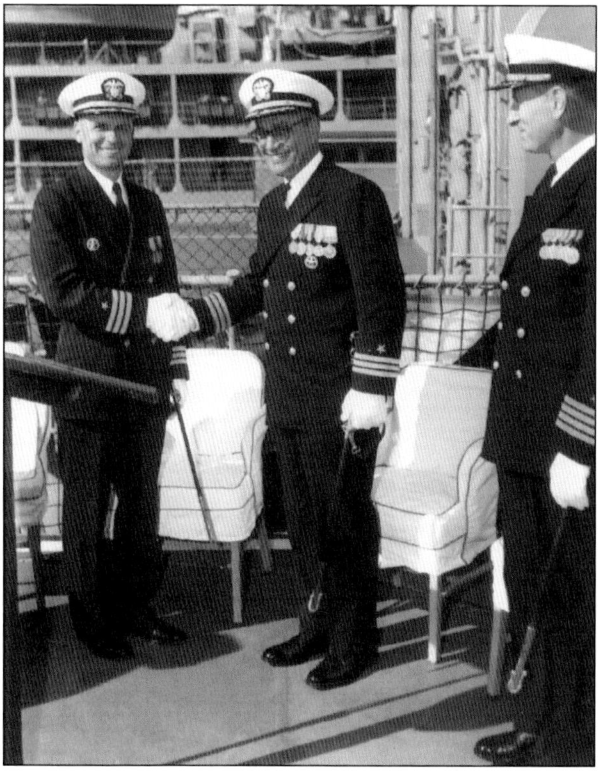

On October 4, 1963, Commander Mikhalevsky was relieved as commanding officer of the *Kennedy* by Cmdr. John V. Peters. This photograph was taken during the Change of Watch Ceremony. Shown here are, from left to right, Mikhalevsky, Peters, and Capt. George F. Britner, commander of Destroyer Division 102. Commander Mikhalevsky then reported to the US Naval Academy, where he taught operations analysis. (Courtesy of Dr. Peter Mikhalevsky.)

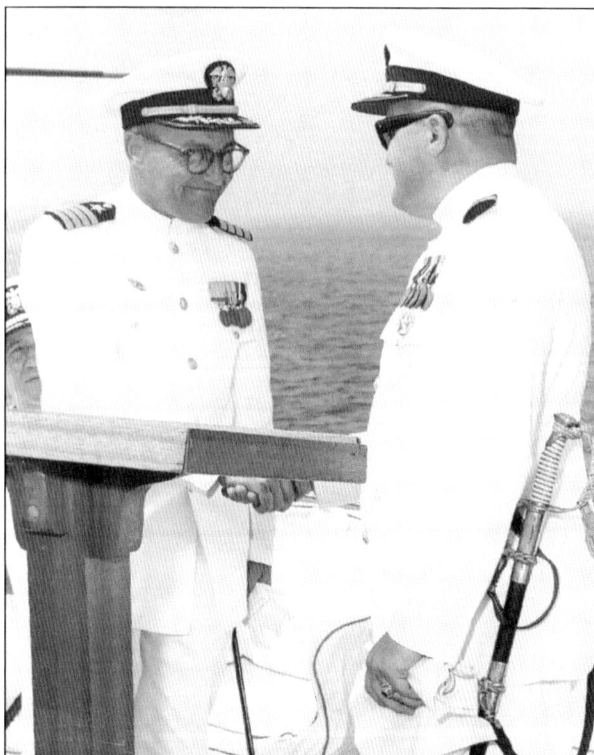

In October 1964, the *Joseph P. Kennedy, Jr.* participated in the largest amphibious exercise since World War II, Operation Steel Pike I. Over 90 ships from the navies of the United States and Spain landed over 30,000 Marines and Spanish soldiers on the coast of Spain. In 1965, the *JPK* helped qualify two new Polaris submarines and then underwent a three-month overhaul in the Boston Navy Yard. On July 14, 1965, Cmdr. James W. Hayes Jr. (right) took command of the destroyer from Commander Peters.

Sailors stand at attention on top of the DASH hangar during the Change of Watch Ceremony. This photograph provides an excellent view of the ship's electronics mast. The mast enabled the ship to conduct electronic warfare to interfere with the operation of an adversary's weapons systems. The destroyer had both Electronic Support Measures and Electronic Counter Measures.

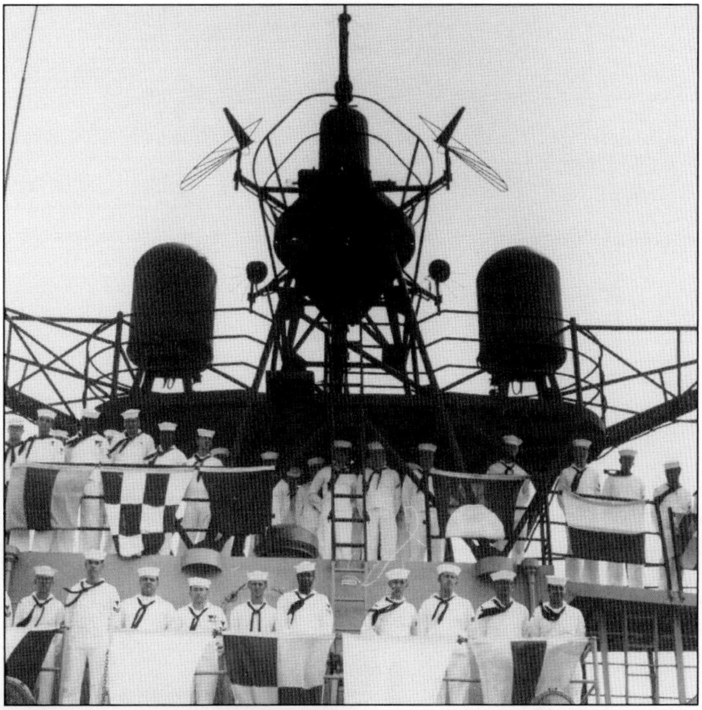

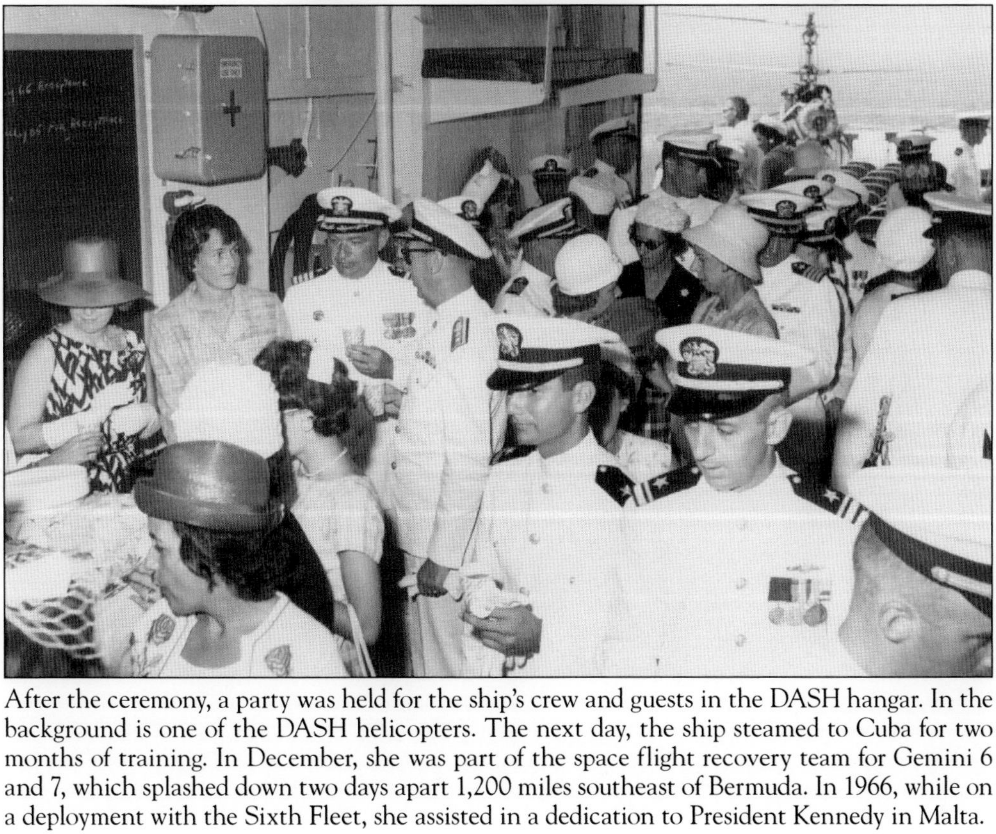

After the ceremony, a party was held for the ship's crew and guests in the DASH hangar. In the background is one of the DASH helicopters. The next day, the ship steamed to Cuba for two months of training. In December, she was part of the space flight recovery team for Gemini 6 and 7, which splashed down two days apart 1,200 miles southeast of Bermuda. In 1966, while on a deployment with the Sixth Fleet, she assisted in a dedication to President Kennedy in Malta.

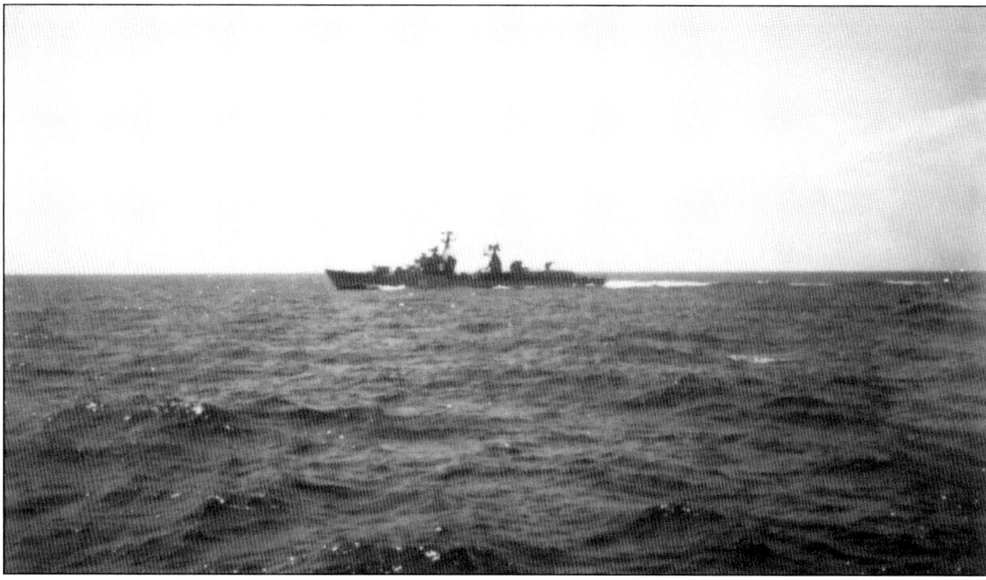

The Soviet Mediterranean Fleet was established in 1963, although it was tiny compared to America's presence in the area. However, by 1967, the Soviet Navy was a permanent presence in the Mediterranean, and both fleets would find ways to harass each other. Russian warships were notorious for attempting to disrupt aircraft carrier flight operations and underway replenishments. The *Kennedy* kept a close eye on the Soviet destroyer seen here. (Courtesy of Steve Wallace.)

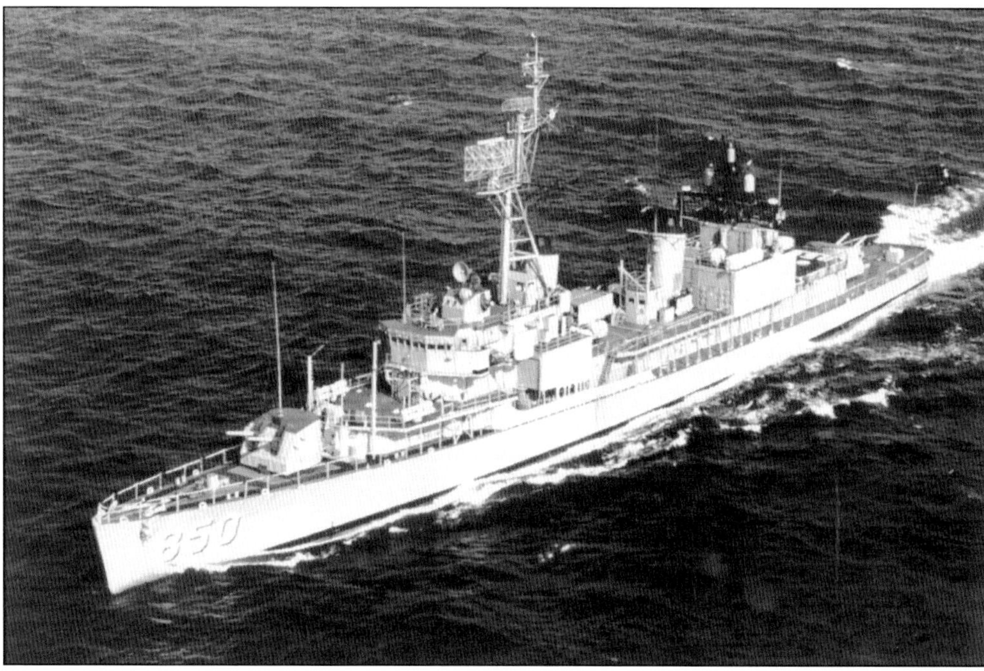

From December 1968 to April 1969, the *Kennedy* was overhauled and received the latest improvements in weaponry, communications, and electronic systems. The destroyer left Newport for Guantanamo Bay for refresher training. This aerial photograph of the *JPK* underway in Narragansett Bay on June 4, 1969, was taken by Photographer's Mate First Class Frederick W. Gotauco. (Courtesy of US Navy.)

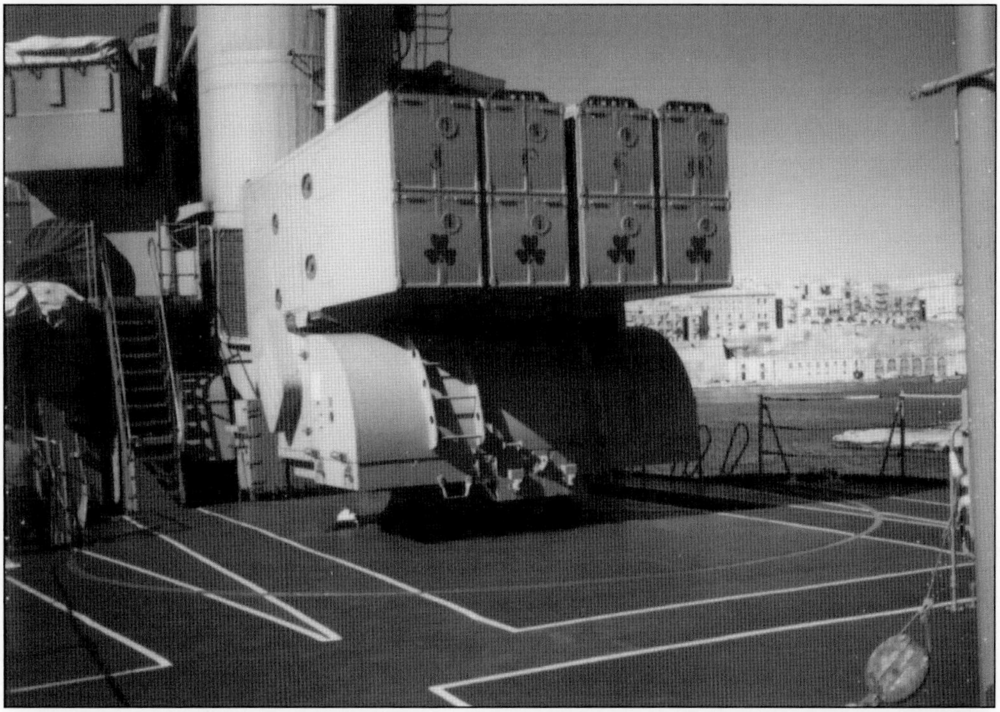

In September 1969, Cmdr. T.A. Rogers became the destroyer's new commanding officer. In November, the *Kennedy* left for another deployment with the Sixth Fleet and made ports of call at Malta, Spain, Italy, and Turkey. It also participated with the French navy in antisubmarine exercises. The *Kennedy* is shown here docked at Valetta, Malta. The red danger circle around the ASROC launcher was panted with camel-hair brushes, as were the white guide lines. At upper right is the decontamination sprinkler. (Courtesy of Steve Wallace.)

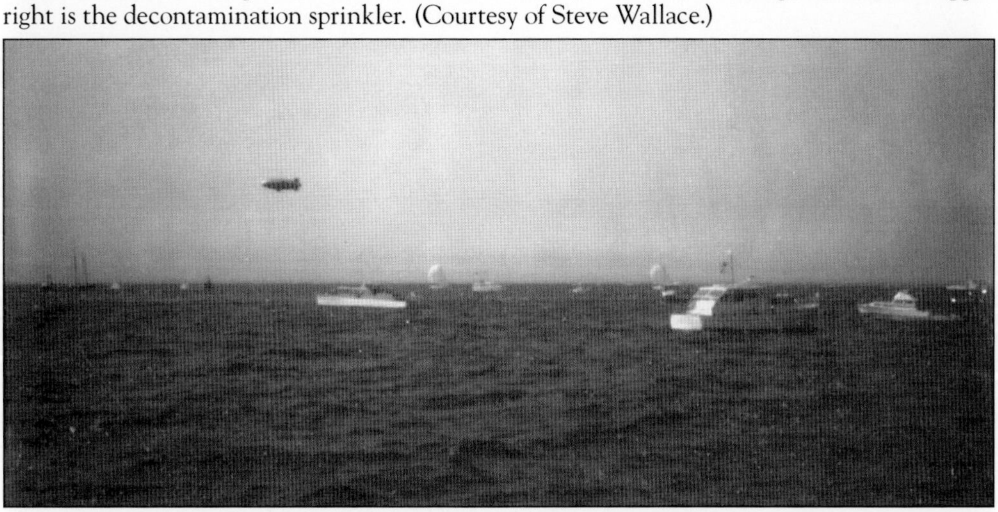

After returning home in May, the *Kennedy*'s crew enjoyed a month's liberty before heading to the Caribbean for a month of training exercises. In September, the *Kennedy* once again hosted numerous distinguished American and foreign guests, including former First Lady Jackie Kennedy, for the 1970 America's Cup races off Newport. In this photograph taken from the ship, many pleasure boats can be seen in the distance. The American *Intrepid* defeated the Australian challenger *Gretel II*. (Courtesy of Steve Wallace.)

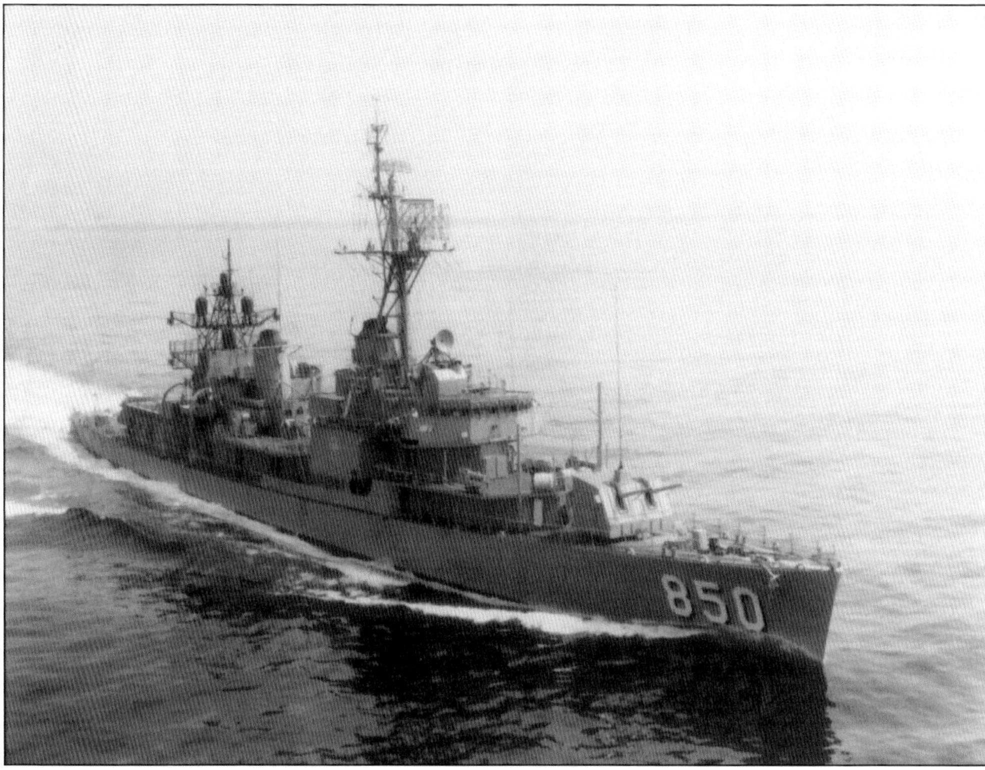

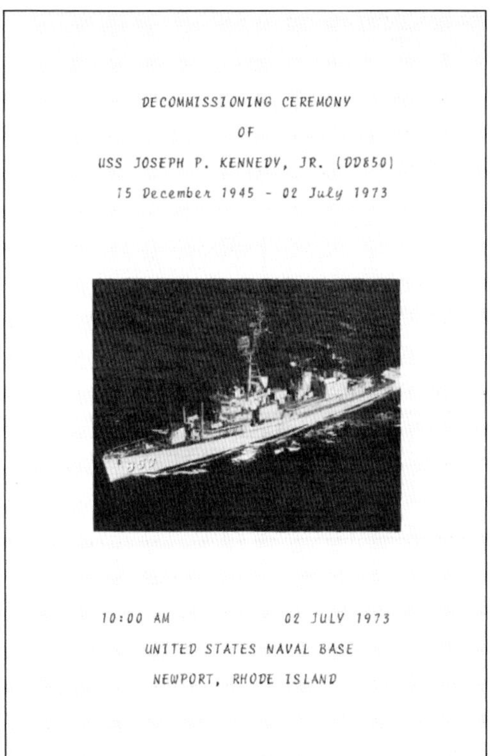

DECOMMISSIONING CEREMONY

OF

USS JOSEPH P. KENNEDY, JR. (DD850)

15 December 1945 - 02 July 1973

10:00 AM 02 JULY 1973

UNITED STATES NAVAL BASE

NEWPORT, RHODE ISLAND

In February 1972, the *Kennedy* participated in Operation Snowy Beach, an amphibious operation conducted off the northern coast of Maine, in order to determine the effectiveness of the Navy–Marine Corps team under extremely cold weather conditions. In April, she steamed to the Caribbean to participate in Operation Lantreadex-72, a high-intensity antisubmarine warfare exercise with surface ships and submarines of the Atlantic Fleet. (Courtesy of the US Naval Institute.)

On June 13, the Jay Pee, now a member of Destroyer Squadron 24, left Newport for her 11th and final deployment to the Mediterranean with the Sixth Fleet. For six months, she took part in amphibious and antisubmarine exercises with ships of the French, Italian, Greek, and Turkish navies. On her way back to Newport, she encountered a ferocious storm that damaged the ship. She arrived home on December 18, 1972. On July 2, 1973, after serving her country for 28 years, the *Kennedy* was decommissioned.

Instead of being sent to the scrap pile, the *Joseph P. Kennedy, Jr.* was donated by the Navy to join the *Massachusetts* and *Lionfish* at Battleship Cove to become a museum ship. Arriving in January 1974, she was placed outboard of the *Lionfish*. The *Kennedy* offered visitors the ability to examine the Navy's transition from World War II to the Cold War.

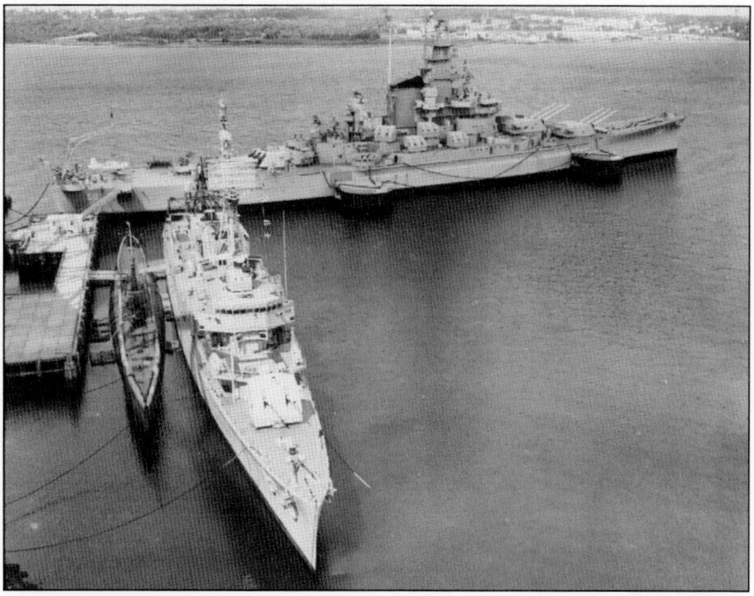

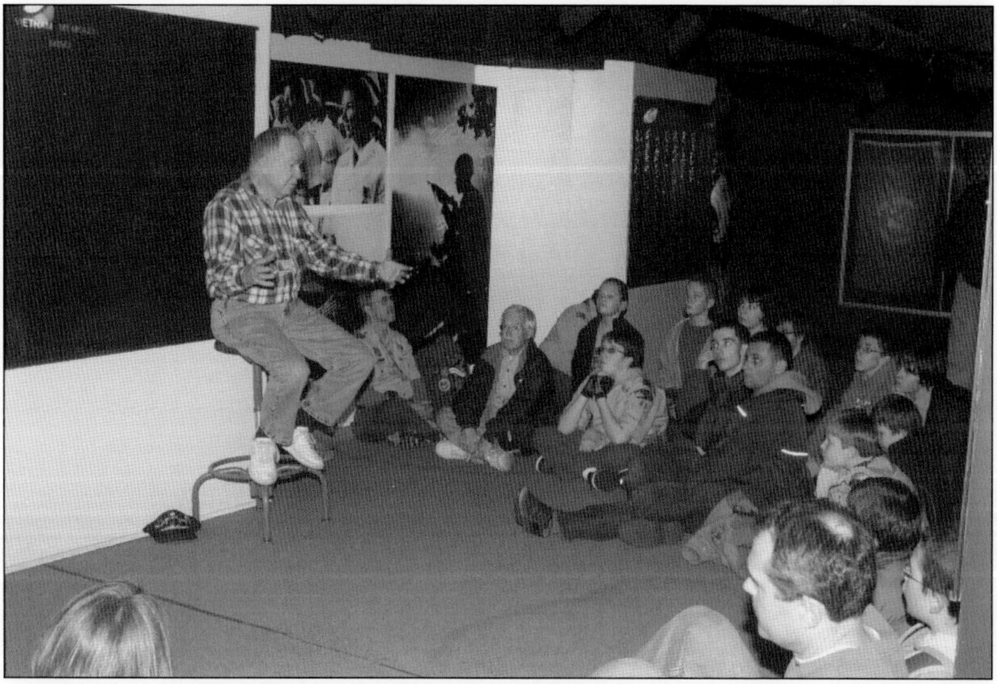

In 1973, the Commonwealth of Massachusetts passed the Korea-Vietnam Memorial bill. Originally planned to be built onboard the *Massachusetts*, the memorial was relocated to the *Kennedy* when it was learned that she would be coming to Battleship Cove. Like the World War II Memorial on the battleship, the Memorial Room in the *Kennedy* lists all the Massachusetts residents killed in the Korean and Vietnam Wars. Retired Navy Lt. Cdr. James Mulvihill, a former destroyerman and longtime volunteer, conducts a "Meet the Veteran" talk with Boy Scouts. (Courtesy of Ted Hayes.)

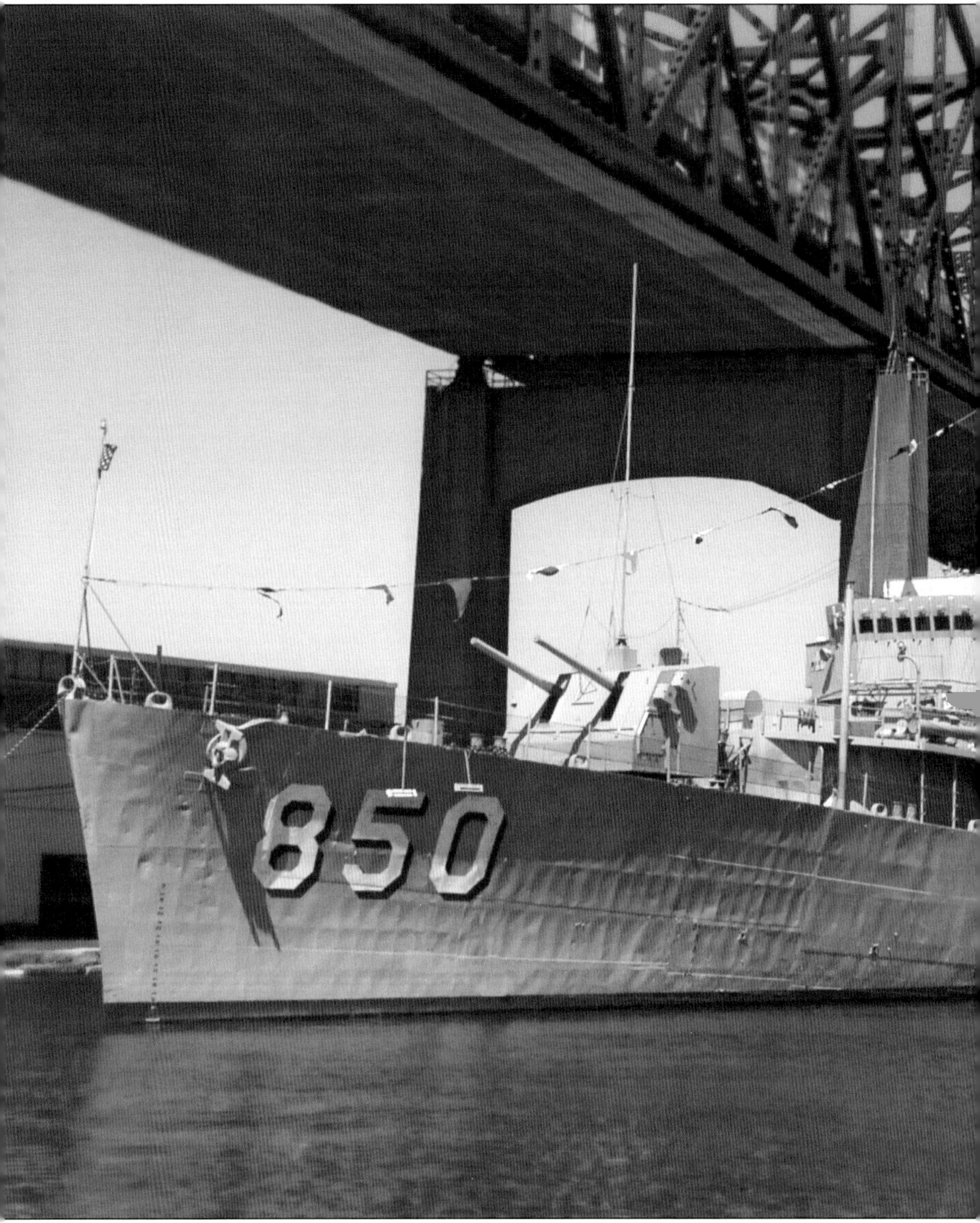

In 1976, Tin Can Sailors Inc., the National Association of Destroyer Veterans, was founded on the *Kennedy*. The association strives to support destroyer veterans through its *Tin Can Sailor* newsletter, supports museum destroyers with grants and volunteer labor, and supports the active fleet with copies of its newsletters. In addition, it makes contributions to Navy Relief. Since 1979,

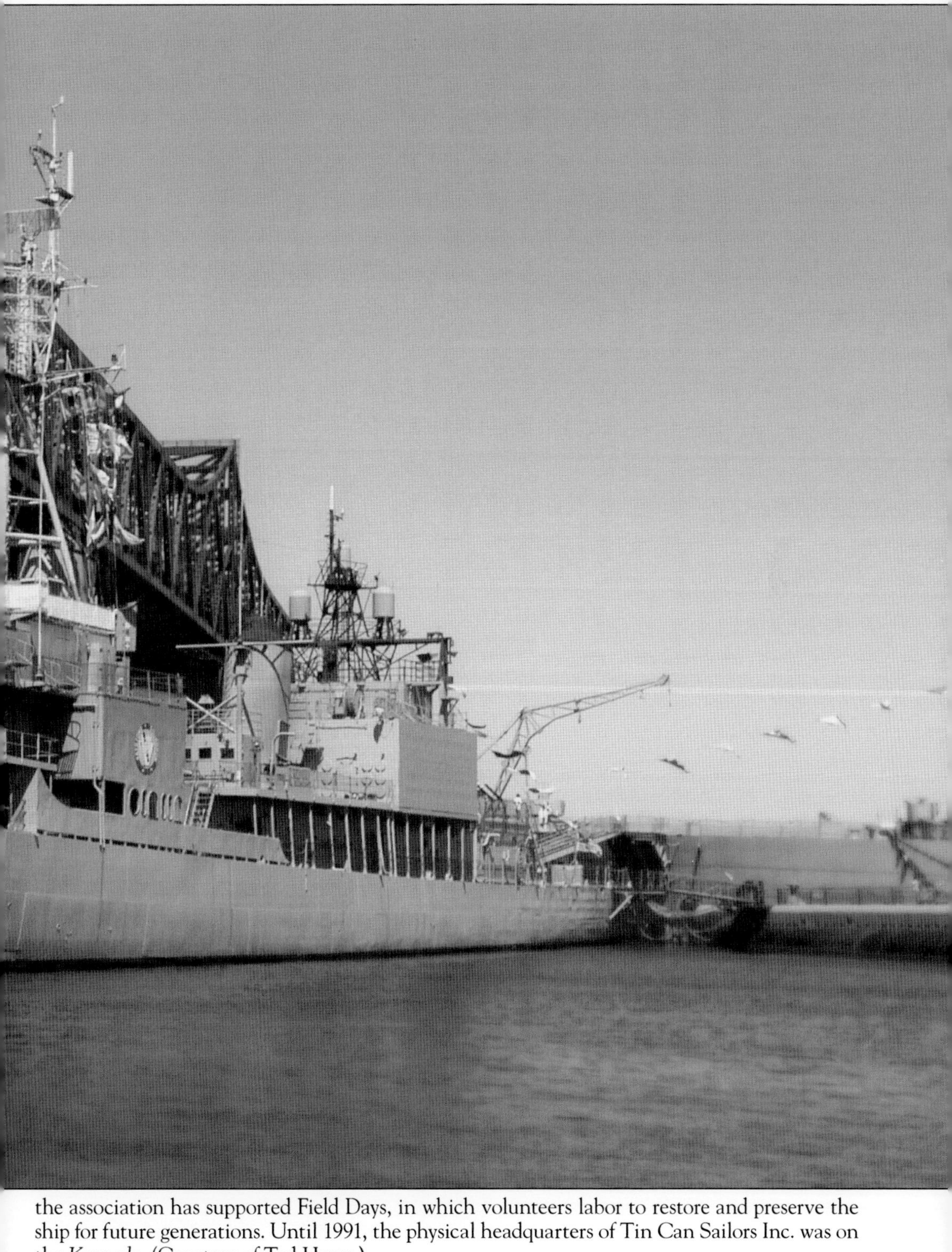

the association has supported Field Days, in which volunteers labor to restore and preserve the ship for future generations. Until 1991, the physical headquarters of Tin Can Sailors Inc. was on the *Kennedy*. (Courtesy of Ted Hayes.)

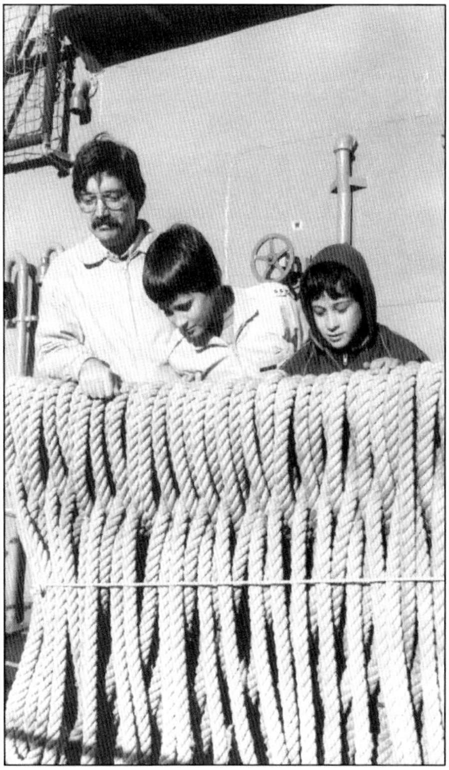

A father and his two sons tour the *Kennedy* on a frigid day in December 1984. Unlike some museum ships, the vessels at Battleship Cove are open all year long. The harsh New England weather takes a real toll on the ships, making volunteers a necessity in prolonging the life of the exhibits.

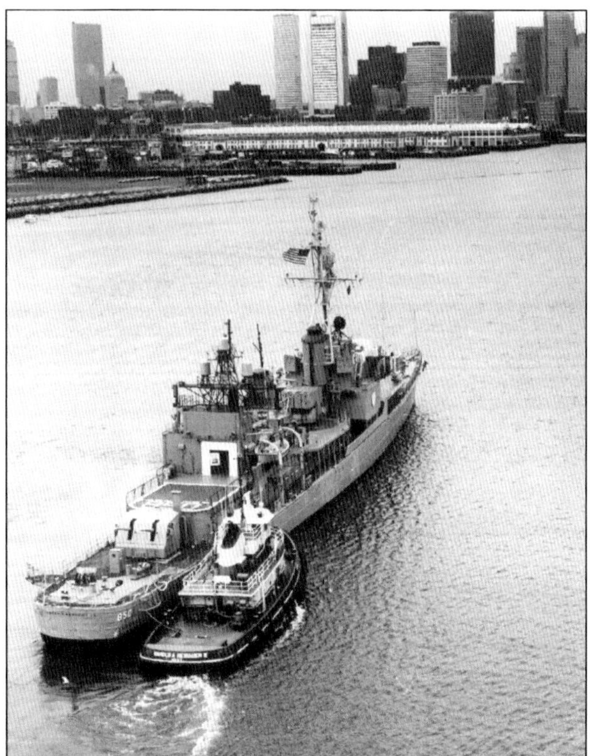

In 1986, the organization completed the Arleigh Burke National Destroyermen's Museum in the aft section of the *Kennedy*. After the Navy's superintendent of ships survey discovered that the destroyer badly needed hull restoration, she was towed to Boston in November. On December 10, she entered the dry dock and returned to Battleship Cove in March 1987. She was designated a National Historic Landmark two years later.

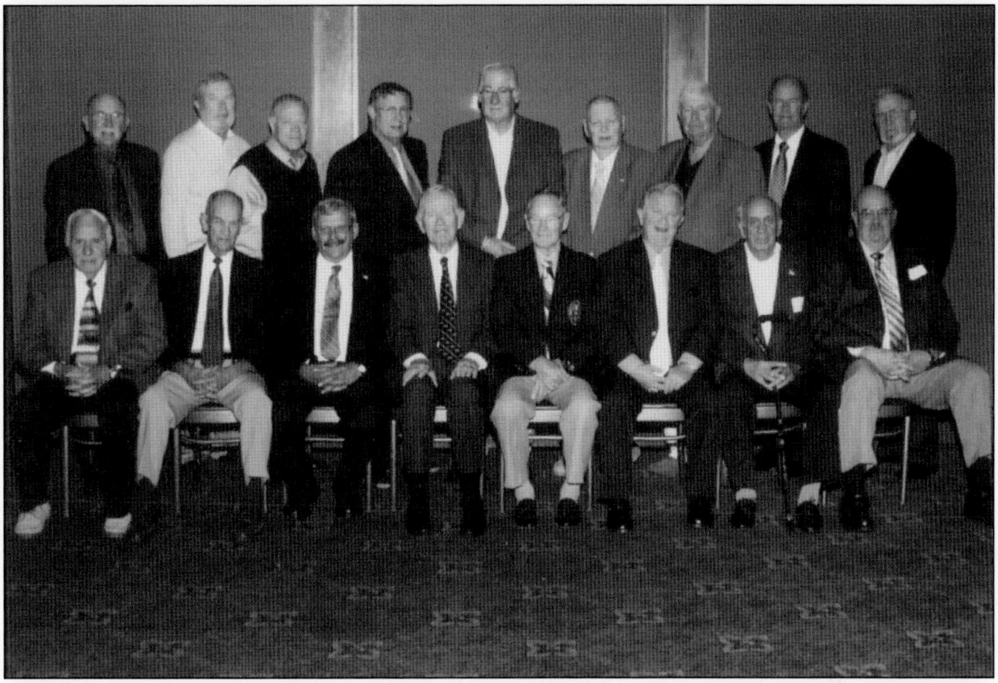

This is a group photograph of former *Joseph P. Kennedy, Jr.* crewmembers during their 19th reunion at White's of Westport on October 4, 2013. Every October, they meet for fellowship and to honor their deceased shipmates. Anyone interested in the *Joseph P. Kennedy, Jr.* can join the association. Membership includes a copy of the newsletter. (Courtesy of La Torre Photography.)

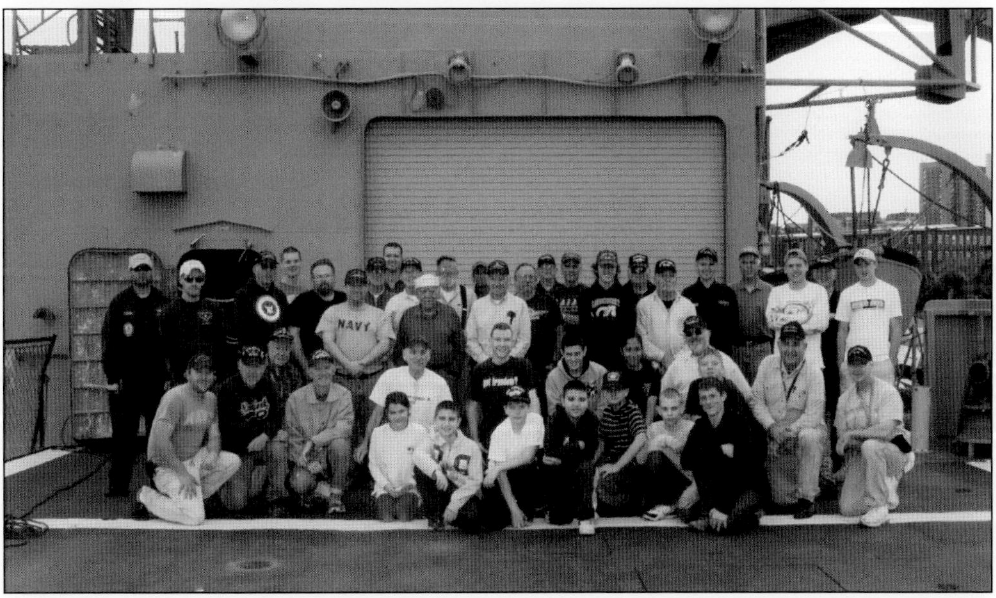

During the most recent Weekend Field Day, volunteers pose for the group photograph on October 19, 2013. Volunteers included former destroyer sailors, Navy veterans, active Navy sailors, Naval Academy prep students, the ship's own Sea Scouts, and civilians. The weekends are held each May and October from Thursday to Sunday. Volunteers sleep in the same racks and eat in the same mess as the ship's sailors used to. (Courtesy of Ted Hayes.)

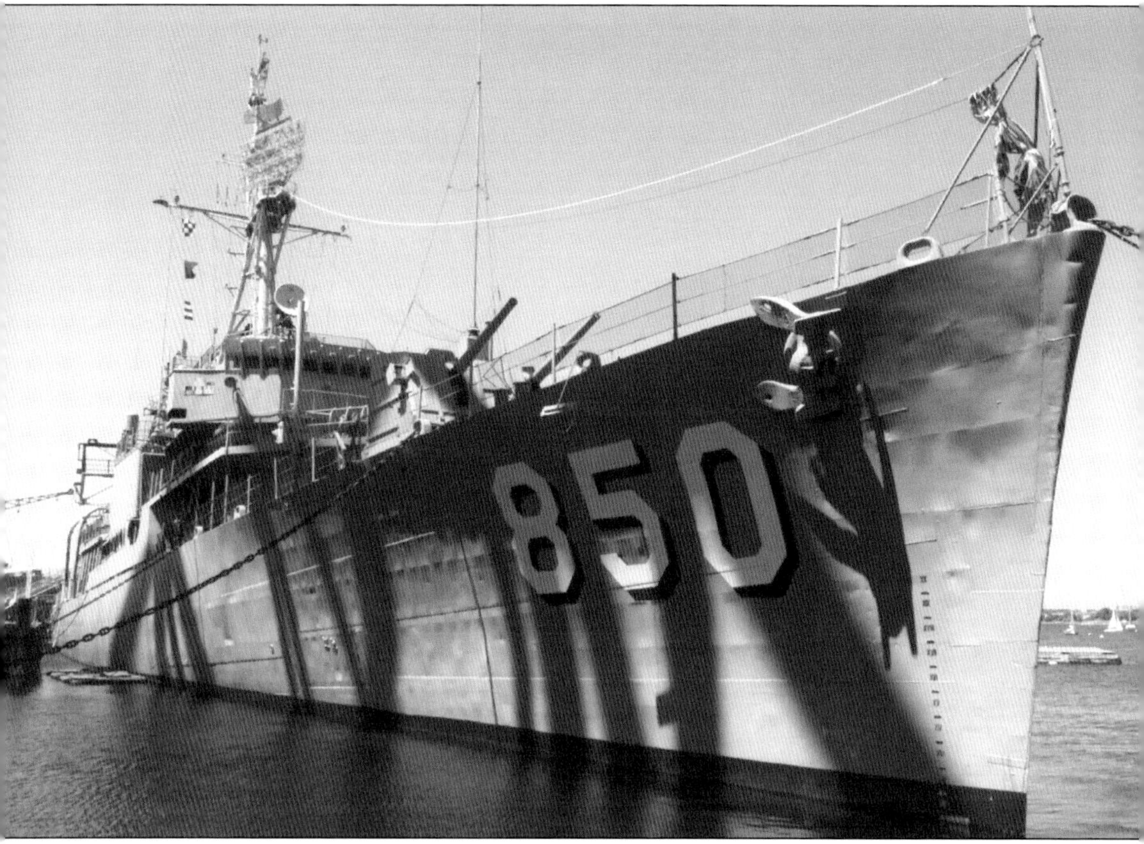

The *JPK* appeared on the big screen in the movie *Thirteen Days*, which hit theatres in December 2000. The docudrama highlights the Cuban Missile Crisis from the perspective of President Kennedy, Robert Kennedy, and Kenneth O'Donnell. In the film, she appeared, albeit briefly, as herself and as the USS *John R. Pierce* (DD-753). The Jay Pee is the last Massachusetts-built destroyer in existence and the only ship of her type restored and presented in a US Navy Cold War/Vietnam-era appearance. Today, the elements are her greatest enemy, as she currently needs to be dry-docked for hull repairs. The *Kennedy* serves as a memorial to all destroyermen. (Courtesy of Ted Hayes.)

Five

GIMICK AND PT-BOATS 796 AND 617

In the 1970s, Battleship Cove partnered with PT Boats Inc. founder Jimmy "Boats" Newberry to tell the story of PT-boats in World War II at the museum. In subsequent years, two PT-boats opened to the public, and the National PT-Boat Museum was created on the *Massachusetts*.

First, Newberry loaned the museum what was guessed at the time to be a Japanese suicide boat. In 1975, this craft was viewed by the public on the fantail of the battleship. Only decades later would museum staff discover its real name and purpose.

Also in 1975, *PT-796* arrived at the Cove after being restored by a dedicated group of volunteers. Opening to the public a year later on a concrete pier, she had been towed as a float to resemble *PT-109* in the inaugural parade of President Kennedy in January 1961. She now resides in an authentic Quonset hut. *PT-617*, nicknamed "Dragon Lady," served her country for only months before she was sold by the government. Saved from destruction by PT Boats Inc. in 1979, she was completely restored and opened at the Cove in 1985. In honor of Jimmy "Boats" Newberry, the building that houses *PT-617* bears his name.

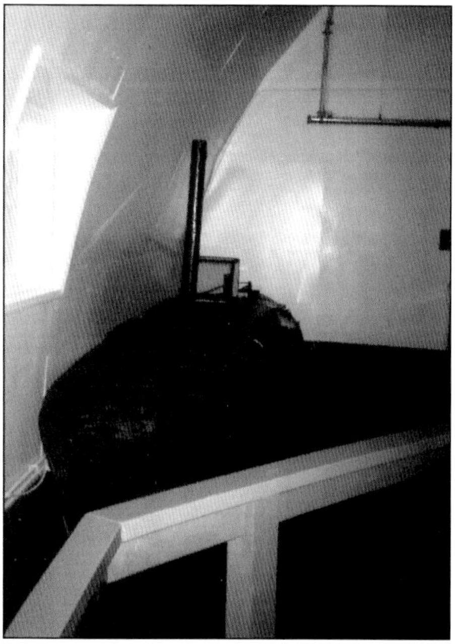

Jimmy "Boats" Newberry, a prominent Memphis, Tennessee, businessman and World War II PT-boat veteran, founded PT Boats Inc. in 1967. In the early 1970s, he acquired what he thought was a Japanese suicide mini-submarine and loaned it to Battleship Cove in 1975. It was first displayed on the fantail of the *Massachusetts*, then was moved indoors to a building that would become known as Newberry Hall. (Author's collection.)

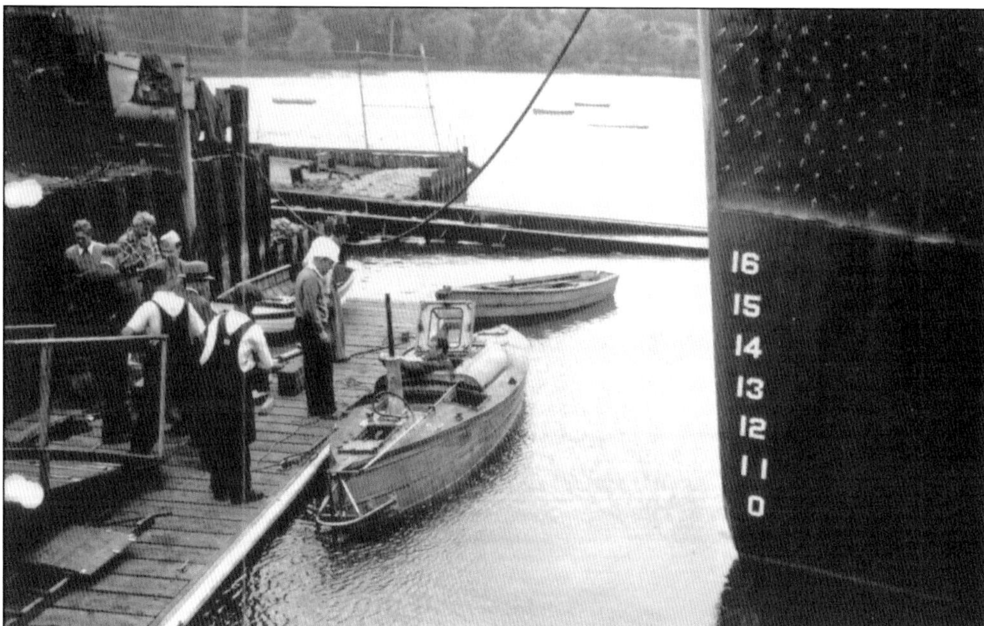

Extensive research and the declassification of CIA documents in 2011 led to the real identity of the semi-submersible and its intended use. This vessel was designed and built during World War II by the Office of Strategic Services (OSS), which later became the Central Intelligence Agency. In June 1945, the OSS completed only two of these semi-submersibles, and they were called GIMICK. Just shy of 20 feet in length, the GIMICK could carry one pilot and two passengers. Its hull was made of plywood, but the crew compartment was made of metal. Powered by gasoline, it had a top speed of six knots and was just over five feet in width. Here, OSS personnel train for Operation NAPKO in the summer of 1945 at their Catalina Island facility off the coast of Southern California. (Courtesy of PT Boats Inc.)

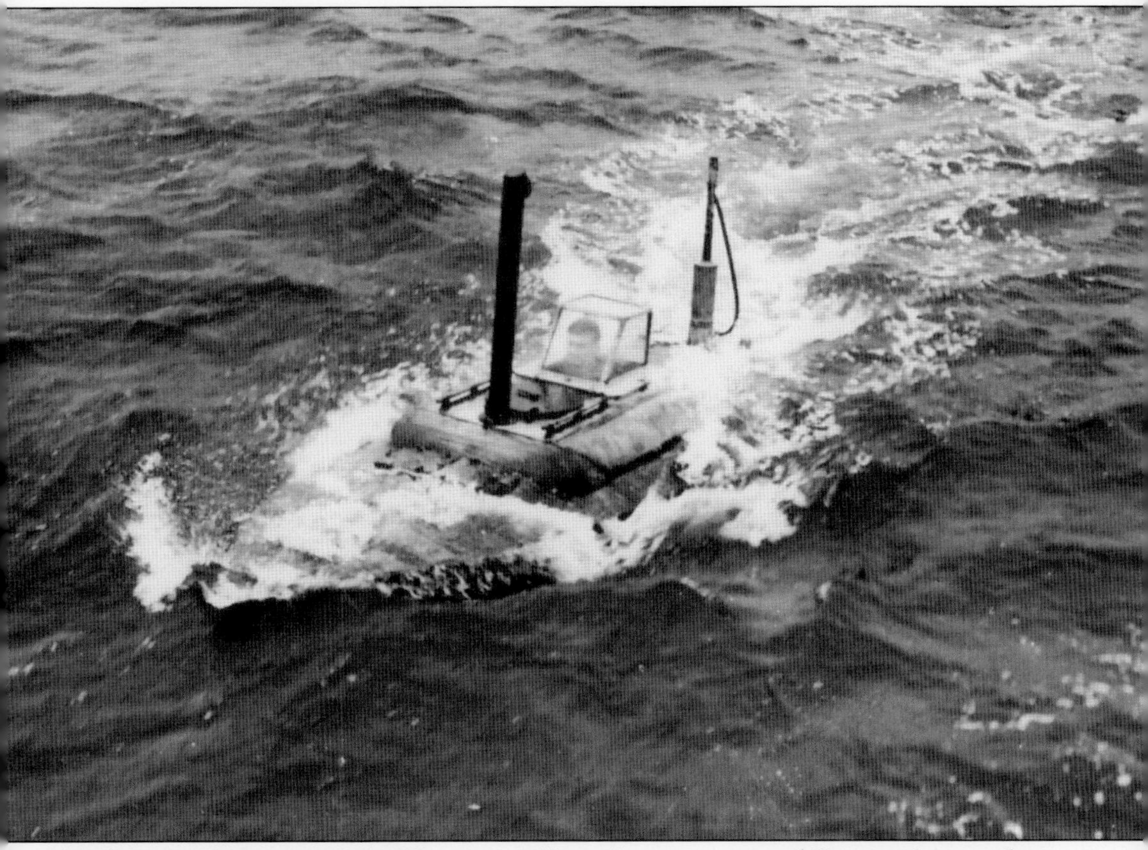

The objective of Operation NAPKO was to infiltrate Japanese-occupied Korea with spies who would eventually make their way to Japan. Once inside Japan, these operatives would conduct sabotage activities and collect intelligence that would be used for Operation Olympic, the invasion of Japan that was scheduled for late 1945. The GIMICK would be piloted by an OSS agent, and the operatives would be recruited Korean Americans or Koreans recently freed from the Japanese. The GIMICK would be transported by a mother ship across the vast Pacific, then the OSS pilot and two Korean operatives would cruise toward the coast with only the topside deck above the water, as pictured here. Operation NAPKO was planned for August 26, 1945, but was cancelled when Japan surrendered. (Courtesy of PT Boats Inc.)

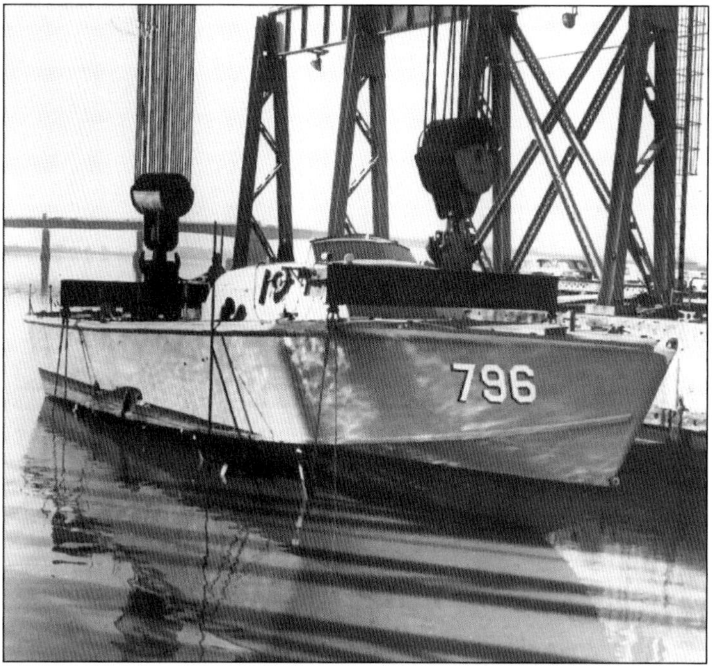

PT-796 was built by Higgins Industries in Louisiana and completed on October 26, 1945. Reclassified as a Small Boat a month later, she was 78 feet long and had a top speed of 41 knots. Although not the same type of boat skippered by John F. Kennedy, it was decided she would portray the famous *PT-109* for his inaugural parade in January 1961. After being pulled from the water and renumbered, she was placed on a trailer for the parade. (Courtesy of PT Boats Inc.)

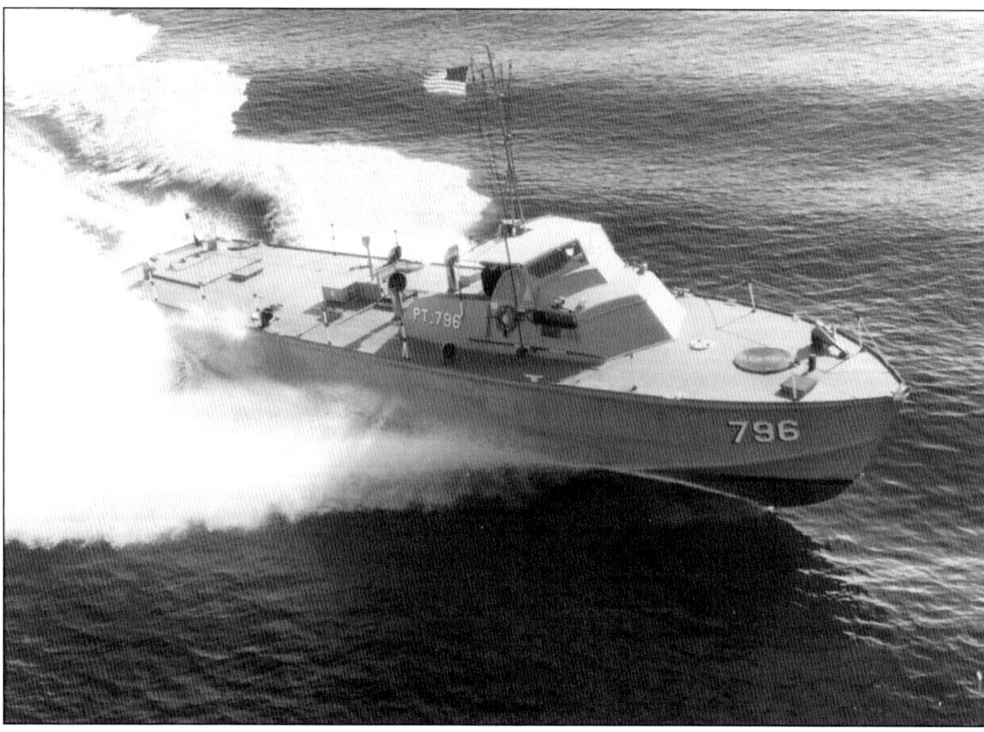

Nicknamed "Tail Ender," *PT-796* was later assigned to a Navy ordnance testing station in Panama City, Florida, and performed high-speed towing work in the development of specialized equipment for Vietnam river patrols. She was decommissioned on July 7, 1970, and was later acquired by PT Boats Inc. In 1973, Battleship Cove and PT Boats Inc. worked out an agreement to bring the boat to Fall River. (Courtesy of PT Boats Inc.)

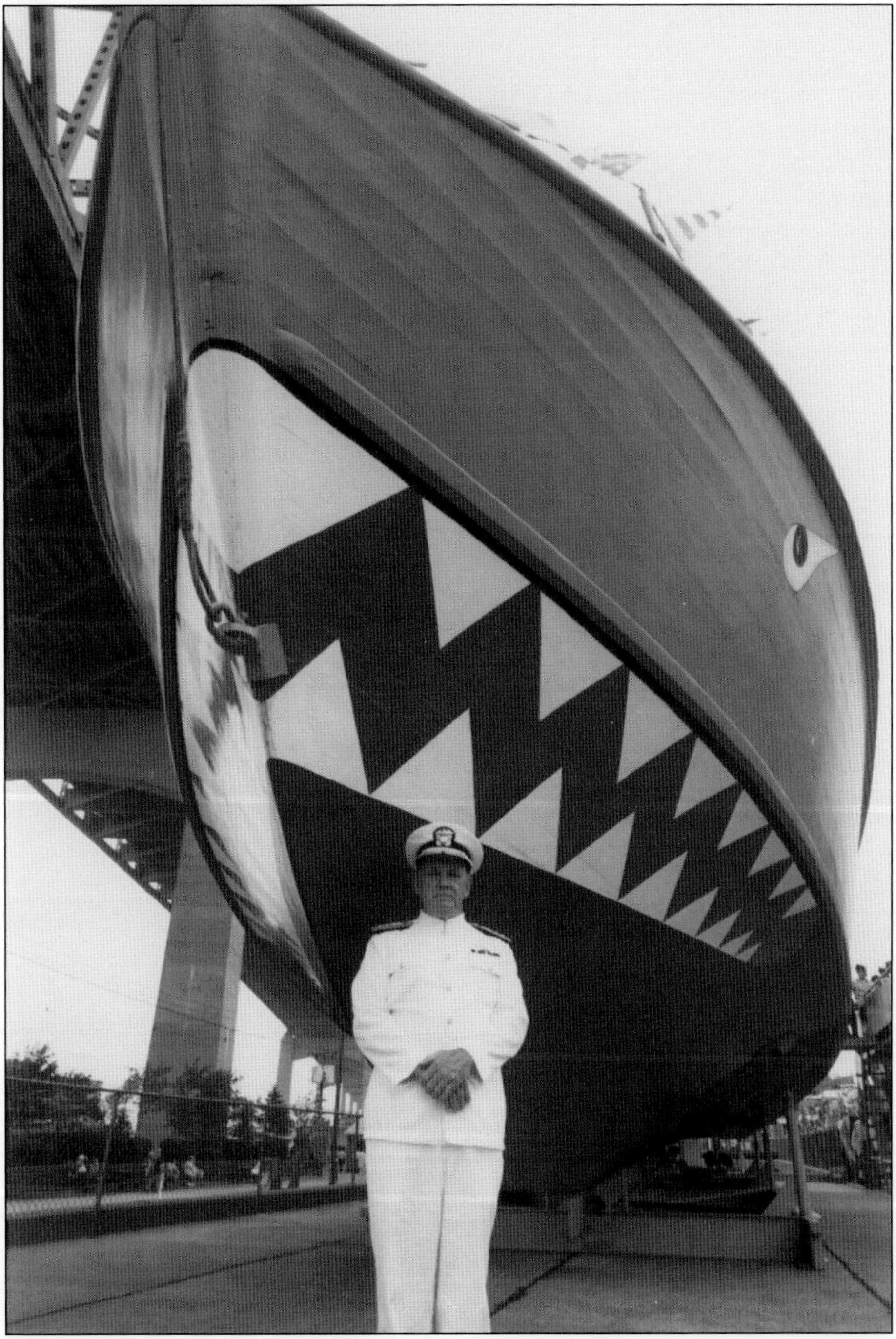

In 1975, it was decided that the National PT-Boat Museum would be built on the *Massachusetts*. The *PT-796* arrived under her own power on August 14, 1976. She was officially opened to the public on September 5, 1976. Vice Adm. John D. Bulkeley, pictured here, worked closely with J.M. "Boats" Newberry to promote PT Boats Inc. He received the Medal of Honor for evacuating Gen. Douglas MacArthur and Philippine president Quezon from Manila Bay to the southern Philippines aboard his PT-boat in 1942. (Courtesy of PT Boats Inc.)

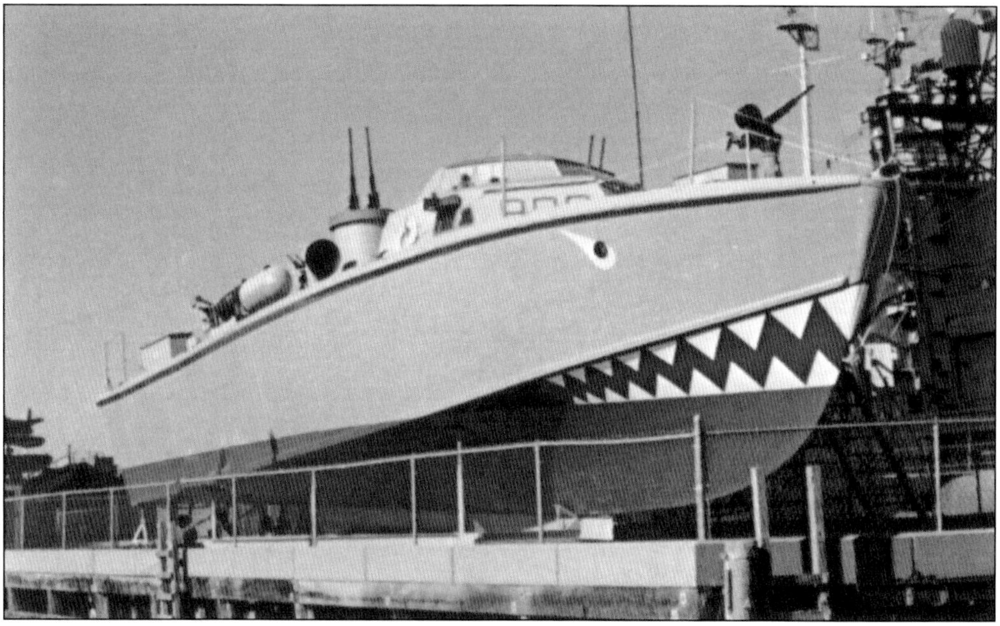

The *796* was initially displayed on a concrete pier adjacent to the *Kennedy*. Later, the museum obtained an original Quonset hut from Rhode Island, and she was soon placed inside to protect her from the elements. She became a National Historic Landmark in 1985. (Courtesy of PT Boats, Inc.)

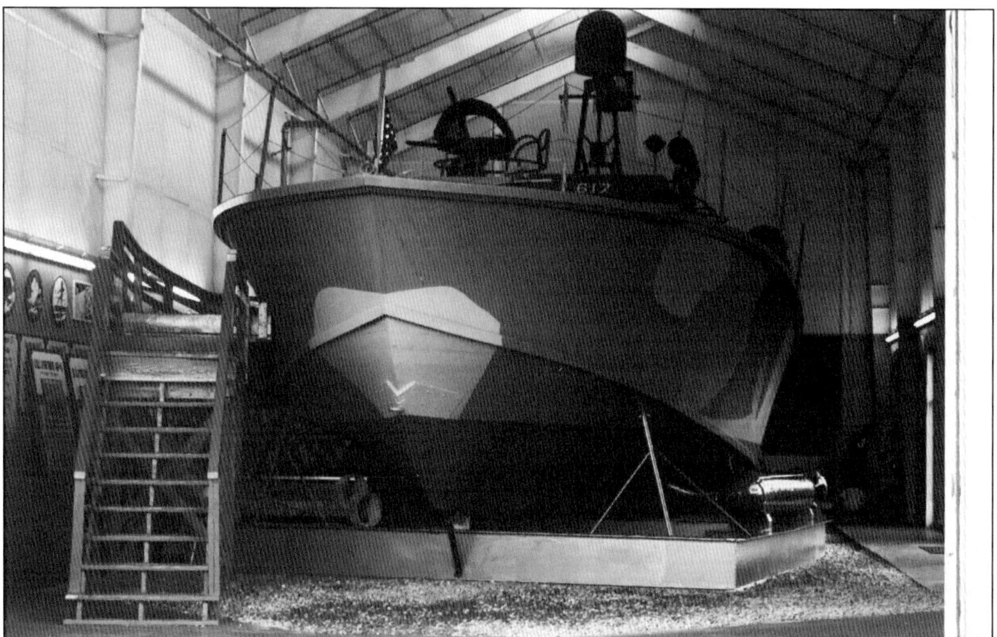

Visitors cannot walk on the decks of either PT-boat, which are instead accessed by a walkway on their starboard side. *PT-617* was built by the Electric Boat Company of Bayonne, New Jersey, on September 21, 1945, and was assigned to Motor Torpedo Boat Squadron 42, the only squadron commissioned after World War II. In October and November 1945, she participated in the Victory Loan Bond Drive. Nicknamed "Dragon Lady," she was placed out of service on January 28, 1946, and was sold on October 23, 1947. (Courtesy of Ted Hayes.)

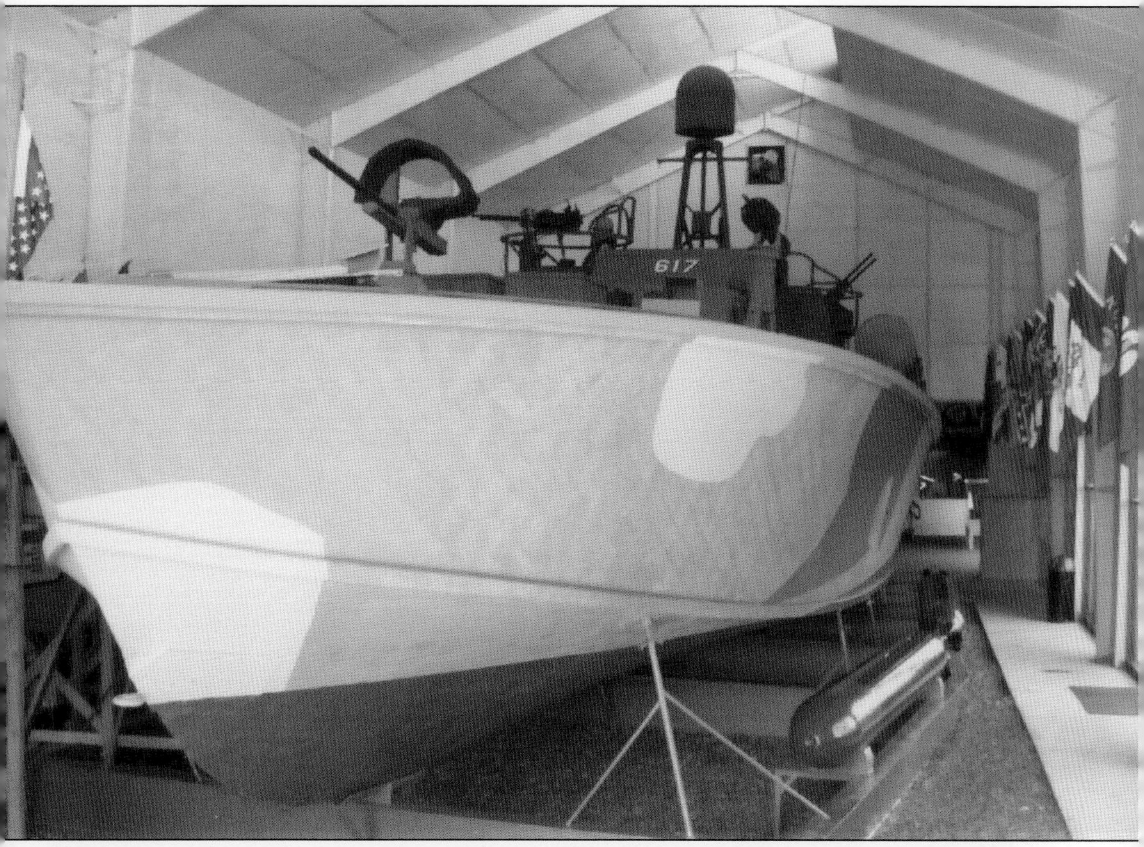

After being used as a pleasure yacht, and later a salvage boat, *PT-617* was bought by PT Boats Inc. in 1979. It was brought to Melville, Rhode Island, in 1981, and considerable work and funds went into restoring the vessel to its World War II configuration. On September 1, 1985, *PT-617* officially went on display at Battleship Cove, and a year later, Newberry Hall was built around it. She became a National Historic Landmark in 1989. (Courtesy of PT Boats Inc.)